ID0258045

Priceless

Priceless

CHARLIE DANIELS

MY JOURNEY
THROUGH A
LIFE OF VICE

HODDER &
STOUGHTON

Author's note: All names have been changed
to protect the innocent, and the not-so-innocent.

Copyright © 2006 by Charlie Daniels

First published in Great Britain in 2006 by Hodder & Stoughton
A division of Hodder Headline

A Hodder & Stoughton Book

2

A CIP catalogue record for this title is available from the British Library

Hardback ISBN 0 340 89976 X
Trade paperback ISBN 0 340 92396 2

Typeset in Sabon by Hewer Text UK Ltd
Printed and bound by Clays Ltd, St Ives plc

Hodder Headline's policy is to use papers that are natural, renewable
and recyclable products and made from wood grown in sustainable
forests. The logging and manufacturing processes are expected to
conform to the environmental regulations of the country of origin.

Hodder & Stoughton Ltd
A division of Hodder Headline
338 Euston Road
London NW1 3BH

To my darling daughter –
My most beautiful and priceless treasure
My unconditional love always
Mum X

ACKNOWLEDGEMENTS

....

This book would not have been possible without the help of my agent, Judith Chilcote; Rowena, Helen and all the staff at Hodder and the following writers who tutored and inspired me along the way: Jean (formerly of Swarthmore Writer's Circle, Leeds), Allegra Taylor, beautiful woman and wonderful healer (especially for helping me write through the deepest darkest moments), Jonathan and Julie Myerson, Helen Carey.

Thanks also to Andrew Crofts for endless patience and hard work in editing the final manuscript.

And, finally, to a group of very special friends for their enduring support and encouragement – Angie Allen, Maureen Gardner, David Awty and Richard M.

Love, light and many thanks to you all.

If you are inspired by this story, you might consider supporting one of the many charities working tirelessly with sex workers. Genesis, a well-established voluntary sector organisation with a Leeds citywide remit, is one such group that is particularly close to my heart.

Their mission is:

'Provide support, advocacy and information to women of all ages that are involved in, at risk of becoming involved in, or wishing to exit prostitution, whilst raising awareness in the wider community. We believe in the unique worth of every person and are committed to providing a confidential service based on respect and trust, which encourages women to realise their potential and fufil their goals.'

To make a donation, call 0113 24 0036.

Charity No. 1048606

CONTENTS

....

Prologue: We've only just begun . . .   1

1. Street Life   5
2. Happy Days   11
3. First Heartbreak   16
4. Getting a Reputation   21
5. Stray Bitch   26
6. Home Truths   30
7. Lost and Found   39
8. Secrets and Lies   47
9. The Bullet   61
10. Lessons in Love   73
11. School of Life   97
12. Mona Lisa   110
13. Stars in My Eyes   124
14. Suffer Little Children   138
15. The Bodyguard   153
16. Moth to a Flame   159
17. Trials and Tribulations   164
18. Band of Gold   180
19. Pond Life   193
20. Amazing Grace   216

21. Inside Out   225
22. Phoenix From the Ashes   234
23. Rat Race   247
24. All the World's a Stage   263
25. Queen of Tarts   274
26. The Queen Is Dead. Long Live the Queen.   289
27. The Start of Things to Come   296
28. Full Circle   301
29. Life Is a Beach   306

PROLOGUE:
WE'VE ONLY JUST BEGUN . . .

....

The local chemist on our estate knew my mother. She also knew that I was just seventeen. She passed me the test in a paper bag, speaking only to tell me the price.

Later, in the privacy of my bedroom, I watched the plastic stick intensely. As the tiny window turned a different colour – so did I. I couldn't breathe! A wave of nausea that I'd come to recognise swept over me.

Who was the father? Probably that one-night stand I'd met at the Little Angels concert. I wouldn't even have known how to begin tracing him! All I knew was that he had long dark hair. There were other possible candidates, but he was the most likely one.

I wasn't going to have an abortion because of a detail like that. I was a teenage, pregnant, ecstatic girl and I was going to keep my baby. At last there would be someone I would love to love me back unconditionally, someone who wouldn't desert me.

It didn't matter to me that I lived in a twelve-storey concrete dump, with scraps of carpet strewn about the floor and a piss-smelling lift that never worked. It didn't matter to me that I hadn't finished college: I couldn't see how education was going to help me.

1

All I had to do now was convince my mother that this wasn't a disaster and wasn't confirmation of all her worst fears about me. It seemed incredible to me that in the 1980s and living in the area we lived in she still had conservative ideas about sex being reserved for marriage.

Even now I remember the look of horror on my mother's face when at twelve I wistfully wished for either a motorbike or a baby. I'm sure she couldn't decide which option was worse.

I was dreading the hell-and-damnation judgement that she was bound to hand out. It took me two weeks to face her with the confession. Predictably, she immediately became hysterical and started screaming at me as if I'd done it on purpose to spite her.

'I only ever wanted the best for you . . . You never listen. You think you always know better . . . don't expect me to sort it out for you . . . I knew it! It's history repeating itself!'

But whether she liked it or not, I was about to give her a grandchild. Life for both of us would never be the same again.

Before you read on, I wish to reclaim a little language. In the same way that gay men recently embraced 'queer' I wish to reclaim 'whore' and 'brothel'. When you reclaim a word it becomes less derogatory and more honest. Use of these words is not meant to cause offence, especially to those in the industry, but merely to remove the sting that outsiders would wish to attach to them.

1
STREET LIFE

....

'*Where all the streets are paved with gold, And all the maidens pretty.*'

George Colman

It was dark. The air was damp. Freezing mists were descending rapidly. The orange glow of the street lamps dimly lit the huge run-down Victorian buildings that loomed tall and grim like stone monsters. Broken windows and derelict yards lined this notorious street.

The faint sound of traffic could be heard in the distance, broken only by the sound of our heels clicking up and down the hard, wet pavement. Donna was trying to light a fag but was hampered by the wind and drizzle. My feet felt like two blocks of ice. I drew in my head and arms and, as I breathed out, condensation hung in the air.

Headlights approached. Donna stood tall and let her coat fall open to reveal more of her hourglass figure. A shiny brand-new Mercedes crept up slowly beside us and its tinted electric windows whirred down. I stood frozen to the spot, whilst Donna leaned in and flirted, making full eye contact with the driver. She got in the front and sat brazenly discussing the price of a blow job. She turned to me abruptly. 'It's OK, you can get in'.

I climbed into the back. Half embarrassed – half terrified. As the car pulled away its engine purred. A man's stare met mine in the driver's rear-view mirror.

I was starting to wonder what I was letting myself in for. How had I got myself into this position? Donna and I had used up all of our social security: usually we would borrow nappies and baby milk from each other but this week we'd both hit rock bottom at the same time. Neither of us had anyone else to turn to. This wasn't living – it was surviving. Every day seemed more difficult than the last. Lucy, my gorgeous baby girl, seemed to go up a size in nappies every other week and they were getting more and more expensive. The packaging showed some well-dressed doting mother and a smiling baby in a designer outfit. I didn't even mind that my life wasn't like that as long as I could just manage the basics. There I was, dressed in one of Donna's suits that buried me – I didn't own anything half-decent to wear. My stiletto shoes badly needed reheeling and my cheap underwear was no longer white, it was a paler shade of grey. I was sick of ever-increasing piles of red reminders and having to scrape pennies from the back of the settee. We were living hand to mouth and the very little we had to do even that with was disappearing faster and faster all the time.

I hated being a scrounger but neither Donna nor I had much choice. Both of us had tried to get credit at various local estate shops – without any success. The month before we'd ended up borrowing cash that we couldn't pay back to the loan man. Everyone knew he was the one man on our estate you didn't mess with.

The driver's eyes were reflected in the mirror again. I turned my head and stared out of the window. Donna seemed a very streetwise thirty-year-old. I thought I'd lived until I met her. Now I knew I was just a green eighteen.

Donna had previously worked in a sauna/brothel and she was talking about going back, but to get the job she would need to go for an interview. With no money to get to an interview that might lead nowhere anyway she'd suggested to me that she'd pay me ten pounds to accompany her on 'the beat' for her safety and so that I could get the money I needed for nappies.

I remembered the warning that I'd had from the girl who'd introduced me to Donna a few weeks before, a school friend of mine who'd babysat Donna's kids a few times: 'Don't you get involved or you'll end up on the game!'

Donna and I were both lucky to know this girl. She was a good friend who was great with kids; she had all of them with her at Donna's house that night while we went on our mission.

I found Donna mesmerising. I'd never met anyone quite like her before. She was the closest friend I'd ever had. No one had ever shown me the attention she did and I felt safe with her. I loved it that she would ask me to talk to her while she was in the bath. I'd never even seen my own mother naked and at first it had seemed strange but it also felt like a privilege. Donna seemed to have something I craved so much. I didn't know then that it was sexual charisma – all I knew was that everyone she worked her charms on seemed to be very receptive. Her eyes were captivating; they were a pale grey-blue but they changed colour according to the light. She was very good at making eye contact and her body language – even with women – always appeared sexy and alert. I used to watch in awe as she spun everyone within a mile around her little finger like a witch casting a marvellous spell.

The car pulled into a dark yard. Donna sat, deliberately twirling the curly blonde ringlets that fell around her face. She seemed quite cool and chattered incessantly to the unremarkable man. She seemed very confident, not at all uneasy in this environment – I wished I could feel the same.

The man parked up and switched off his engine. I felt sure that the others could hear the pounding of my heart. Donna abruptly finished with the flirting and demanded the money up front. I was a little startled at first. It seemed very sudden and I wouldn't have dared but, as she told me later, '*The bastards can never be trusted.*' The man put up no protest: Donna smoothed her hand up his inside leg and it had the desired effect. He reached into his inside pocket for his wallet. I felt awkward and stared hard out of the car's window.

Then I heard the sound of his zip coming down. Donna's head disappeared from my line of sight, although occasionally I could see the back of it slowly rising and falling as the man's breathing became heavier. I'd never seen anybody do anything like this before. It seemed amusing that the guy didn't appear to mind me being there, but as his stares via the mirror continued it dawned on me that he was getting off on it. I tried not to look in the mirror but I felt his gaze burning into me again.

Suddenly there was a loud bang. Donna's head shot up. We all turned to see where the noise had come from, but it was only a fox, searching out his supper from a nearby bin. I loudly released the breath I'd been holding and the activity in the car continued. Donna's head started to move faster as the man began to breathe harshly. Then he abruptly stopped Donna and turned to face me, almost breathless. 'Let me touch your tits!' he gasped.

Unusually for me, I was speechless! Donna – not one to miss an opportunity – wasn't. 'It'll cost you . . .'

I shot Donna a stare. I had now been thrown into the lion's den and I wasn't sure I liked it. Wasn't I only supposed be there for 'moral support'? We'd never discussed anything like this and yet she'd seemed very quick off the mark. The man turned around and looked at me directly. 'You've never done this sort of thing before, have you?'

Was it that obvious?

He produced a crisp ten-pound note and waved it at me. I swallowed hard. The first thing I thought was that another tenner on top of the one Donna was going to give me would come in very handy right now. But at the same time I couldn't help thinking that either he was going to make me feel cheap or I was going to make him feel cheated because in those days I had a chest as flat as my grandma's washboard. I snatched the money quickly before he could change his mind. A tenner for a quick feel seemed like a bargain. Taking the money was easy. How many times had I let men touch me for free and not even received any pleasure in return? Without realising it at the time, I had just made a decision that was to change the course of the rest of my life.

2

HAPPY DAYS

....

'There are secrets in all families.'
George Farquhar

When I was a child I lived with my family in a council house on one of the more picturesque estates in Sheffield, at the side of a park and a farm. My father was a painter and decorator and mostly worked away from home. Very proud of his roots, he was a stereotypical Yorkshireman complete with large flat cap, broad North Country accent and a sense of frugality. He had a nightly ritual of emptying out all his pockets and 'coppering up' and would even write down the few pence he spent on gum. That, among other things, used to wind my mother up but it amused me, as did the fact that he smoked a pipe just as his own father had done.

Our house seemed to be permanently saturated with the aroma of clean, damp, fresh laundry hanging from a rope pulley in the kitchen. The odour would mingle with the smell of the night's meal on the boil. My mother was always ironing – she was the Queen of Steam! If that dry metallic smell hit my nose when I returned from school I would disappear into the world of toys in my bedroom, where I would dig out some long-lost object worthy of my attention, because once my mother got going there was no stopping her. She would iron socks, knickers, hankies – even my dollies' dresses. I would imitate her with small toy sets: I wanted to be the one who performed all the daily tasks, although that novelty soon wore off once I was old enough to do them for real. And besides, she never really got much thanks for it. The tiny amount that my father gave her to keep house didn't seem much reward either. My pocket-money job was to polish my mother's collection of brass ornaments that she kept on the mantelplace.

My brother was already grown up and I also had a teenage sister. My sister had Sam, a black-and-white puppy. I had a half-dead goldfish that Dad won me at the fair – my brother called it 'Jaws' after a movie he'd just seen at the pictures.

Our home was like millions of others. In the lounge was an orange-and-brown stripy settee. On the fireplace stood a photo from those happy early years. In it I'm at my brother's wedding, in a horrible green dress with a patterned trim. I have knee-high white socks and Milly-Molly-Mandy-type buckle shoes on. One of my feet is turned inwards and my mum is trying to smile for the camera and straighten me up at the same time. My eyes are red from crying because I've just stuck my thumb in my dad's lit pipe. My legs are red because I had just repeated the words 'shotgun wedding' and been smacked for it. My brother looks smart but uncomfortable.

I am very bored. I don't want to smile – I want to pull faces and go to the party. When we get to the reception I have fun running and hiding under the tables with all the other kids. There's lots of food but I have to sit at the kids' table, I can't sit with Mum and Dad. Mum keeps coming up and wiping my face with her tissue.

My Uncle David takes me onto the dancefloor and I sit on his shoulders while he sways drunkenly and my mother shouts at him. My dad puts my little feet in their buckle shoes on his toes and we dance together. I giggle and love it. The cake has canary-yellow icing (well, this *was* the 1970s!) and I want to take the bride-and-groom figures off the top and play with them. But no one lets me touch the cake.

Christmas Day was the only day of the year we ate in the lounge on a covered table, and that made it feel even more special. We didn't have a dining room; we usually had our meals in the kitchen. The year that I was four was my first white Christmas and I was very excited. I didn't know what to do first – frolic in the snow (in my favourite red wellies) or madly rip open all my presents (and then play with the boxes). My mother usually did the cooking but that day both she and Dad created a fantastic meal together.

Then, as we watched *The Wizard of Oz*, Dad grumbled about 'only three bleedin' channels 'n' same rubbish on every year!'

Indignantly he sank into his armchair and snored vigorously as if to show his displeasure. I popped a peanut up his nose, and everyone except Mum (who said I was doing something dangerous) screamed with laughter as he grunted and sneezed the peanut out like a bullet.

Dad was only slightly roused by our hysteria, which fuelled our laughter even more.

My Nan, my mum's mother, was a mixture of the late Barbara Cartland and Dame Edna Everage. Ethel loved to wear fluffy jumpers and bright fluorescent lipsticks. On other occasions, despite being in her late seventies, she would wear jeans – that was Ethel, unpredictable. She was constantly knitting – and airing immovable opinions on everything and everyone. To disguise the ravages of time she would cake on face powder and dye her white hair. The colour on the dye packet said 'chestnut' but somehow it came out a lurid orange – which was ironic because Ethel was very judgemental about other people's style decisions and used to roundly curse punks, or anyone who was a bit different.

Ethel had worked for years as a bus conductress. In retirement she collected glasses from her fans down at the Transport Club. On those nights she never had to buy a drink and she'd still go home sloshed. She'd don her fake-fur coat and large diamanté brooches and whatever else she felt like throwing on. With her raucous humour she'd be the life of the party, entertaining them all till closing time. Although her eccentricity was her greatest charm, she was in many ways a 'typical York-shire lassie' and woe betide you if you dared argue with her! She had a quick stubborn temper, which would dissolve as fast as it flared up. She liked to be loved. She liked to back the horses and to guzzle the rum and the whisky, and her conversations were often punctuated by the sound of her rudely rasping wind.

We all loved her dearly – despite the fact she always drank her tea cold, slurping and dribbling it down her front. Tea to Ethel was an essential part of the daily ritual. To her it was life-giving. Tea for company, tea for sympathy and for any other reason she could think of. There will never be another Ethel: sometimes I feel her presence watching over me and my daughter Lucy. We shall always miss her.

3
FIRST HEARTBREAK
....

He was handsome, a real gentleman.
Her love for him was pure, unselfish.
He was her protector and hero.
'I have to leave':
Quizzically she looked at him.
'I won't be coming back this time.'
The first man to break her heart was her father.
She was five years old . . .

Charlie Daniels

I was sat on the floor playing with my favourite dolly when my mum asked me to go over to her. She put her arm around me tightly and said; 'You know I love you just as much as your brother and sister, don't you?'

I nodded solemnly, staring up at her with trusting eyes.

'Well, you have to be a big brave girl because there's something I have to tell you.'

Nothing could have prepared me for what came next.

'Remember how at the doctor's they kept giving you the wrong surname?'

I nodded again.

'Well, that's because you didn't come from my tummy, but another lady's.'

It was already a day that I would never forget. Then another blow landed.

'And your daddy is moving out. We still love you but we don't love each other any more.'

The break-up of what had seemed until then a happy home was traumatic enough but the bitterest, cruellest blow of all was still to come, albeit unintentionally, from my father. He stood with his suitcases, ready to leave for the last time, hampered by my frantic and hysterical attempts to prevent him from going. I clung to his leg, a tiny limpet on a solid rock, screaming wildly, purple with pain and rage.

'Don't go, Daddy – I still love you!'

'I have to go, I'm sorry.' His throat constricted, choking him as the words escaped.

'Then take me with you!' I threw myself at him in desperation. I'd have done the same if it had been my mum: I was torn. I just didn't want to be deserted by either of them.

He turned around to face me and said something that to him was just straightforward yet to me was life-shattering.

'I didn't sign for you – your mother did.'

What did he mean, 'sign for me'? Was he talking about the registered parcels he used to send home when he was working away?

Even once I knew the truth, I never thought of my family as my 'foster' family. To me they were the real deal. After my brother got married and Dad left, my sister went off to university. She and Mum had fought endlessly after Dad went: she wanted to be with him and resented my mum for winning custody of us kids. My dad had shacked up with a much younger woman, younger than my brother but older than my sister. Mum was very hurt by that. She was never the same again. I went to visit Dad and his new woman once, but it didn't work out – there was too much hurt between us.

Now it was just Mum and me left and she seemed to lose the will to live. She stopped wearing make-up and bothering with her appearance. Her blonde hair went grey and even her blue eyes seemed to grow dull. Her depression increased: now there were whole days in bed and a string of illnesses, all somehow linked to the sadness that filled her. On her better days she was neurotic and housework became an obsession, as if she was trying to wipe away the memories. In her efforts to stay clear of the pit of despair she started on tablets: pink ones, blue ones, Valium, Ativan – bottles and bottles of pills.

'For my nerves,' she would say if anyone asked.

Mum's behaviour grew worse with every passing year. Although it came to seem normal to me it was still agonising to live with. I would never know what to expect when I arrived home. There would be occasional days of sunshine, when she would be warm and bright and full of life again and we would laugh and joke and play fight. But such times were rare. I would sneak into the house quietly from school, treading on eggshells, and on those good days I would feel instant relief that my old mum was home.

Other days I would make the mistake of running

home, full of excitement and joy, only to find the house in total darkness. All the curtains would be drawn to shut out the rest of the world. Mum would scream and shout at me whatever I did or said. At the bottom of our stairs was a door. Dad had put it on when I was a baby, to stop me crawling up. He'd fixed a bolt at its top. By now I had started to react to Mum's bad days. Sometimes I would lie on the floor just kicking and screaming. When she yelled so did I, and I would blame her for my father leaving – we would goad each other to fever pitch. There were times when she couldn't even scream, let alone cope any more, and so she would make me sit on the stairs in the dark with the door bolted. That was the worst and she knew it. Once I crept up to the toilet because I needed a wee, but all the floorboards creaked and gave me away so it ended with her red angry face an inch from mine. After that I always just sat there, perfectly still.

Once Mum broke down in the middle of making tea. On the small transistor radio one of the songs – 'Everything I Own' – that she'd played endlessly since Dad had gone came on. It resulted in her collapsing on the floor in a heap, sobbing. I tried to console her by telling her that I hated my dad for what he'd done to her, but she responded by screaming at me and saying that I didn't understand anything.

I came home another day to find her in the bedroom – this time I couldn't rouse her. She was hanging off the end of the bed, lifelessly clutching an empty pill bottle. As a sensible ten-year-old, I knew exactly what to do.

Keep calm. Think. Ring for the ambulance. Give

Mummy's full name and address to the nice lady on the phone. The lady asked me if Mummy was still breathing. I thought so.

A neighbour took me into her house as they took Mum's limp body away in the ambulance. I knew it was my fault. I couldn't make Mum happy. I was a naughty girl. I couldn't love her enough. I knew this because that morning before I'd gone to school we'd had a row. I told her that even if Daddy didn't love her any more she should be happy because I loved her more than anything. It didn't even matter I came from that other lady's tummy, she was my only true mummy and so I was mixed up and hurt when she turned around and said it didn't make any difference and that she wished she were dead. I would be twenty-seven years old before I understood the deep abyss and roller-coaster ride of depression. Back then, all I knew was that I couldn't make her happy.

Physically Mum recovered from the overdose, but the depression lingered for even more years. The two of us were locked head-on in a collision course, bound for serious mutual resentment and inevitable destruction.

4

GETTING A REPUTATION

....

'*The purest treasure mortal times afford / Is spotless reputation . . .*'

Shakespeare

By the time I was twelve I thought that I was pretty much a grown woman. So Mum and I were trapped in a constant battle of wills. While most kids were struggling with acne and braces I was turning my attention to other things. I would leave the house looking like a schoolgirl but as soon as I was out of sight I would take off the clothes that Mum had put me in, cover my clock in enough make-up to plaster a ceiling and slip on a lethally short skirt. I can't have been that subtle about it because Mum soon cottoned on and would call me back into the house, vigorously smudging the make-up around my face with a cold, wet flannel. I soon learned that waterproof mascara is only waterproof once it comes *off* your eyelashes.

Mum would send me off to school in a duffel coat and plastic boots with laces. She called them 'Derry boots', whatever they were. They were bloody awful and I looked like a fisherman in them. When they started to leak, she would put Mother's Pride bread bags on the inside to keep my feet dry. When everyone else was wearing pretty little ankle socks she would insist that I wore thick patterned ones pulled up to my knees. When all the other girls were wearing the latest skirt styles, mine were always an unflattering A-line. I just felt awkward – a total geek – and the other kids singled me out even more. I was bullied and called names, even spat on a few times.

Rather than withdrawing into myself, though, I became louder in my quest for attention, drawn to other loud characters and misfits. I had one particular friend, a tomboy skinhead called Tuz, who had the same ambition as me: to be different.

I was also developing an interest in boys, and one in particular. His nickname was Remy and he was a seventeen-year-old skinhead. He must have known that I was crazy about him, although he paid me no attention at all until one night when he asked if he could escort me home from the youth club. He was waiting outside for me, smoking and trying to look hard. I was only allowed to go to the club if I walked there and back with a girlfriend. I knew Mum would be furious if she found out I was with a boy but it was too tempting an offer to refuse. I was in love and couldn't believe my luck.

We cut across the pitch-black school fields and sat chatting on the school steps for a while. When Remy kissed me it took my breath away, but then he shocked me by thrusting his tongue violently into my mouth. I pushed him away, asking him to slow down.

'You know you want it,' he responded angrily. 'Don't fuck me around!'

He started fumbling with my top, popping the buttons, and I felt panicked. Then his hand shot up my skirt and I tried to fight him off, realising that something was very wrong. At that point the only other person who had ever been near my knickers was Mum on washday.

'You're just a little cockteaser!' Remy snarled. 'I'm only doing this for a bet, anyway.'

I was hurt and confused by the sudden change of mood. The next thing I knew I was pinned against the wall, his free hand around my throat making me choke and splutter.

'You stupid little girl!' he shouted angrily and, in a final vicious act of savagery, he stabbed his fingers inside me so sharply that it sent a shock wave of pain through my entire body. I felt my skin tear and a trickle of warm blood ran down the inside of my legs.

Emphasising his point with a sharp slap across the face, Remy warned me that he'd kill me if I told anyone what had happened. Then he let me go. I stumbled home as fast as I could, dashing straight upstairs past the living room, where Mum was watching *Hill Street Blues*. I was too frightened to tell her because I knew how angry she would be that I hadn't come home with my friend as I was supposed to. So she never knew what happened that evening until years later.

But everyone else seemed to know and the other kids started shouting 'Slag!' and 'Slut!' at me when I walked past the bus shelter, jeering at me by my surname as if I didn't have any other name. I hadn't done anything wrong but already I had a reputation.

The boy who took my virginity lived on the next estate. I was just thirteen and he was seventeen. He had dark greasy hair and his fringe seemed permanently in his face. He was on a mission to conquer me since I'd now been labelled 'tight' and 'a tease' because I hadn't lived up to my earlier labels of 'slag' and 'slut'.

Like many other girls I caved in to pressure, not lust. He had coaxed and cajoled me for weeks. I wanted a boyfriend. He wanted to stick it in me and fuck off. And he did. The event itself was painful, brief and unsatisfying. I was left feeling empty and hostile towards him – and a complete idiot for giving in.

I was called the estate bike well before I earned the reputation. I was lost, unable to work out what it was that the world wanted from me. I only ever wanted love, approval and warmth but I had no idea what would be the best way of winning it. All I got for my naivety was a series of men of all ages who would tell me whatever I wanted to hear so that they could get into my knickers.

Head games.

Pushing. Pulling.

'Will she, won't she?'

And, most of the time, she did.

I felt an instant gratification whenever any boy showed any interest in me. I didn't crave the actual sex act, whatever it might involve, just the attention that came with it. It was like a quick hit of adrenalin for my low self-esteem. My superficial self-confidence and strong character meant that I came across as being brazen, while underneath lay bottomless pits of insecurity. At that stage I was never the instigator of sex, but I used to get giddy around boys, which meant that they almost always responded sexually.

Like most young girls I was romantic and believed that one day my prince would come, that I would marry a wonderful man and live happily ever after. But after my first few sexual encounters I began to accept that this sort of raw experience was probably the reality of how my life was going to be. Despite my apparent confidence, my self-esteem had been slaughtered and I started to think I was worthless.

5
STRAY BITCH

....

'All women become like their mothers. That is their tragedy.'

Oscar Wilde

Everything I did seemed to be wrong for my mother. She was always on the warpath. Not for any logical reason that I could work out. I had come to resent everything about her: the mood swings, her endless days in bed and her total lack of lust for life – it was all pissing me off. I wasn't able to be myself, like my friends could. Not allowed any make-up or modern clothes, I felt like a teen geek because of her. She thought that she was protecting me, keeping me 'her little girl'. I hated it and I was starting to hate her.

I dreaded going home. I couldn't bear Mum yelling at me and lashing out. More and more frequently our heated discussions turned into screaming matches and physical battles. I so badly wanted to hit her back, although I knew that I shouldn't, but she just kept pushing me further and further and I got more and more aggressive with my reaction until I forced her to breaking point.

I could cope with the physical pain, but mentally I was close to snapping.

Mum seemed to have done nothing but store up anger and bitterness since the day my dad had left. The constant illness and depression seemed to make her totally unreasonable.

One night when I was thirteen we were in the kitchen together and things started to become more than heated.

She was in my face again, shouting me down. I couldn't bear it any longer: I could feel my fists clenching and my blood starting to boil. She pushed me against the sink, knocking the wind out of me.

'You're turning into your real mother! You're going to be a slag just like her if you don't watch it!' she yelled.

Smack! My hand slapped her face. I was instantly sorry for what I'd done – but I didn't want to back down. She glared at me angrily, recoiling and holding her cheek.

'You'll pay for this . . .'

'Yeah? Well, so will you!'

I was mixed up. I didn't know whether I should scream or cry.

My brother must have driven like a bat out of hell as soon as he heard what had happened. I nearly jumped out the window as he burst through our door. I was in total shock. His face was dark and glowering like an impending thunderstorm.

'Get down to my car – now!' he boomed.

He was usually a gentle man, but that day his voice was deep and loud like a factory foreman's. I sat beside him in the car, my knees shaking uncontrollably. I'd never seen him that way before and it scared me. We sat in silence.

Finally he spoke his mind.

'You just don't realise how lucky you are . . . I know things aren't always easy, but you'd better shape up!'

I looked down at the car floor.

'Look at me when I'm talking to you!'

My eyes welled with tears as I looked up but he didn't stop . . .

'You came from shit!'

I had never heard my brother swear.

'She's *my* mother – if you ever lay a hand on her again I'll kill you! You've been given a good home and all you've ever done is bite the hand that fed you!'

His rejection tore me apart. Sensing my obvious distress he softened his tone a little, but it was too late. The words were out and couldn't be taken back.

'Look, I know what she can be like . . .'

But he didn't know, not really, because she wasn't the same woman he'd lived with before he went away to start his own family.

My heart felt as if it was cracking wide open. The truth was out. All those years when I thought he'd loved me as his baby sister I'd just been some stray bitch they'd taken pity on. It felt as if he'd snatched away my entire identity, right there, in the front seat of his car.

Even now I still think of him as my true brother. It's in my heart that one day at least he will just say that it is so, but both he and our sister have broken off all contact with me. So they have no way of knowing how proud of them both I am.

My brother was always ambitious and has stood by his family and raised the two lovely girls that I once knew as my nieces. I'm only sad that once my life went off the rails I never saw any of them again.

I cannot forget those words he said to me. But I still love him, forgive him and assert my right to be his sister through unconditional love.

6
HOME TRUTHS
....

'And he who gives a child a home / Builds palaces in Kingdom come.'

John Masefield

The day when Mum finally threw me out was fucking awful. She rang social services and demanded that Joel – my social worker – should come for me immediately. As is the case for most foster children, I had had a social worker for most of my life. Joel tried his best to support me and even tried to give me a hug. But what I really needed was my mum's love and cuddles. I needed to know that however cross she was with me she still loved me. He seemed just as bemused by it all as I was. I liked him: he reminded me of Tom Baker when he was Doctor Who. He even wore the same endless multicoloured scarf. By the time he came to fetch me my mum had put every item of clothing, every toy and every other thing I had ever possessed, into black bags. He was a very laid-back man but that day he had a strange expression on his face as we silently stuffed as much as we possibly could into the back of his clapped-out mustard-coloured estate car.

'I'm sorry, I just can't fit anything else in.'

I stared at him in silence but he didn't seem to understand – my pain wasn't about 'things'. Physically it felt as if she had reached right inside me and wrenched my guts out. It hurt me that she felt that at any time she could just give me back to the system. As difficult as it had been for both of us, she was all I had and now I knew I couldn't even rely on that. I couldn't believe that this wasn't all a bad dream.

Thankfully the children's home wasn't completely unfamiliar as I had been there once before when Mum had been in hospital. On that first visit Joel had shown me around and had introduced me to everyone. I'd returned to Mum full of surprise, having expected to be incarcerated in the orphanage from *Oliver!*

'You won't believe it,' I enthused. 'It's just a big house with a big telly and a pool table . . .' (Not that I could play pool.) '. . . You get regular pocket money – more as you get bigger! And a clothing allowance so you can get new clothes!'

It wasn't that I was ungrateful for what my mum did for me. I think I was just genuinely surprised by how nice it was – but of course it didn't beat having a mum.

My words had been taken as an insult.

'*You like it so much, go and live there.*'

But now I stared out of the car's rear window as my home slowly disappeared.

As we pulled into the drive of the children's home there were some kids playing footy. I recognised a couple of them from my previous visit. They stopped and stared, partly, I guessed, because they were surprised to see me again and partly at the car so fully loaded with all my stuff. I felt ashamed and guilty, as if I didn't deserve any of it. The deputy head was on duty that day and the first thing she did was throw her arms around me and bury my head in her huge bosom. I shook with relief – strange as it seemed, I felt safe. I cried my eyes out, until I finally lost my voice.

During the following years love was replaced by care, but there was real warmth with all the staff. I spent most of my teenage years going back and forth between my foster mum's place and the children's home. I didn't know if I was coming or going and it was an emotionally charged time but I can honestly say that I look back on my time at the home with fondness. Luckily I was able to continue going to the same school, so at least there was some continuity.

It was nice to have playmates. I'd always been such a loner. In the home we were all pretty much like a big family, apart from the occasional falling-out or scrap in the garden.

On my original visit, I'd made a new friend, whose real name was Jason but who we all called JJ. He was a handsome black kid who was hilariously funny and really good at impressions, modelling himself on the then-popular Eddie Murphy. The first time I'd ever seen him he was on the front lawn, spinning around – upside down, on a piece of lino. Apparently doing something he said was called 'break-dancing'.

JJ would cheer me up with his vivid impressions of the staff and their mannerisms. He'd spent his entire life in care because social services had said he couldn't go to white foster parents and that his 'cultural needs' would be better served with a black family – but one had never become available. One of the black lads in the home next door said it was because if he did Jason would 'turn into a coconut'. I struggled with that one until someone explained that he didn't mean an actual coconut but someone who was black on the outside and white in the middle – but at that time I still didn't get it.

As the years went by, kids came and went. Sometimes you thought your heart would split when you had to say goodbye. I never got used to that bit.

When I came back to the home from school, instead of worrying about what mood Mum was in I would now be wondering who would be on duty. There was one member of staff who we only knew for a brief time, but she had a devastating impact on us all. She was a young woman, petite, timid and shy. We used to laugh and tease her because she'd do wacky things like wear rainbow-coloured wellies and put colours in her hair to match. She wasn't much good at being assertive so we all used to give her the run-around, which wasn't very kind really. So we all felt guilty and responsible when we heard what she'd done. This oddball woman who was only in her twenties, who wouldn't have hurt a fly, had locked herself in a garage and gassed herself. We were all reassured that it wasn't our fault and that we were the one thing she had held out so long for. She'd had a complex life with many twists and turns and had been badly disillusioned after the end of her first disastrous lesbian relationship. (Yes, that revelation was a bit of a talking point with us narrow-minded kids.)

The staff formed genuine attachments with most of us and were careful not to cause bitterness or resentment with unfair judgements based on personal feelings. If they did have favourites, most of them kept it well hidden. However, one woman came to work there who did upset the equilibrium. 'Mrs B' was a short-tempered woman. She was the only member of staff I would see handing out the odd slap. It was as bad as being at home when she was around. Back then we didn't know that we could do anything about it – I'm not sure whether any of us would have rocked the boat, anyway. She *definitely* showed unfair favouritism – always towards the boys. She had daughters and made no secret of the fact that she'd always wanted a son.

At one time a cute blond-haired eight-year-old boy joined us. He might have had the face of an angel but in reality he had severe behavioural difficulties. As Mrs B grew more and more obviously attached to him her judgement became coloured. She would let him get away with murder and occasionally stick up for him even if he was obviously in the wrong.

But for all her faults she did possess some redeeming qualities. She was a damn fine cook, that being her original profession, and she could make a silk purse from a sow's ear, so to speak. She was always the one who would mend your uniform, sew buttons on or make new curtains for your room.

One time I came home from school and Mrs B was on duty.

'The book,' she said – the Communications Book was a sort of diary, kept in the office for the staff – 'says you've booked an extension for Monday night so you can come home later after your school disco.'

'Yes,' I said, 'but I don't think I'll be going.'

'Why ever not?'

'I don't have anything decent to wear.'

All the clothes I'd brought from home were old-fashioned: nothing modern, and all my clothing allowance from the home had already been used up. I showed Mrs B the pathetic ra-ra skirt and boob tube that I'd attempted to make in sewing. She wasn't the first person to laugh at my efforts. Apart from the state of it, it didn't leave much to the imagination. I'd always been picked on at school for my gawky image and now I was suddenly dreading the party of the year.

In those days there was a thing called 'the clothing order book', which was the old way of doing things before allowances were introduced. The home could revert to it in 'emergency situations' but it was a humiliating experience, which was why it was eventually done away with. The matron of the home had offered to let me use it, but the idea alone gave me nightmares. You could only go to the one store and all the staff there would know that you were from the home. Half would watch you like a hawk just in case you were a thief from one of the 'naughty' homes and the others would look at you and smile patronisingly, or pat you on the head. One once asked me 'How is the orphanage?' But far worse than all that were the clothes themselves, which were really formal and stiff-looking, and when you wore them the other kids would laugh at you.

But Mrs B had a plan . . . 'I'm sure we can sort something out by Monday,' she said brightly.

Maybe, I thought, she'll bring something that belongs to one of her daughters. I cringed at the idea of yet another outdated hand-me-down. I'd had enough of my sister's old things, which were always out of fashion by the time I got them.

The following week I came home from school and Mrs B had a huge old pan bubbling on the stove. She produced a smelly disintegrating old lime-green dress that she'd found in a second-hand shop. I didn't bother to look at it properly when she pulled it out of the bag – I just ran to my room and cried. Unaware of my reaction, Mrs B submerged the dress in the pan full of water while the other kids watched in amazement as she added a palm-size tin of 'Midnight Blue' dye. The dress was then hung up in the boiler house to dry. The next day she took it home, where she made several layers of netted underskirt and repaired it until it was like new.

On the disco night, she presented me with the finished dress. I was expecting the worst and I couldn't stop myself from gasping when she pulled it out of the bag. She had created an exquisite full-circle off-the-shoulder ball gown in taffeta – it was stunning. She'd even dyed a pair of full-length gloves and a stole to match. She then made me up in glamorous 1940s-style make-up and piled my hair onto my head in a tousled 'bun'. I was transformed, no longer the ugly duckling.

We stopped off at my foster-mother's house on the way to school to show her. She had tears in her eyes and told me I looked like Audrey Hepburn – not that I knew who *she* was!

'Wait there,' Mum said and disappeared upstairs, coming down carrying a little box. 'Here, wear these: they're real pearl-drop earrings that Dad bought – no wonder they say pearls for tears.'

We both laughed at the silly superstition and she

carefully put them in my ears, the perfect finishing touch. I felt so proud when I got on the bus and for the first time the driver asked me my age.

Would *he* be there? 'He' was Ian. Everyone in school fancied him. I'd had a huge crush on him for over a year, which meant that if another boy at school had looked at me I would never have known it.

I walked apprehensively down the school corridor. The other girls had on the latest teen fashions and looked pretty good, but I felt like a million dollars. Everyone turned to stare and my heart almost stopped. Then I realised that it was because they were wondering who I was. They hadn't even recognised me!

I guess there will always be kids who are more popular than the rest – I had just never been one of them. Mostly I'd got attention from being with the wrong crowd or being loud. My first dance made me feel special – it was with my form teacher, who could see that I'd entered alone (not in a pack like the others).

After the dance the head of my year served me a cola in a plastic cup. As I put the 20p in a tin he called out my name. I wondered what I'd done wrong.

'I didn't recognise you!' he said. 'You look so different!'

I thanked him, blushed and started to walk away, hugely embarrassed. He shouted after me.

'I really mean it, and do you know what? You're the best-dressed lady in here!'

'Lady!' No one had ever called me that! I wanted to cry. I had never even been noticed at school before. I'd always been the one with the pudding-basin haircut and freckles, a turned-up nose and a big gob. Tonight I was a Hollywood starlet and I loved it.

I wasn't the only one who underwent a change that night. My tomboy mate Tuz wore a skirt and make-up for the first and last time in her life. We stuck together all night, causing shock waves with our transformations.

A male voice came from behind. 'I'd like the next dance, please.'

I turned around to face Ian. I thought my head would explode!

'Can I just go to the toilet?' I said.

'Cool,' he said, and winked.

I ran off up the corridor. Everyone had seen him come over to me and I was embarrassed.

The toilets felt like sanctuary. I carefully lifted my skirts to use the loo and sat down, the cubicle seeming to spin around me. I washed my hands in the tiny pot-sink and had to force myself to concentrate. I fixed my face in the small mirror over the sink, took a deep breath and held my head high as I tried to walk out with confidence.

Ian took my arm as we moved onto the dance floor. I floated, as everyone stood back smiling. It was right there and then that it all turned into the high-school prom scene from the film *Carrie*. The whole school was laughing at me! As I spun around to run off, I discovered my faux pas. After I'd been to the toilet I'd tucked my dress into the back of my tights – *and* I was trailing toilet roll all the way back from the loos. I ran from the hall in floods of tears, my balloon of self-confidence cruelly punctured. From that day forward the only pearls I ever wore were the proverbial pearl necklaces the clients showered me with.

7

LOST AND FOUND

....

'*Man . . . still bears in his bodily frame the indelible stamp of his lowly origin.*'

Charles Darwin

A few months after my disaster at the disco my social worker made an appointment to come and see me. I knew from the way everyone was talking to me that there was going to be something different about this visit. For a start, we had our chat in the matron's office – that never normally happened! I sat on a little wooden chair, staring around the room as if it was the first time I'd ever been through the door. Us kids weren't usually allowed in there. I was fourteen years old by then.

Joel just didn't seem his usual happy self: more solemn and preoccupied, he sat in the big chair across the desk from me. I stared at his balding, bespectacled head. He was wearing a bright knitted jumper with an unironed shirt underneath. He produced a tatty orange cardboard file from his worn leather briefcase and nervously flicked through it. It suddenly hit me – maybe I was in deep shit! My head started banging.

'I don't really know how to say this,' he said in an awkward bumbling sort of way.

'Am I in trouble?'

'No, no! Erm . . .' He fiddled with his ear. 'Your mother wants to see you.'

Now I was confused. He cleared his throat before he dropped the bombshell.

'Your natural mother, the one who gave birth to you!'

I didn't know what to think, or how I felt. I had recently been given access to my files. Joel had sat down with me as I had read all about why my birth mother had had to give me up. It was a sordid story and there had been lots of hints as to what sort of woman she was, but I hadn't been ready to take in the whole picture. There was so much about it that I still didn't understand. Everyone who is parted from their birth parents dreams that they were rich and beautiful, and fantasises that one day they will return to rescue their children from their dull or unhappy lives. No one wants to lose that little ray of hope, and now I was able to tell myself there was a chance that it was going to happen to me. She had realised the mistake she had made in giving me away.

By the time the long-awaited day arrived, when I was going to meet my 'real' mum, I was feeling almost sick with excitement. The matron fussed around me all day and the lounge in the children's home was laid out with a nice spread. I was wearing my best outfit. In the room sat the matron, my key worker, Joel and me. There were two empty chairs.

When Doreen walked in through the door I suddenly

felt a deep fear grip me. Who was this woman? No way was *she* my mum – surely there had been a mistake. I only hoped that the other kids hadn't seen her or I would die of embarrassment. Her long dark greasy hair looked like it hadn't been cut in years. She wore a tatty old dress with buttons missing. The sandals on her feet revealed the dirt under her toenails. Her feet must have been freezing – it was February.

In with my mother came another surprise, a scruffy little urchin who looked about eight years old. She was extraordinarily pretty, a real-life blonde-haired angel, and so painfully shy. She looked at me and smiled. As soon as I saw her sparkling blue eyes, I swear the whole room filled with sunshine. She looked like a young Hayley Mills.

'This is Amanda,' I was told. 'She's your half-sister.'

I had a half-sister? I looked at her and then at Doreen. Couldn't she have cleaned herself up to meet me? And she was so loud!

The other kids were playing outside. Were they laughing because of what they could see and hear? I felt my face burning with embarrassment.

Doreen dramatically ran over to me, bawling and sobbing. She grabbed me hard, pulling me out of my chair and trying to hug me. I just stood there, trembling, not knowing what to do, not knowing how I should feel. She didn't seem to understand that I wouldn't be as emotional as her. She pulled away, shaking my shoulders slightly while looking into my face.

'Moira, Moira!'

Who was Moira? It was the name she had put on my

birth certificate and I hated it. It felt and sounded so alien to me. My mouth was dry and I couldn't find any words. I tried to look into Doreen's brown eyes. One kept focused on me but the other had a cast and wandered. As she finally let go, I just stood there, moving my body weight from one leg to the other until Joel finally saved me.

'Why don't you both relax a little?' he suggested. 'Take a seat.'

In all the hours I'd spent imagining what this meeting would be like, I had never come close to picturing the emotional scenes and melodramas that Doreen played out as she filled me in on my background without me even having to ask.

'Your father was involved in gang fighting,' she shrieked, launching straight into her story. 'He was killed in cold blood . . . decapitated!'

Her story didn't sound quite the same as the one in the file I had read, which had simply said that my real father had been killed and had not given any gory details. I asked her why she had given me up as a baby.

'No!' she shouted. 'You don't understand! Social services wronged me!'

Doreen explained that she had given birth to a boy before she'd had me. He'd been born in the 1960s when single mothers had not been the norm. The file I'd read had insinuated that she was an unfit mother. The baby died and Doreen said that he'd died of an infantile convulsion – a fact, she told me, that I could check with the death certificate. In fact, the file showed little documented evidence apart from such judgemental comments as Doreen being 'a promiscuous woman of dubious character'.

When my foster-mother had tried to adopt me, social services had noted that Doreen was somewhere in Scotland, a fact she vehemently denied.

'When you were a baby it was the beginning of the 1970s,' Joel explained. 'Social services were not as regulated as they are today. In those days workers would sometimes bend the rules a little – in the interests of the child.'

He looked a little embarrassed as he turned towards Doreen.

'Look, I know it's not right – and I hate to admit it – but it's possible that the social worker concerned felt the need to protect your baby. Perhaps because you opposed the adoption.'

Doreen carried on ranting and Joel and I just stared at each other blankly. To be fair, there were some other serious inaccuracies on my file that made Joel suspect that some 'do-gooder' working in social services had deliberately changed the records on paper to ensure that I was taken away from Doreen and put into a safe place. Joel reckoned that this plan could've been aided by making her seem a worse mother than she actually was.

Maybe Doreen giving me up had been a blessing in disguise for everyone, including me. But I was confused about how I felt. She certainly wasn't the sort of mother I had been fantasising about coming to rescue me and I was very unsure whether I would ever want to live with her.

What did she expect from me? Did she think that I

would instantly love her? That we would start over again? Did she think I would feel a bond? I couldn't even call her 'mother': to me she was only 'Doreen', let alone my 'real' mum!'

Now that she'd made contact, Doreen wanted me to visit her and a few weeks later Joel and I pulled up outside her house on one of the most notorious estates in Sheffield.

'We'll be lucky if the wheels are still on the car when we come out,' Joel muttered as he locked the car, glancing nervously around him.

It was the sort of place where kids do crime for kicks and television producers make well-meaning social documentaries about it all. Burned-out shells of cars decorated what green spaces there were, and old furniture had been casually dumped at the roadside to be claimed later by someone else or set on fire by the kids.

When we got to the house my natural gran was there. It was the first time that I'd met her. She was slim, frail and had a strong Belfast accent. She was also stone-deaf. I wondered if that was why Doreen shouted so loudly all the time, or maybe it was Doreen who had deafened Gran in the first place!

Most people would have had a tidy-up when they were expecting visitors but not Doreen. Newspapers were stacked to the ceiling in the lounge. Why? She didn't have a dog or a real fire! I thought the carpet was plain brown until she moved a chair and I could see that really it was pink with flowers. I should have realised its condition by the way it squelched when I walked on it.

I cautiously went up the threadbare stairs to the toilet. I liked the duck-egg green colour on the bathroom walls. But there were black handprints where she had got out of the stained bath. I didn't sit on the toilet seat. My foster-mum had always told me to be careful on other people's toilets, but this was the first time I'd taken notice of that warning. I wanted to wash my hands in the chipped pot-sink but there was no soap, the sink was thick with grease and the only towel-like object was dirty, dry and encrusted.

As I came out of the bathroom my curiosity got the better of me and I crept towards the door that I assumed must lead to Doreen's bedroom. She hadn't offered to show me around when we arrived and the suspense was killing me. Amanda appeared silently at the top of the stairs, probably hoping to get some time on her own with her new-found big sister. She didn't say anything but she must have sensed my disgust at the state of the house. She quietly pushed open Doreen's bedroom door for me to look inside. As the stench hit me I clapped my hand over my mouth and nose.

I saw a long shiny 1960s dresser – well, the front of it, anyway, because the top was completely covered in inches of cigarette butts. Dust hung in the air, sparkling like glitter with the light from the window. Amanda told me that Doreen had bragged that there was one butt for every morning of her life, since the day she'd started smoking. No wonder her fingers were so yellow.

In the corner a pile of clothes sat rotting like compost. I discovered that Doreen had a habit of buying second-hand clothes when she got her giro every other Tuesday.

The dirty clothes then went into a pile to be recycled, worn again at a later date without being washed.

Amanda then led me into her own tiny room. It was the tidiest one in the house and as she saw my surprise she told me that she cleaned it herself. She had a single bed with an old green candlewick bedspread. There was one doll and a few books and games all neatly stacked in a small pile under the window. Nothing like my bedroom at my foster home, which resembled Hamley's toy store and was serviced by my foster-mum.

'Where are all your other toys?' I asked. Amanda just shrugged.

We looked out of her window at some kids hanging around outside.

'They shout at her, you know,' Amanda said, 'when we go down the street.'

I looked at her, this delicate flower on a lonely rock, waiting for her to go on. But she fell silent and I found it hard to imagine what her life must be like.

When it came time to leave I promised I would stay in touch. I really did want to get to know Gran and Amanda better, but I didn't really want to see Doreen again. In all honesty, I was repulsed by my natural mother and didn't want anything more to do with her if I could help it.

8

SECRETS AND LIES

....

'All happy families resemble each other. Each unhappy
family is unhappy in its own way.'

Leo Tolstoy

I sat in front of my careers teacher with my gaze fixed
firmly on him in eager anticipation. He didn't give me
any eye contact in return – he was too busy shuffling his
papers around. God knew how many girls like me had
passed in front of him over the years.

'Well,' I said in answer to his question, 'I'm not sure
exactly, but I know I want to do something different.
When I lived in the kids' home I was chairperson of The
Young People in Care Group – I enjoyed that! Oh, and I
loved the lunchtime photography club!'

He had only asked the question out of habit: he hadn't been
listening to my enthusiastic replies as I proudly listed my
interests and achievements. He didn't want to hear how Ethel
had given me my first camera for Christmas a few years before
and how much I had subsequently enjoyed the school camera
club. His tone now turned to one of frustration.

'Get real, girl. What type of shop would you like to
work in?'

He'd already put my file away and was looking at his watch. Many years later whenever I thought about his remark I smiled ironically. I often wonder what he would have done if I'd known what I know now and replied, 'A knocking shop!'

Throughout school I'd never appeared academically brilliant, but I possessed bags of superficial confidence and enthusiasm. My reports were always full of comments like: 'Great potential, lacks concentration – needs to talk less and listen more.' (Maybe it should have read 'Enthusiastic oral contributions!')

I finished school with only two 'O' levels and with a place at college lined up. The course was a very basic social-care one – which I later found out only enabled me to be an overqualified care assistant. It wasn't what I had really wanted to do but, like most kids, I listened as adults 'brought me down to earth'. Why does everyone have to be brought down to earth so soon? Why can't they be allowed to fly after their dreams, at least for a while?

I left the home at just turned sixteen. Foolishly, I couldn't wait for my freedom. I'd spent a few months living in the flat attached to the rear of the home. The idea was supposed to be that this way I would get used to non-domestic bliss and work out how to look after myself so that I could survive on my own.

The first flat I had after that was on the top floor of a tower block. It was on the same estate I'd grown up on. A tiny two-bar electric fire greedily gobbled electric tokens, which I could barely afford to replace. For the first year I had scraps of carpet strewn around the cold tiled floor and all the furniture was second-hand, but I was as happy as a pig in shit. I finally had my own place and could come and go as and when I pleased, without having to endure my mum's disapproval or worry about the rules of the care home. I was independent, with none of the restraints and boundaries that I had found so irksome as a child.

That was when I fell pregnant with Lucy and when I first met Donna. I had no idea how I was going to be able to earn enough money to keep myself and a baby alive, let alone get us out of this terrible flat and into something half-decent.

Ethel must have known I needed to talk the day I went round to break the news that I was pregnant.

'Put kettle on, then,' she said, 'I knows tha's got summat on thi mind.'

Tea served, I sat nervously waiting for the opportunity to tell the grand matriarch my news – when suddenly, in true Ethel style, she piped up with, 'Well! So I hear you've got a bun in the oven – are you getting married, then?'

I wasn't and I told her so. I felt as if I was playing out a scene in a 1940s melodrama. I braced myself for the lecture.

'I'll knit in lemon, and it won't matter if it's a boy or a girl!'

What! Did I really just hear that?

'But, Nan . . .' I was gobsmacked!

'Oh, I know your mother doesn't approve, she's already made that clear, but you can't shut t' barn door after the hoorse has bolted!'

My mother's view was: 'You've made your bed, now

49

you have to lie in it!' She had made it clear that if I was so stupid as to let myself get pregnant and too stubborn to get an abortion, then she was washing her hands of me. She had said a few more things about how I was turning out.

I was totally stunned at Ethel's reaction. I felt a great surge of love for this tiny, powerful woman who was now my closest ally. She looked at me with her head cocked sympathetically to one side.

'She shouldn't 'ave said that, though; I mean, that about you turning into your *real* mother. Cruel, that – your *real* mum might of made mistakes an' all but her mistakes, see, they was *our* gain.'

And with that Ethel grabbed me and smothered me in her luscious luminous sticky lipstick, my cheek now stinging scarlet. Strange, those words – *real mum* – because to me Pam was my mum and Doreen – well, she was my birth mother. But there was no denying my connection to Doreen when I looked in the mirror.

'I fell on (got pregnant), tha knows, befoor we wa married, like.' Ethel dropped another surprise bomb.

I looked at her closely: my mother had never let that one slip.

'Tha knows what's up wi' thi mother?' I had a feeling she was going to tell me. I liked it when she confided in me as if I were an equal. 'During war, when she was little like, her dad wasn't around, see . . .'

I looked at her, trying to work out what she was trying to tell me as she stared at the floor.

'Well,' she went on eventually, 'things weren't always

so easy like, an' we 'ad to do what we 'ad to do, if tha knows wot I mean.'

I didn't and it must have shown on my face.

'Well,' Ethel sighed, realising that she was going to have to spell it out. 'Yer mum, she had a lot of, shall we say . . . *uncles* like, and sometimes I'd sleep wi'landlord just to pay rent – but tha mustn't tell 'er I told thee!'

I was flabbergasted and strangely proud she had confided in me.

'An' we lived in hovels an'all, they were all crawling, them places. Mostly we all lived in one room. And there were times we 'ad to do a runner an' all! Moved from pillar to post, she was!'

Suddenly I knew why my mum had lived in the same house for so long, and it also explained her zest for cleaner living.

I loved Ethel, my Nan, so very much: we were great friends and came to rely on each other. We had a secret conspiracy going against my mother. We used to sit in the taproom of the local and I'd run out of the back door of the pub (even when I was nine months pregnant) and into the back door of the bookies to put a bob on Nan's *round robins* and we'd feel dead chuffed that we'd got away with it – like kids nicking candy. Ethel loved me, and later my baby, unconditionally.

At just turned seventeen I made a discovery. I didn't exist! Well, not to the government, anyhow. There was no National Insurance record for me. I was presented with a stark choice. I had to make my name legal, but it could be any name I fancied.

Because I'd never been formally adopted, 'Moira' and my birth mother's surname were still on most of my records whereas 'Julie' (or 'Juliet' at college) and my foster-family surname were on the rest. I had three choices. Either I could revert back to Moira – a name I had never used – or I could stick with Julie, but I would have to sign a change-of-name deed to do so. Or I could reinvent myself – and that's how Charlie Daniels was born. 'Charlie' was the name Donna used on the streets and I thought it had an exciting ring to it. I also figured that it wouldn't hurt to have people think it was a man's name occasionally.

Meeting Doreen and reading my social-services file had opened up old wounds and made me think about the past. I became desperate to know more about where I had come from, especially after listening to Doreen's rantings about my father. If my dad had been murdered then I wanted to know how it had happened. I decided I would start the hunt by finding out who'd killed him.

I spent hours in the library, painstakingly trawling through microfiches, newspapers, phone books, electoral rolls and anything else I came across, with no result. I'd carefully noted all the names that I'd found in my father's obituary and had all the cuttings from his murder. He had been only twenty-one years old when he'd died on 2 January 1970.

One day I was sitting in the staffroom of the day-care centre where I was a student on placement. I hadn't told anyone there, apart from a woman called Sadie, anything about my mission to find out about my father. I don't know why I chose her, apart from the fact that I liked her and we got on so well. There are some people you just feel you can open up to, and others you know you can't.

'Norie!' Sadie rolled the name around thoughtfully. 'I'm sure my son works on the bins with a young lad who has the same surname. Maybe he's a link. It's not as if it's a common name.'

You wouldn't believe such a coincidence if this book were fiction!

The following week Sadie came in to work and told me that the boy was a distant cousin of mine. Although she couldn't get an address for me, he had told her where one of my uncles drank every night.

The pub that my investigations had led me to was a smoky old hole. I felt like I'd landed in some parallel universe – sometime in the 1950s. It hadn't had so much as a lick of paint for years. The dark wooden bar still had an original stained-glass panel and the carpet was red, patterned and threadbare.

As I walked in everyone stopped what they were doing and stared at me as if I had no right to be there. The landlord's stare roamed over every inch of me. His attempt at flirting was hilarious, but he said he knew the man I was looking for and promised to send him over to me when he came in.

I hadn't told him why I was there and I'm sure he thought it was a blind date. He kept winking at me from across the room and I was trying not to look his way. Many different men, mostly in overalls, were coming in and out. I kept scanning the room through the choking smoke and sipping nervously at my glass of wine.

Someone put the jukebox on and it was loud. It made

everyone in the bar jump. The landlord left the pint he was pulling to turn it down. That was when the man walked in. I knew immediately that he was the one. I just felt it. All the hairs on the back of my neck stood up. And it wasn't as though we looked alike because we didn't.

The man went to the bar and waited as the landlord mopped up the spillage from the pint that had just run over. They chatted and laughed as he got served and walked away. The landlord had said nothing. Maybe I was wrong. Then the landlord shouted to him across the pub.

'Oh and – 'ow could I forget – there's a babe sat over theer, asking for you.'

I wasn't sure what to be first – embarrassed or terrified.

The man walked across to me, smiling eagerly. He had greasy longish hair and milk-bottle-bottom glasses. He sat down practically on top of me and put his hand straight on my knee. I quickly removed it. The landlord was polishing a glass but I could see him straining to watch.

'So, what can I do for you then, me lovely? Do I owe thee some money?'

I laughed politely at his joke.

'I'm Doreen's daughter. I was born Moira.'

At first he looked at me blankly, shaking his head. But then, we were talking about seventeen years ago.

I told him her surname but he continued to shake his head.

'Raymond – your dead brother . . . I'm his daughter.'

His head jerked up and he stared at me intently. 'I didn't even know Raymond had a daughter.'

As we sat together I showed him all my cuttings and told him the tale that Doreen had told me.

'Nay,' he said, shaking his head. 'It weren't quite like that.'

But he didn't offer to go any further. He called me Moira, which felt strange – only Doreen had called me that.

I didn't sense any bond between us, just a feeling that I had reopened a previously closed and painful chapter that he would rather forget. There was no mention of future meetings and I couldn't think of any more questions. I was so shaken by the episode that I didn't even think to ask what other relatives I might have or whether my father's parents were still alive. All I wanted to do now was meet the man who had killed my father, making me a stranger to my own flesh and blood.

Some time passed and I had almost given up on my investigations when a name jumped out at me from the newspaper. My brain started ticking. I wondered why I had never thought to do this before. I picked up the phone, my hand shaking as I rang directory enquiries and gave them the murderer's unusual Irish surname.

A few more enquiries and I was making a call that had my heart thumping.

' 'Ello,' a gruff voice answered.

'Er, hello . . . Can I speak to Sean, please?'

There was a slight pause. I heard a dog bark. 'Speaking,' he said, tentatively.

'You killed my father.'

'Pardon?' Mr Gruff spluttered.

'I said, *you* killed my father.'

His voice filled with panic. 'Who is this – is this some kind of sick joke?'

He's going to hang up, I thought. 'No joke! I'm Raymond's daughter.'

'Raymond din't have a daughter!' By now he was almost squealing.

'Don't fucking tell me Raymond didn't have a daughter, because I'm her. I'm here – your worst nightmare and you robbed me!' Where did that anger suddenly come from?

He was silent for a moment. I was afraid he was going to put the phone down. Then he cleared his throat. 'I didn't know, I mean . . . that he had anyone.'

'My mum was pregnant when you killed him.'

And, as if he'd waited for this call his whole life, he wailed this awful, soul-wrenching noise. I snapped back into reality – enough drama now.

Between crying and sniffing, he told me what had happened – or, at least, his version. No decapitation, no big gangland murder. He said it was an accident. My father had been drunk and fighting with someone else.

'Don't fucking lie . . . I want to know what happened . . . I want the truth!'

The truth? Could I take it?

His voice quietened. 'He died choking on his own vomit.'

I felt as if I'd been hit in the chest with a cricket bat. I took a deep breath. I didn't hear most of his apology. I felt as if I'd broken him.

'Look, I served a long stretch for this – how old are you?' he asked.

'Seventeen,' I said. We both paused a minute.

'I just want to get on with my life now. I've done me time.'

I felt my fury rise again. 'Yeah? Well, my dad's dead and you dunnit, so you'd better look out for me!' I slammed the phone down.

I sobbed my eyes dry. I tore off the cover of the cushion I was sitting on and bawled into the naked pad. It was over now. Years later, I wished I hadn't closed the conversation that way. I should have forgiven him. But at seventeen I wasn't ready. I was too confused and too full of hurt. I'd had two fathers in my life: one had been taken away from me before I'd even been born, and the other had left me a few years later. Although I had now managed to get a better picture of what had happened to my natural dad, there was nothing I could do to bring him back or undo what had been done in the past. He hadn't even had a chance to know me, let alone love me.

I had a frustrating feeling that I would never have all the answers. The more I shone a light into the dark corners of my past, the more things ran straight at me and then away, beyond my reach. It was like wading through thick smog and pricking myself on lots of sharp objects. I knew they were there but I just couldn't stop myself from carrying on.

Part of me wanted to dig up all the bones, lay them out, put flesh on them, make sense of it all. But I couldn't because the flesh had rotted away years before I came along. All that was left now were the scattered remains, blowing in the wind. Another part of me wanted to pack everything away into neat compartments and fasten down the lids.

Years later I tracked down some more of my birth father's relatives. According to them, my birth mother's version of events had not been completely wrong and yet, technically, neither had the killer's. Funny how there can be two sides to any story, as well as the truth . . . Apparently, the coroner's verdict did record my birth father's cause of death as choking, but his face was so unrecognisable from having his head kicked in that he had to be identified from the tattoos on his arms.

At the same time as I was trying to cast some light onto my past, I was also trying to work out what to do with my future. The baby was due any time now, and then I was going to have to think seriously about how to earn some money. Most of the jobs I would be equipped for paid about five pounds an hour and I didn't fancy trying to support myself and a child on that.

I'd got on well at college – I'd already passed a handful of exams – but when I got pregnant I gave up going to classes. The two bus rides combined with morning sickness had made it impossible. I didn't believe I was clever enough to get a job that would even cover the costs of childcare. Men had always used me and I'd let them. It didn't seem so unnatural to use that to make a living. I didn't want to sink into the background, I didn't want my child to have the same start as me – I wanted an extraordinary life for the both of us.

*   *   *

I loved my baby from the moment she was a tiny seed in my belly. I knew she would be special, beautiful and precious. As soon as I knew she was in my life I wanted her and she changed me. Even when I was carrying her I felt so special. I glowed and was the most radiant I have ever been in my life.

She wanted to come out early and gave us all a scare – for a while I thought I was going to lose her before she was even born. That experience brought me closer to my own mother at a time when I needed family the most. For ten weeks, in the hospital, I didn't dare move for fear of hurting my baby. Just to break the boredom Mavis, a special midwife, would come onto the ward and fetch me to her classes three times a week. By the time Lucy was ready to hatch I'd been so often that I was the one taking the class!

When everyone else's husbands simulated contractions by squeezing their wives' ankles I felt bad because I knew that Lucy would never have the joy of a father. I laughed so hard when they suggested that I 'share' other ladies' husbands. They then squeezed for us too!

Mavis was there on the day when Lucy finally arrived. Mum was there too, keeping me calm and mopping my brow. She kept talking to Lucy while she was still inside me. The triple dose of breathing classes had paid off and I got through many hours relatively comfortably.

Then the pain came like a train and hit like a hurricane. I felt close to death. Lucy's head engaged. I gave my hardest push until I could give no more and Lucy took her first gasp of air, entering a room full of welcoming faces in a gush of wet sticky love. While she was still in her protective coat of blood and wax they placed her on my deflated tummy.

As if in a scene from a movie, 'We've Only Just Begun' by the Carpenters came over the speakers as my foster-mum cut the cord, linking all three of us for life. She might not have given birth to me but she helped bring Lucy into this world. I stared down at the tiny bundle in my arms in wonderment. 'A baby, I've had a baby' was all I could say – as if I'd had a lobotomy too!

Nan and a nurse nudged each other, waiting for me to announce that it was a girl. But I'd always known! Lucy didn't even cry. Her big saucer eyes with spider-leg lashes flicked up and it felt like they had penetrated my soul, moving me in immeasurable ways – I knew from that day forward everything I did would now be for her.

Later they cleaned us both up and Mum went home. A nurse came in and took Lucy away for a sip of water. I'd tried to suckle her at two in the morning but we were both too tired to learn right then. I really wanted to feed her myself. At seven a.m. I was still sat bolt upright, weary-eyed, waiting for her to return. The nurse had put her down in the nursery, thinking that I would sleep. But I didn't want to miss watching and hearing her first night, breathing at my side.

I knew that day that I wanted always to be there for her – right behind her, around her heart and under her skin. At last I had found someone else apart from Ethel with whom I could share love unconditionally.

9

THE BULLET

....

'*Now this is the law of the jungle – as old and as true as the sky; And the Wolf that shall keep it may prosper, but the Wolf that shall break it must die.*'

Rudyard Kipling

Once I started working on the streets with Donna I couldn't believe how much money I was making. I'd previously been living on thirty pounds a week and now I could make a couple of hundred in one night's work. Being paid for sex seemed like some kind of validation, a confirmation that I was attractive. Not only did I now have money for the electric meter, I could even afford to go out and buy myself some new clothes and nice things.

It was exciting, going out at night under the orange-glow street lights, watching the other girls and the pimps fighting, the strangers coming and going in the shadows. But it was frightening, too. I had arrived as a wide-eyed innocent, constantly shocked as the truth of what was going on around me was revealed. Surely that nice guy couldn't be a pimp? The girls weren't really taking drugs, were they? I can't believe that girl actually did it without a condom! Each time Donna would laugh at my naivety and set me straight.

Working like this was no better or worse than the sort of thing I'd been doing for free before. The sex didn't worry me at all: it was always over fast, there was never any real intimacy – a blow job here, a quick screw or hand job there. We gave punters 'fish-and-chips'-style menus through the car window before getting in. 'Twenty pounds for a blow job, thirty for sex, forty pounds all-in.' There was never any foreplay or role-playing, just clinical relief and on to the next one.

I once asked Donna why we didn't kiss clients. She just pulled a face and said she reserved kisses for her kids and her lovers, and then she got really annoyed with me when I pointed out that she used the same mouth to suck cock with! But on the streets no one ever did ask for a kiss.

Fear didn't come from what the clients might ask me to do. It came from what else might happen while I was out there, unprotected in the dark. Would I be beaten up, robbed or even murdered? You had to live on your instincts, just like an animal in the jungle.

With one customer I just knew, the moment the locks on the car doors snapped down, that he was different to the others and that I would be in trouble if I didn't do exactly as he told me. He drove me to an area I didn't recognise, under some arches. There was something about the way he looked at me and spoke that warned me I was in danger, and I knew it was pointless asking for my money. At a moment like that I could see the one and only possible advantage to having a pimp behind me, a man who would have been watching out for me. But I always worked independently and had no intention of ever doing otherwise.

I didn't consciously feel dirty or humiliated by the job in any way because I made sure that there was always a layer of rubber between me and the client before I was penetrated, which somehow made it less personal. But I did always like to get in the bath after a night's work, and I would completely submerge myself under the water for a few seconds, like a sort of ritual cleansing. I would come back to the surface feeling reborn.

Night after night Donna and I went back on 'the beat'. For all her apparent self-confidence, she didn't know much about the streets – I knew even less. Only two weeks earlier I'd thought that saunas, massage parlours or whatever were actually performing legitimate public-health services. I had no idea they were just fronts for brothels.

Gradually I became aware of a change in our friend-ship without being able to understand why it was happening or what I could do about it. At first we stuck together for mutual safety. Then Donna began insisting that the clients wouldn't put up with it and said we should split up. I was so naive I hadn't realised she'd been pissed off with me, even on that first night. Un-known to me at the time, she had imagined that she could mould me into what she wanted. To her I was too foolish to understand the ways of the world; someone would have to bring me down to earth. Donna had decided that a new arrangement had to be made . . .

'I think you should look after me a bit better,' she growled one night. 'I am showing you how to go on.'

'Aren't you doing so well?' I asked my friend with genuine concern.

'*Actually* I'm doing *very* well,' she snarled. 'You forget how I've looked after you!'

Obviously I just wasn't getting the point. My head was buzzing with conflicting thoughts. Why had Donna suddenly become so aggressive with me?

'Have I done something to upset you?'

'I think you should start giving me money – if it wasn't for me you wouldn't have any!'

I couldn't argue with her on that score: she was right. Things hadn't been sweet for me recently. A few nights before my neighbour told me she'd seen my ex-boyfriend 'moving out'. He was just a lad from the local estate, a skinhead – I can't even remember his name. I'd wanted to have someone in my life and so I'd trusted him and given him a key. Now I just felt stupid. I didn't have much, but what I had he took; a few new baby items that had been bought for me by the staff at the kids' home, a TV and video, a second-hand microwave and an old music centre. After only a couple of nights' work I'd already been able to replace everything except my one most treasured possession – my mother's wedding ring.

I needed to think about getting insurance, but right now just sorting the essentials out was my priority. I'd rung the police on my ex so he wasn't likely to return, and Donna was the only other person who knew I had a flat full of new electrical items.

'What do you suggest?'

I was thinking she'd ask me to pay for the taxi yet again.

'How about paying that electric bill I've just got in?'

I was horrified – it was a huge bill, well over three hundred pounds! I didn't want a confrontation but I had a strange feeling about this. I might have been naive but I wasn't stupid. If I agreed to this what would she ask for next?

'Look, I think that's unreasonable, to be honest – if you ever need to borrow anything . . .'

Donna stalked off to her corner without saying another word. I felt it was only a matter of time before I parted company with my new friend. I wasn't comfortable with the situation but lacked the courage to tackle it head-on. I thought that perhaps I should give up street life. I had almost everything I needed now; no matter how hard it would be I would try and manage back on benefits.

Donna only dated black guys and had introduced me to a few recently. These were not decent, hard-working professional guys, they were what she referred to as 'ghetto men'. It seemed that most of the working girls were with 'ghetto' black or Asian guys. Sometimes they discovered they were unwittingly sharing the same men – which would end in tears or, occasionally, bloodshed.

After quieter nights girls would turn up covered in bruises. Were they immune to the pain? I wondered, or did the vast amounts of drink and drugs that most of them were on mask it? Maybe this also explained why some of them looked a lot older than they actually were, as if the street life had weathered and hardened them beyond their years.

With time the streets had become familiar but they

never felt safe. The more I found out, the more dangers I realised there were. It was always a hostile terrain and now I wasn't even sure who the enemy was. I was already avoiding the other street girls as much as possible and now I was going to have to avoid Donna as well. I would soon learn, the hard way, never to trust any of them.

Sometimes on the beat I felt like a foreigner. A couple of the white street girls used to try speaking the Jamaican patois street slang, and I needed to learn it fast if I was going to survive.

Most of them had several kids from different fathers, proudly reeling off a list of names. I noticed that the same ones kept cropping up. I couldn't understand why the girls went on working for the men; it seemed a pretty pointless exercise, lying on your back with one man to give the cash to another. If the men were so desperate they should cut out the middle-woman and sell their own arses. But the point was that the men weren't desperate: all they had to do was sleep with these women, who were the ones who supported *their* children. Often they would take hard-earned money from one of their women in order to be seen making a magnanimous gesture to another. The saddest thing was that the girls honestly thought they were loved.

Donna didn't work for anyone. But she did have two mixed-race children to support, each from a different father. Jasmine, the eldest child, was five years old. Joseph was eighteen months old and still wore nappies. He had brain damage and sadly would never be any different. I admired the way Donna tried to cope, even though she was a single parent. I wondered what life for them would have been like had the children gone into care, like social services had suggested.

Sometimes, when there hadn't been any incidents for a while, Donna and I would relax and become complacent, almost forgetting how dangerous the beat was. Donna had settled into her new environment with ease, even making a few friends among the other girls. She enjoyed the flexi-hours as opposed to working practices in the saunas, which operated twelve-hour shifts – plus in the saunas you also had to pay the management a cut of whatever you earned.

One night, as we had been getting off the bus, Donna had given me a warning. 'Listen, I've heard *she*'s back out of prison – you'd better be careful.'

I knew that *she* was Betsy because I'd heard about her from other girls as well as from Donna, who'd met her before Betsy had gone to prison and knew her brothers from the clubs she frequented. At only four foot six Betsy had a legendary reputation. She was petite in stature only. She came from a family that also included six Jamaican brothers, all of whom would frequently be seen on the beat, picking her up or collecting their own girlfriends. She told all the girls that she'd never turned a trick in her life, but Donna knew different. Betsy robbed clients. She also had a nasty habit of 'taxing' the other girls.

I went to my favourite corner. It was a well-lit cobbled street around the back of the maternity hospital, of all places. Molly MacDonald had beaten me to it. She'd heard that this corner had become a hot spot. She looked around fifty and had yellow bleached hair with jet roots. I could never understand a word she said. This was partly because her nose had been broken more times than a boxer's but she also had a thick Glaswegian accent and was always drunk. As soon as she opened her gaping mouth the smell of cheap whisky would blow you away. Her permanently shaking hands were covered in tattoos and the lines on her face bore witness to the severity of her life.

I walked further down the street and stood against a wall, waiting for something to happen. I recognised a few clients already driving around, looking – most of them were in old bangers but there were the usual elite set as well. At first it had puzzled me that the fancy men didn't go somewhere upmarket. It was soon apparent that some didn't want to pay for comfort, while others got a kick out of the excitement and danger. They were always the ones you had to watch. The guys in the beat-up Cortinas were usually more straightforward, only there because they couldn't afford anything better.

An hour and a half later I'd earned over £200 and wanted to go home. Donna was nowhere in sight. A large new BMW pulled up. I walked over to the driver's side and leaned into the window, noticing the smell of new leather. The large man looked me up and down and asked me to stand back so he could get the full view.

'How much?' he barked.

'Forty pounds, all-in.'

He was bulging out of his expensive suit. 'I want to hire it, love – not buy it!'

Before I had a chance to 'renegotiate the deal' he sped off up the road.

Tight bastard. Rich men never like to part with it. This was too much – I felt cold and miserable. I watched as he pulled up a little further down the road. Molly came out of a doorway and got in with him. Molly would charge him twenty pounds. They deserved each other.

Just then another figure emerged from the shadows. Dressed in a full-length leather mac, it was Betsy. I started to walk away but it was already too late: I'd been spotted.

'Gimme a light.'

'Sorry, I don't smoke.'

She mimicked my voice. She must have thought I was trying to wind her up. 'Gimme – a – light!'

I looked around nervously for Donna. The predator instinctively sensed her victim's discomfort. Betsy scanned me up and down, making an assessment. She could tell by looking at me that I was a good earner. For the second time in a few minutes I felt like cattle on market day.

'Who ya mahn, then?' Betsy could speak in a broad local accent but she found her street voice the most intimidating.

I shuffled and looked down at the pavement

'The Bullet – from London!' Could she tell I'd just made that up?

Betsy sneered and spat on the floor. 'Mi know ov im, he ain't nuthin!' I still couldn't see Donna. 'Who you looking for, gal?'

My stomach lurched and twisted itself into a ball. I suddenly found that I had a nasty taste in my mouth and my chest felt like it had turned to stone. I was paralysed with fear.

Betsy grinned, showing a mouthful of gold teeth. I remembered Donna's tale of how she'd had them made from all the gold she'd 'taxed'.

'How much you got, then?' Betsy whispered and took a step closer.

'Sorry?'

'You deaf or daft, gal?'

'We've just come out, I've only been here five minutes . . .'

She knew I was lying. She'd go along with this silly girl's nonsense for now, priming me to savour later. As she walked off I reflected: there was no way anyone was taking anything off me, *especially* not another woman.

I walked around the block, trying to find Donna. Instead I found a couple more clients, including a wealthy Irish gypsy who paid me almost entirely in Irish banknotes. I went back towards Donna's corner and saw her – Betsy was there, too. I couldn't hear what they were saying and I was very worried about Donna. Suddenly Betsy turned around, saw me and ran at full speed. She leaped on top of me like a black panther, her mac billowing out like a cape behind her. My face hit the deck as my ankles were pulled from under me. I could feel warm blood oozing from my head. I tried to fight off the hands that were now tearing at my pockets. I started to see stars and then I guess I must have passed out for a minute.

When I came round Donna was stood over me. 'You all right?'

Her quiet enquiry suddenly changed to a shout – 'Quick! We'd better go – *they*'re here!'

Before I had time to ask who she meant, or scrape myself off the floor, Donna had disappeared, leaving me to face two guys in a Peugeot. This night couldn't get any worse.

'Get in the back.' The copper wasn't in the mood for pleasantries. As the car drove away the two of them talked as if I didn't exist.

'New blood! Should be interesting – got a name?'

Donna had told me before that the best thing was to keep quiet until I could get a solicitor.

'We got a statement earlier from another girl – says a girl fitting your description robbed her.'

I was thinking, how can that be? Haven't they got it the wrong way around? But still I said nothing. The copper turned to his partner. 'Haven't we got better things to do than sort out an argument between tarts?'

The car reached the edge of the beat and stopped for traffic lights. It was then that I saw Betsy step out of a doorway, having waited for the car to pass, putting one finger to her lips. Her other hand slid across her throat in a chopping motion. I knew full well what her signals meant – say anything and she'd cut my throat.

The lights changed and we drove away. Only later did I discover that Donna, who I still thought was my friend, and Betsy split my money between them that night.

Once I was at the police station I got myself a solicitor and was out several hours later. Mystery Girl had dropped all charges. Lucy usually stayed with the sitter overnight at Donna's, but now I couldn't wait to fetch her. I knew it was late but I desperately wanted to talk to Donna as well. She wouldn't answer the door although I was sure that I could see the light from the TV flickering through the lounge curtains. It was like she was trying to avoid me but I couldn't work out why, so I gave up and went home.

As I got to my flat door I had to stand for a minute in shock. There it was, half on, half off and splintered wood everywhere. I knew that Donna was the only one who knew I had replaced all my stuff, but I still wasn't ready to accept that my best friend could actually have turned against me. Not for the first time that night I had been well and truly fucked.

10
LESSONS IN LOVE
....

'Keep thy foot out of brothels, thy hand out of plackets, thy pen from lenders' books and defy the foul fiend.'

Shakespeare

If the entrance into the 'sauna' was anything to go by, my immediate instinct should have been to run, but I forced myself to keep going. I had to get off the streets and this was the best option I could think of. It was too dangerous to be out there night after night. I'd only been working there a few weeks, but I still knew that I was lucky not to have got into more trouble than I had. I also knew there was a limit to how much I could earn working with punters in cars. Having got a taste for what money could buy I wanted more, and I wanted to earn it in safer surroundings.

My relationship with Donna had deteriorated badly and I had begun to realise that she was ripping me off. As far as she was concerned I owed her big time and she was going to make the most of it. I didn't think I was better than anyone else but she accused me of putting on 'airs and graces' because I was always polite and spoke nicely, and she was constantly reinforcing the point that I knew nothing about pain and survival. It even annoyed her that I had worried about the street girls who were on drugs when I didn't even smoke cigarettes. To her it was sickening. I was just a silly young girl, an amateur next to her, and she made it clear that she wasn't going to play second fiddle. That was why I couldn't understand why she was so angry with me when I suggested we should keep our distance. I was so green that I never realised she had manipulated me for her own devices.

The sauna looked as if it was back in the 1970s instead of the late 1980s. There was mould in the hallway. A revolving cage groaned and clanked as I pushed my way through into a dingy damp room that I presumed was a lounge. Once through it I was unsure if the cage was to keep unwanted visitors out or me in. Still, however depressing this was it had to be safer than a punter's car in the dark or a deserted street at night. The newspapers had recently been full of a gruesome story. Parts of a woman's mutilated body had been found in black bags on wasteland. I read the front page in front of the lady in my paper shop.

'Ah! That's why,' she said matter-of-factly. 'She was a whore!' With that she walked away to continue stacking shelves.

I looked down at the photo. It wasn't a family portrait, it was a police mugshot – some people don't even get dignity in death! Staring back at me was a younger, barely recognisable Molly MacDonald.

But however frightened I might have been of life on the streets, I had one even greater fear. It wasn't death.

Death didn't scare me as much as the thought of being forced to live on the same council estate all my life, struggling as a single mum on benefits, my daughter having to wear hand-me-downs and being bullied for it, or being pushed around by people who intimidated me, and of not having control of my own life. I wanted something better than that for Lucy, and for myself, and the only place I could see to get it was the sex industry.

The owner of the sauna was waiting for me. He was about forty, slim and unshaven.

'Hello there! I'm Dick. You've come for an interview? What's your name?'

'My working name's Chrissie.'

He sent me to a cupboard-like room to get changed. I knew from what Donna had told me that the saunas were very different from the streets and the competition would be much stronger so I had used some of my hard-earned money from the streets to invest in some 'tools of the trade'. I emerged a few minutes later wearing a sheer baby-doll negligee, seamed stockings and suspenders. I finished the look off with a little tasteful silver jewellery and fluffy high-heeled slippers. My hair was done up in a bun with curled ringlets at the sides.

He stared at my nails intently, noticing that they were nicely manicured.

'Come upstairs with me,' he said, 'and I'll give you a *proper* interview.'

I knew exactly what he meant. Donna had warned me a long time ago that this happened. I guess it is one of the reasons men like him work in the business.

'Okay,' I said. 'But if I give you more than a massage you pay me the difference.'

He paused only briefly to consider this new arrangement and then, with obvious enthusiasm, said, 'Deal!'

He showed me to the stairs, insisting that because he was a gentleman he would follow behind. He viewed my G-string and stocking tops bobbing about in front of him, his excitement clearly visible as we entered the dark green room. There was no bed. This was not a hotel and we were not lovers. Instead, there was a high bench with a stiff threadbare towel barely covering a ripped plastic cover.

A fusty smell offended my nose. The light in the room was very dim. The gaudy flowered curtains were closed and a tiny table lamp with tassels sat on an old chipboard table.

He turned away from me silently and undressed, snagging his clothes as he threw them onto a dilapidated wicker chair. As he turned back he dropped his pants to the floor. He looked at me proudly as if waiting for some praise for his beloved erect cock, like a five-year-old might look to his mother, but I couldn't think of anything appropriate to say.

He clambered eagerly onto the high massage couch and lay face down. I stood to one side, motionless, unsure if I should get undressed yet. I decided to wait until instructed. I tickled and caressed him, knowing nothing about massage. But he didn't seem to mind.

I tried to think of something clever or witty to say but my mouth was frozen and my mind was numb. He turned over and yawned. Was he relaxed or bored? At least his manhood was still stood to attention: if he was disappointed then it wasn't showing. I flushed red as my youth was confronted with his confidence and I felt inadequate. Should I show him affection or just give him sex? Perhaps I should at least show a little interest. I started to talk about life outside of work, but somehow chatter seemed more off-putting and I decided to go back to being a silent seductress.

I could smell the mixture of cheap talc and the sweat from the last body that had lain on the butcher's slab. Stray pubic hairs curled on the rug below. This was the raw truth, the here and the now. Although I had a condom ready, in other ways I was far from prepared. Life was just a little bit too much in my face: would it all be worth it in the end?

Nothing in any of the encounters I'd had on the streets, or before that, had taught me anything about the arts of lovemaking. Everything was basic, matter-of-fact and over in a flash. I knew nothing of foreplay or seduction, but I was eager to learn. He squeezed a tit and I tickled his balls – he was no more accomplished in the arts of sensuality than I was. I knew nothing about who he was or what he wanted or needed. All that mattered was the money. While I stroked him I planned what I would spend it on. His fuck would pay for a week's groceries.

He asked me to remove my knickers and leave the rest of my gear on. He had to show me how to put the condom on properly rather than leaving him to do it for himself, and then I scrambled on top of him. I balanced precariously, ready to ride him to death – and it was a sudden death because he rapidly reached his climax. He appeared to care little for my lack of polish: my youth and my lingerie had proved to be enough stimulation. He got off the couch happily and jumped into the shower. I was left with a full condom and purse, one for the bin and one for the bank. As always I felt fine, knowing nothing more than a condom had penetrated me.

I showered for a long time since there wasn't a bath. The cubicle door was hanging off – but then, so were half of the greasy grey tiles. I remembered Donna telling me, 'Bring your own toiletries, them places don't provide fuck all!'

I got the job and it wasn't long before the work started to seem like a familiar routine. At the beginning I worked mostly with a girl called Cheryl, and it wasn't long before I could see that I was starting to get on her nerves, just as I had with Donna.

One day the sauna hadn't been as busy as usual and Cheryl was looking at the clock again. Time really crawled if you didn't have any customers. I came back into the room and let out my seventh customer of the day. Cheryl got up from the couch and looked into the mirror. Her roots badly needed doing. Her hair was no longer blonde: it was more yellow. She touched at the sides of her eyes where fine lines now appeared. She looked far older than thirty-two. She bared her discoloured teeth and polished away the lipstick on them with a cigarette-stained finger. Piercing green eyes shimmered in the mirror. Once she had been beautiful.

My customer blushed as I gave him a quick kiss on the cheek and he stuffed a five-pound tip into my hand as he dashed out of the door. Cheryl looked me up and down suspiciously.

'I hope you don't kiss the clients in the room.'

I guess that really would have been too much for her to compete with!

'Look, please get off my case, it was only a peck – besides, why shouldn't I?'

'It's not allowed, that's all – everyone knows *whores* don't kiss.' She said the words sharply, as if she wasn't a whore herself.

But you perform oral sex, I thought. What's the difference? But I didn't push it. She was so abrupt; she hadn't said a single nice word since I'd arrived. The more clients I did the more she sat with her back to me, smoking one cigarette after another, staring blankly at the TV. I tried to sit opposite her so that I could chat to her, in the hope of winning her over. She sat with her arms folded and legs crossed, silently smouldering.

The phone rang. Cheryl reached over lazily and lifted the receiver.

'Good afternoon, Cheryl speaking.'

She had a very husky voice and flirted well with customers on the phone.

'Well, I'm twenty-five . . .'

Chezyl reeled off a long and highly elaborated description of herself, making sure that she repeated her own name. The caller must have asked who else was working because then she changed her tone, giving a rapid description of another girl. After she put the phone down it dawned on me that I was the other girl, although I can't say the intro was particularly flattering.

'Go and sit in the bloody changing room,' she snapped. 'I don't want to sit with you. Stay in there a while, give someone else a chance!' She launched further into the verbal attack. 'You're a fucking tout! Smiling all over the place, taking them by the hand when they pick you – it's not done like that!'

I felt like shit. I hadn't meant to piss her off or to take all the clients. I mean, she didn't even wear stockings over her unshaven legs and she didn't seem to care enough to touch up her hair or make-up. I'm sure she would have done much better if she'd smiled a bit more, or tidied herself up a bit.

I walked silently into the cramped room and took out my lunch box. I bit half-heartedly into the cheese sandwich. I wasn't really hungry. My stomach was turning over like a washing machine. Was I really tough enough for all this? Was I going to end up like her, as hard as concrete, working for years like a robot?

I'd thought I would quit after my time on the streets, but I just couldn't. The money was too bloody addictive. If I went on benefits I'd be expected to live on a measly few quid a week, and it made me feel like a scrounger. The other working girls had said I was crazy when I signed off, especially as I now had to pay all my own rent. Unwittingly I'd just ensured that I couldn't quit now, not until I had a plan.

It wasn't going to be easy; some days I just didn't feel I could handle the stress of it all. All day long I was acting, wearing masks, pretending to be someone I wasn't; pretending to be feeling things I wasn't feeling, that I liked people I didn't really like. One minute I had to act the dominatrix, the next the little sex kitten or sex siren.

It could be emotionally draining, dealing with some people. Some of them would be awkward and would spend the whole time making me feel like a piece of shit, but I had to keep going because I knew there was going to be fifty or sixty quid in it for me at the end. I was as trapped by my new-found relative wealth as I had been by my previous poverty.

If someone was a bit smelly I had to coax them into having an 'assisted shower', going in with them so I could wash them properly. Most of them loved that. The worst thing was when clients insisted on giving me oral sex, because it felt like the most intimate thing to do. It would make my skin crawl, not having any rubber between me and their tongues. It was impossible to convince myself at moments like that that I was one part removed from the act.

Then there was the added strain of dealing with Cheryl if she was being funny. Then there were the days when Dick would come for the rent and they would all be sucking up to him. I could see why some of the girls kept leaving and coming back and ultimately had to fall back on benefits, mostly for the sake of their children.

I heard the cage bang. Another gent had come in. I peeked into the lounge where Cheryl was all over him – cheeky bitch, after the lecture she'd given me. But it was to no avail. Despite her efforts I heard the cage go again as he left. Cheryl muttered something about him only coming in for a look, but I felt sure that she'd scared him away. Just then Dick came storming towards me.

'Where the fuck were you?'

'I, well I . . .'

'What the hell are you doing in here?'

'Cheryl said—'

'Cheryl said what?' she snarled, suddenly joining in.

'Well, about, you know, giving someone a chance and everything.'

She flounced off in disgust and threw herself back onto the sofa.

'Hey! I'm the boss here – don't listen to that old slapper!'

I was shocked. I felt sure she would have heard him. I turned away from him as my mascara started to slide down one cheek. I grabbed my bag and began thrusting my things into it.

Dick instantly lowered his voice: 'Aw, come on, I didn't mean it!'

'Stop shouting at me, then!'

I turned and stared him straight in the eyes. He backed down, shrugging his shoulders apologetically.

The cage went again and I walked purposefully into the lounge. Cheryl looked up and groaned. A small breeze woke all my goose bumps as a bubbly brown-eyed woman made her entrance.

'Huh! I might as well fuck off now!' Cheryl shouted.

The girl threw back her hair and laughed, dragging a huge sports bag in with her.

'Same old miserable cunt! Don't change, Cheryl!'

I was stunned at the language but the delivery sure cheered Cheryl up: she seemed to respond to it and softened a little. Dick told me this was Tania – one of the more popular ladies. Apparently she was half Italian.

She spun around to face Cheryl. 'Stick kettle on, then, Chez.'

Cheryl sloped off. By now she had changed into her carpet slippers and her tatty stilettos lay discarded on the floor. Tania bounced over to me; she looked in her early thirties. She had an energetic, childlike way about her.

'Now, what do we got here?'

Dick gave her a smile. 'A bit of competition for you at last, a bit o' class.'

She grinned. 'Marvellous! Got a name, young 'un?'

'Chrissie.' She made me feel welcome for the first time that day.

'New to all this, then? I thought so. I've seen less green in Kermit the Frog!'

I laughed nervously. How did she know?

'Don't worry, love. I'll show you a few tricks!'

I knew straight away that I'd just met my next sexy mentor. None of the girls on the streets had ever bothered to pass on any tips on how to please the punters, possibly because they didn't know any. But Tania knew a lot and didn't seem worried about sharing them with me over the coming months, even though I was potentially her rival. She was so confident that she never appeared threatened, unlike the other women.

Cheryl and Tania had a lot of catching up to do; they hadn't worked together for years. The conversation turned out to be very revealing. Cheryl was with the same guy she'd been with for the last ten years. He was not a pimp. He sold jewellery and was a six-foot black guy. He was an expert in martial arts – but not a troublemaker – and he called himself 'The Don'. The girls sniggered about that bit and from what I could gather it was some sort of reference to him being rather well endowed. She also said that she was sure he was still seeing a couple of his 'baby mothers' and that he had ten different children by seven different women.

Cheryl had two daughters from a previous relationship, who were now in care, and she had a son by Don. She also confessed to having other lovers, including her latest, who was several years her junior.

Tania and Cheryl started to go out together straight from work to small illegal drinking dens known as 'blues clubs'. Donna used to go to the same sort of places. They were dark seedy rooms where ghetto guys played loud reggae and smoked weed from dusk till dawn. Sometimes they were held in people's dark and decrepit basements, sometimes in small industrial units, anywhere where they could get away with it. There was always something going on in a blues club.

I went with them a couple of times, but there was always trouble and I felt on edge. One night Cheryl asked me to babysit for her instead. I took Lucy with me.

Cheryl lived on a really rough estate in a high-rise similar to the one I'd just moved out of. Once Lucy was born I'd been able to persuade the authorities to move us into a maisonette, which wasn't at all bad. I still didn't have a regular relationship. All through my life boyfriends and lovers have arrived intermittently and have been transient. In most cases they would come home to screw me, hang around a few weeks and then disappear. I might have been learning a lot about sex in my job, but I still knew nothing about relationships or how to sustain them. I've never been courted and I have never courted anyone. Because I saw myself as worthless the men in my life saw me the same way.

Everyone I passed as I approached Cheryl's block was half covering their faces with scarves or hoods or baseball caps and moving about furtively. There were people throwing rubbish out onto the streets and there was dog shit everywhere. Cheryl's flat badly needed decorating and there were piles of rubbish all over the place.

I went babysitting for her several times after that and one night while I was there Don came home early. Even though I knew he was many years older than me I couldn't have guessed his age. I'd heard that he'd been known for being violent when he was young. He had a certain charisma about him and I instantly felt a 'chemical' attraction.

'My son often talks about you,' he said, 'after you've been round to babysit.'

'Yeah?' I grinned, pleased at the thought. 'That's nice.'

'Yeah.' He smiled. 'You know, I think Cheryl is jealous of you. She's always bitching. It was her *asked* me to come home early.'

My hands went clammy as I listened to his words.

'She asked me to sleep with you, so's to get you working for me, so we could get money from you.'

I knew that Don wasn't a pimp, not actively. One or two of his 'baby mothers' were on the game and would willingly give him money, but he never made them. As I listened, however, my mouth went dry as I realised I was back in the danger zone that I'd been hoping to get away from. I didn't want to be in anyone's power, not even with this apparently kind man. Within a few minutes of talking we had connected mentally; he was very deep and clever. He was older than a lot of the guys I met, and more relaxed as a result. He told me he liked the fact that I wasn't jaded like Cheryl and that I saw the sauna as a stepping stone to a better life rather than a dead end. The tension between us electrified me in a way that I had never experienced before. I was unable to resist the temptation and we soon entered into an explosive relationship.

Cheryl had no choice but to maintain that she knew nothing about the affair since she had instigated it in her attempt to manipulate me. In her own world she thought she had me 'all sewn up'. She started treating me like her underdog and encouraged everyone else to pick on me behind my back but I was willing to put up with it because I was in love with Don. He was the first person to actually make love to me instead of just having sex, and I sometimes found that hard to cope with. I would get overcome with emotion.

Tania was one of the best hustlers I ever met. She had this knack of judging how much a guy had in his wallet: she could squeeze every last penny out of him and he'd still come back begging for more. She taught me how the game was not a job but an art form, where you had to work out the guy's needs or fantasy without asking directly. It might be that he wanted you to be his friend, his mother, his marriage guidance counsellor or his confidante. You didn't even have to have sex with some of them if you read them well enough. Tania was loud and sassy yet she could turn on the charm like a tap. She was totally without inhibitions and on numerous occasions she laughed at my naivety.

One time a guy rang asking about water sports.

'We're not a sports centre,' I told him. 'We're a sauna. You have the wrong number.'

When I put the phone down Tania showered me with a mouthful of tea as she fell about laughing. By the time he rang back she'd put me right and I told him to come in.

So there I was a little later, the caller's head carefully positioned beneath me over a shower tray, trying to piss into his mouth! All the time I was giggling so much that I found it really hard to keep my balance and aim straight. Worse still, I sent the poor bloke home with neck ache because it took me so long to wee, even though I had deliberately drunk pints of water and by now I needed one badly!

One of my regular clients was Ives. He was a big man in his eighties who looked like Father Christmas. He was always outside on the pavement, waiting for us to open up first thing Monday morning, when I was never looking my best. He didn't seem to mind the real me and insisted I saw him before I put on my war paint and work clothes.

'You know, I haven't got that long . . .' he told me one morning.

I looked at his kind face, glanced at my watch and thought, well, it doesn't matter, I'm used to quickies.

'I mean, to live,' he added.

I looked at him again, not sure what to say.

'And I haven't got anyone left now – except you . . .'

I opened my mouth to speak but Ives kept on going.

'So, anyway, I thought rather than pay you every week out of my pension . . .' Now I felt guilty. 'How about I leave you me house when I go?'

It suddenly hit me: he was talking about leaving me his house – in his will! I thought, is he *serious*?

As if he was reading my mind he said, 'We can go to solicitor's next Monday.'

I didn't know what to say, so I just said 'Okay' and we went upstairs into the room as usual. A few minutes later we were up on this high massage bench and Ives was on top of me, at it like a rabbit. Suddenly he stopped, his body went rigid and he started to make this 'ugg ugg' noise – it was then that I realised he'd stopped breathing! *I thought he was coming, but it turned out he was going!*

As he went all still and quiet I started to panic.

'Ives! Ives!' I shook him gently to start with, hoping that he was just mucking about, but his eyes had rolled back into his head and there was no movement whatsoever. He was right in my face. I was pinned down by his entire body weight and couldn't twitch a muscle. Cheryl was downstairs but she must have heard me shouting because she came running up to see what the commotion was about.

'He's dead! He's dead!' I screamed in answer to her shouts through the locked door.

'What?' she yelled in disbelief.

'He's *dead*!'

'Are you sure he's dead? I mean, has he just passed out or something? Give him a prod.'

Cheryl didn't want to believe it and was getting impatient with me, assuming that I was being a silly girl again.

I started to wail as loud as I could manage. Ives felt so heavy and I was shaking uncontrollably. There was a small window behind me – it had bars on it to keep out burglars. To make things worse I knew that the door couldn't be forced either. The sauna had been busted by the police so many times that Dick had fixed the door to open outwards only, so it couldn't be kicked in by the cops in a raid. To make matters worse it was a fire door with a built-in steel plate.

Cheryl, on the other side, was rattling the handle feebly. I was feeling totally trapped.

'For God's sake, fetch someone!' I shrieked. 'I'm going numb!'

Now that I'd had a few minutes to think it through I was terrified that Ives would roll off and hit his head – and I would end up in the dock charged with murder. I stopped making any attempts to move in case I dislodged him.

'Dick and Tania aren't here,' she said. 'There's only us!'

'I just want to get him off me *now*!'

'What shall I do? I can't call the police, can I?' and now she was panicking too.

And then everything went silent for a few seconds, followed by the sound of the cage slamming, and I knew she'd done a runner. A few minutes later, although it felt like a lifetime, there was the sound of a loud engine as a large vehicle drew up outside the window, followed by the noise of breaking glass just behind my head.

'You all right in there, love?' a male voice enquired.

'Of course I'm not fucking all right. What does it look like?'

I was so embarrassed! Next I heard a buzzing noise and when I twisted my head I could see blue sparks flying. Ives's body let out an explosion of gas, making me jump. My nerves were in shreds.

A yellow helmet appeared above me as the grinning fireman who had succeeded in cutting away the bars climbed into the room.

'By 'eck, lass!' he chuckled. 'He died with a smile on his face!'

But I didn't see the funny side of it.

Thankfully, the police didn't seem interested in the 'massage' side of things. But unfortunately for me there were no solicitors, no will and no house and even I couldn't force myself to rob a dead man's wallet . . . I guess I would just have to call Ives my most memorable stiff!

Over the following weeks Tania and I became close. Dick used to put us on together and call us his 'dynamic duo'. I went back to her flat once after work, interested to find out more about her personal story. I felt so at ease with her.

Tania's flat was sparsely furnished and uninviting, which puzzled me because in the weeks I'd known her I'd seen her earning at least a grand a week. I was earning hundreds by then, but not nearly as much as her. Why, I wondered, didn't she make herself a bit more comfortable? In the lounge, over a gas fire, there was an old mantelpiece with photos of two beautiful boys on it.

Tania walked in behind me and saw me looking.

'They're my lads,' she said proudly.

I couldn't believe that she had children and had never mentioned them in all our conversations. I was always talking about Lucy.

'Where are they?' I asked.

'They go to a private school,' she explained.

'Is that why you have to work so hard?' I was impressed. I wondered if one day I would be able to do something like that for Lucy. 'To pay for the school fees?'

'No.' She shook her head. 'They're paid for by my parents – the boys live with them.'

Her parents apparently owned one of the most successful local companies, which made the sparse furnishings of the flat even more of a mystery. I got the impression from the way she talked about her folks that she was the black sheep. I waited as she disappeared into the bathroom to shower and came through in a robe a few minutes later, with her head in a towel turban. She sat over a glass coffee table and opened a small paper package. I watched in amazement as she sprinkled a neat white line onto the table. My heart raced as if I'd run a marathon; I couldn't believe what I was seeing. She looked up at me and asked if I wanted a line but I merely shook my head in disbelief. She put one finger to her left nostril and hoovered a long line up the other.

The mystery was solved. Tania had a grand-a-week

coke habit. It had cost her her husband, her parents' approval and her boys. She was lucky she hadn't lost her mind. The coke, it seemed, was now all that she lived for. The more money she earned the more her habit grew. When she couldn't get hold of the gear she would turn to bottles of brandy. Despite the fact that I was so young, I tried to point out to her what a mistake she was making, but she wouldn't listen to me. Nothing I could say was going to be news to her: she'd heard it all before.

Dick opened another massage parlour over in Manchester and put Tania in charge at ours while he oversaw the new one. Of a night Tania's boyfriend would sit in the sauna or the Jacuzzi waiting for her to come out of the rooms to do more and more lines with him. He looked like a black American footballer and I felt intimidated by his size even though he seemed harmless. I wasn't the only one he intimidated – the punters avoided him too. One night he shocked me by asking me to fuck him. I thought about what I should do. Never mind the fact that I didn't actually fancy him, I was loyal to Tania and decided to tell her – even though by doing so I risked losing a mate.

'You should have done it!' she laughed, and I started to lose what little respect I had left for her.

There were other friends of Tania's coming and going all the time: none of them stayed very long. I thought they just had a buzzing social life – I didn't realise that they were using the premises to deal from, making even more money.

A few weeks later Tania made a surprising announce-

ment. 'I'm pregnant! I'm having that fat bastard's baby!'
She was half laughing and half serious and I couldn't
work it out. 'My mother will disinherit me once and for
all for bringing a black baby into the family!'

'Tania,' I said, shocked by how badly she was losing
the plot, 'I've never judged you but you need to stop
taking that shit – especially now.'

She just threw back her hair and sniffed. 'Yeah, yeah,
soon enough, *Mother*.' I smelled trouble; I didn't like the
look of one or two of the guys who'd been in recently.
They asked a lot of questions and never had a massage. I
had a feeling that we were heading for a fall. Finally I
decided it was time to leave.

The moment I told Tania I was thinking of leaving the
atmosphere between us changed and I found myself
pinned up against the wall.

'Did you think you were clever, shagging Cheryl's
man?' she snarled, her face scarlet with anger.

I spluttered, unable to find an answer, never having
expected Tania to take sides. But she and Cheryl had
been sat in the sauna, which always meant they'd been
at the coke together. I'd recently bought myself a long
gold chain, which she now ripped violently from my
neck.

Damn! I thought. I knew I shouldn't have worn that
for work! I managed to get to the phone and called Don
for help. A quarter of an hour later the cage slammed to
announce his arrival. I packed up my things and silently
got into his car.

'Are you going to move in with me or stay with
Cheryl?' I asked later that day, once we were alone.

'What sort of a life would my son have if I left Cheryl?' he asked.

I knew he was right. If he upset Cheryl too much she would stop him seeing his boy, who was the only one of his ten or so children that he was close to. He knew that if he, Don, wasn't around then Cheryl would leave the kid with anyone, past caring because of her drinking and drugs habits.

So things just continued as they were between us, neither of us speaking of the future any more, knowing that we had none really – at least, not together.

Dick rang me after I left the sauna. He hadn't wanted me to leave and now he offered me a job in his new Manchester brothel. I agreed and when I got there I discovered he was operating from a small discreet flat, which, by comparison with the other place, was surprisingly spotless. One Wednesday morning I found out why.

I was just making a cuppa when the doorbell went. Through the spyhole I could see a towering bespectacled man. I opened the door tentatively.

'Do you want any jobs doing, mistress?' he enquired.

Weird, I thought.

'It's not bob-a-job week, is it?' I asked sarcastically before shutting the door in his face and going back to my cuppa in the kitchen.

'You won't believe what just happened,' I told one of the other girls. But she did, and when the doorbell went again I had to go back and let him in. When I opened the door the second time I expected him to be annoyed at my ignorance, but he appeared to think I was wonderful.

'Thank you, mistress!' He positively grovelled. 'I am at your command – eternally your slave!'

One of the other girls explained the routine. I was to show him into a room where he got changed into an outfit he was carrying in a large rucksack. He would then appear in the kitchen a few minutes later, wearing big knickers, a corset and a pinafore. Luckily, he looked down at the floor as if he was ashamed so he didn't see the expression on my face. He was awaiting my next command and I was trying not to split my sides.

Next I had to instruct him to pick up things from the floor, scrub the shower and bleach out the toilet. Another couple of clients arrived and so I had to usher him into a room out of the way. I left the slave cleaning the skirting boards and polishing the mirrors while I dealt with the newcomers.

Two shags and a blow job later, I went back into the room where the tall guy explained what he wanted as a reward for his hard work – a smacked bottom and a stern telling-off. I really had a laugh! Then I got the biggest surprise of all: *he* paid me seventy-five pounds!

I was at home one evening when the phone rang. It was eleven o'clock at night. Don was there and Lucy was fast asleep. At first I couldn't make out what was being said but I could clearly hear panic in the caller's voice.

'Cheryl, Cheryl – help me, help me!'

At first I passed the phone to Don, thinking it might be something to do with him.

'Sounds like Tania,' he said, passing the phone back to me and looking puzzled.

'Cheryl! Cheryl!'

By now the voice was wailing and I realised that something was very wrong.

'I'm not Cheryl – is that you, Tania?'

'Oh God! Please God, help me – it's everywhere . . . and I can't stop it.'

'Can't stop what?' She wasn't making any sense.

'Am at work. Come . . .'

I left Don babysitting and dashed off in a taxi. When I got to the sauna the cage was open – Tania's boyfriend had 'thoughtfully' left it unlocked when he fled, leaving her behind on the floor, covered in blood. A paralysing fear gripped my lungs and throat, making it hard to breathe or speak. I screamed as I shook Tania but I couldn't rouse her and I could see vomit mixed with blood in her hair. I rang for an ambulance. She was haemorrhaging from every orifice. I clambered into the ambulance with her, screaming at the irritatingly calm paramedic to do something.

The doctors discovered that she'd overdosed on Novocaine, the painkilling cocaine that dentists use. God knows why, maybe she couldn't get the other stuff.

Tough as old boots, Tania did eventually come round and I was there when she did. So it was me who had to tell her that she'd also miscarried her baby.

11

SCHOOL OF LIFE

....

'Fortune's a right whore:
If she gives ought, she deals it in small parcels
That she may take away at one swoop.'

John Webster

Helen was solid and dependable. I didn't have many friends like her. Her house and her two small children were always immaculate. She wasn't much older than me but she acted like a mother figure, always giving me advice.

Whenever she came out with the words 'I know it's none of my business . . .' I knew she was about to poke her nose in. 'I was thinking, if you're going to be a prostitute . . .'

'Working girl, please, Helen.'

'Well, if you're going to do this, I think it's time you did things differently, instead of following Donna's lead.'

Helen had never liked any of my other friends but she detested Donna the most – and they'd only met once. I had been in the post office one day with Donna and we had both homed in on the fact that the girl in front of us had two beautiful mixed-race children. We got talking to her and the girl turned out to be called Helen. We lived on a mainly white estate where there were always skin-heads wearing National Front gear hanging about by our shops. It was unusual to see any black people at all. But mixed-race kids turned out to be the only thing that Helen and Donna had in common.

I thought Helen was just being jealous when she warned me that I'd end up like Donna. She thought girls like Donna gave mixed-race children a bad name, because they made people assume that only hookers had kids with black guys. It had been Helen who had explained to me how Donna had ripped me off with Betsy – I don't know how she found out, I guess everyone must have known except me. I hadn't believed her at first, until I discovered Donna with some of my Irish money and put two and two together. Helen also told me that it had been Donna who had robbed my flat the second time.

Helen continued with the advice. 'Donna suits saunas, but I reckon you'd make a good escort.'

'I wouldn't know where to start – are there any agencies in Sheffield?'

'No, not that I know of. But you could look in *The Sport* – that's where my friend who does it got a job.'

When Helen first found out that I'd gone on the game she'd told me that her friend was an escort. Back then I was still naive and thought it meant going out for dinner and being a professional companion. I soon found out there was very little of that involved. Mostly it was a glorified visiting-prostitute agency where the classier girls worked. I was flattered that she thought I could do the same. She looked me straight in the eye.

'You could earn a lot more money as well as get away from all the shit you've been mixing in. You could work somewhere where no one knows your business – move up a league!'

It did sound tempting when she put it like that, so we bought a copy of *The Sport* and found a big impressive ad for an agency in Brighton. Helen offered to look after Lucy for a week while I went away to work, which I was delighted about because she was such a good mum. I used her phone to ring the agency. The guy who answered didn't even want me to send a photo, which took me by surprise.

'How quick can you get here?' was his only question.

The next day I was on the train to the south coast.

As the taxi pulled up in front of an anonymous-looking bungalow I checked the address again with the driver. It just didn't look like the sort of place someone would be running an escort agency from, more like the home of a respectable retired couple. The address tallied so I rang the bell and a small tubby man in his early thirties opened the door, wearing only a pair of shorts and a big grin.

'Wow!' he exclaimed, looking me up and down. 'You must be Chrissie.'

I guess I was expecting someone different – maybe someone in a suit? When he'd said on the phone that he'd put me up I hadn't realised the agency was run from his home and that was where I would be staying. He showed me around. It still looked like an old couple lived there:

the whole place was covered in plastic flowers and flock wallpaper. It wasn't dirty – just a bit untidy. I noticed he hadn't made up the spare room for me.

We chatted for a bit and I discovered he was a former computer analyst with a big appetite for all things and virtually no personality. I sat in the lounge while he brought me a cuppa and explained how he would put the ad in *The Sport* each week and send out various local girls to the hotels.

'My regulars want "fresh" girls every week,' he explained. 'So, each week another girl comes from out of town and stays with me while she's working.'

It seemed like he was making a reasonable living out of it – but I suspected he was in it as much for the 'perks' as anything else.

The week went fast and my host actually turned out to be quite sweet. He made sure that I was earning plenty and he looked after me well. When he asked for sex I made it clear he would have to pay, which he was happy to do. Put it this way: I didn't feel like a victim but I did feel torn. I didn't like the idea of leaving Lucy behind while I was away, but I did know that Helen was right: I needed to make an effort to 'move up a league'.

There was another thing preying on my mind as well. Don had called to issue me with an ultimatum: him or work. He'd never liked Cheryl doing it and had claimed that it was his reason for not committing himself to her completely. If I wanted him to be with me properly, I would have to give it up. I had thought that maybe I could somehow juggle both, but now I realised it wasn't going to happen. Deep down I guess I couldn't trust that

Don would support me, any more than he could support any of his ten children, and I doubted if he was really ready to leave Cheryl and his son. So I wasn't about to give up my livelihood for him.

Then Helen called, sobbing. There'd been an accident. Lucy had rolled off the settee where she'd been sat, smack down onto one of Helen's son's toys. I couldn't get back home quick enough, crying all the way, and I went straight to Helen's house from the station. When I got there it had been over twenty-four hours since the accident, and Lucy was happy and bubbly, sat on Helen's knee. There was a bruise the size of a ten-pence piece on her face and she seemed quite unfazed by all the fuss. It was Helen who was in a state, her eyes red and puffy. It had been a minor fall, not a major catastrophe, but Helen was heartbroken. As soon as she started to tell me the story she began crying again. Apart from the small mark, Lucy was absolutely fine. As Helen explained what had happened her little boy came into the room waving the offending wooden toy.

'Baby fell! Baby fell on me toy! Baby cry – Mummy cry!'

He seemed very upset about it, too. He'd always treated Lucy like a sister.

I could clearly see that there had been no real harm done. Anyone who has a child knows how many falls and scrapes they get into.

'Look, Helen.' I tried to reassure her. 'I can see it was an accident.'

'But I turned my back, I only turned it for a minute!'

Once I felt I'd put her mind at rest I took Lucy home.

There'd been no harm done, but what if it had been a really serious accident and it had taken me a day to get back to her? The thought made me shiver. From now on, I decided, I would never work out of town again.

I began to see less and less of Don. Even though I still adored him I knew I was never going to have him to myself and I had become resigned to that fact. I started a friendship with one of my neighbours. He lived with his wife and kids in one of the other maisonettes in my block. We had often talked as we passed in the hallway and there had been an immediate chemistry. They were a pretty loud, rough family and he had a sort of roguish appeal. But I hadn't meant it to develop into anything more.

One night the temptation proved too hard to resist for both of us and what started with a coffee and chat in the lounge became a full-blown tryst in the bedroom. We had become so passionate that neither of us heard the front door go – I'd forgotten to drop the catch. A few minutes later we were sat in the dark talking when a tiny bright orange light appeared. We both nearly jumped out of our skins as Don lit two cigarettes and passed one to the neighbour who, bemused beyond belief, simply took it and said, 'Sorry, mate.'

Then, without a word, Don went back downstairs and waited in my lounge, silently finishing his cigarette while my latest conquest quickly pulled on his trousers and ran for the door.

Don and I would never be the same again. Although we remained friends and lovers for over a decade he had decided that I was no better than any of the other women and couldn't be trusted.

A few days later it turned out that Don wasn't the only one who had learned of my affair. Someone was stood at my front door trying to kick it off its hinges. As I looked out of the kitchen window I could see my neighbour fighting with his wife. He was trying to pull her away from the door and she was having none of it.

'Come out now, you dirty f*cking bitch!'

I held my breath and stayed behind the door – she looked like a woman possessed.

'You nasty rotten whore, you gave me a dose and I'm gonna stick you good style!'

The letter box suddenly snapped open and a pair of eyes appeared, followed by a carving knife as she jabbed at the air. I didn't doubt she meant it either and I decided to wait until she'd calmed down.

That was the only time I ever caught any disease and it wasn't from a client. I always insisted that they used condoms, but I had a pretty active private life as well as a professional one and I wasn't always as strict with my rules when it was personal. Somehow, in the early days I'd viewed the condom as what separated work from play. But I soon learned other ways to make the distinction.

A few weeks later I bumped into my neighbour again. He told me that luckily, and no thanks to me, their relationship had survived and had actually become stronger. When I asked him how it was possible I'm not sure I was prepared for the response.

'Once I explained to her that you were just a shag and it didn't mean anything, I think she started to realise how much we would lose.'

I felt deflated. How come I was always the mistress but never the wife? In some ways I guess I wanted what they had but I just didn't know how to achieve it.

A couple of days after the accident at Helen's, I was indoors cleaning the kitchen floor. I'd wrapped Lucy warmly and put her out, just under the kitchen window where I could keep an eye on her and she could get some fresh air. The scorned wife walked past my front door, turned to my baby, who was making happy gurgling noises, and bent into the pram to talk to her. She saw the bruising on Lucy's face but didn't say a word.

Twenty-four hours later there was a loud knock at the door. I opened it to see a guy in a suit flanked by male and female uniformed police officers. The suited man flashed official social-services ID. In a scene from my worst nightmares I suddenly found myself at the centre of a social services child-abuse investigation.

Eventually I was cleared of what they termed *non-accidental injury* – but the main man never apologised for the trauma he caused through his 'you're a prostitute so you're obviously guilty' attitude. I later made a complaint about his conduct. My grievance was upheld and he was taken off the case.

The most harrowing part of the procedure was the examination of my baby for signs of sexual abuse. I felt very sad that she had to go through such an ordeal, although I do understand that it's routine during an abuse investigation. It felt as if this was a violation in itself and yet somehow I still felt guilty, as if it was me who was responsible.

I had already got a reputation on the estate as being on the game. Now I was a marriage-wrecker and a neglectful mother as well; all the gossip made life there impossible for me. They'd already made their minds up about me. I moved to an area where I didn't know anyone.

Social services asked if I would like a regular social worker. Remembering the positive relationship I'd had with Joel when I was in care I said that I would give it a go for Lucy's sake. I definitely needed some support. I was beginning to worry that perhaps I was an unfit mother after all. No matter how often I explained that I kept work and home separate, it seemed as though my current occupation meant people thought my baby was at risk. A tiny part of me was beginning to wonder if perhaps they were right. But what alternative did I have? I seriously thought about giving work up but there was no other way I could make enough money to look after her properly. There were no other jobs I could do that would earn me enough to pay for childcare. If I gave up work we would be back on benefits, and what sort of future would I be able to offer Lucy then? I would be miserable and might end up bitter and frustrated like my foster-mother, and that would be no good for either of us. I became terribly depressed.

I started to think back to when I had met my birth mother, remembering how I had felt about the fact that she'd given me away. The best thing she had ever done for me was to give me up: I could finally see that now. I imagined Lucy ending up with a life like my little half-sister Amanda if she stayed with me. Then I started dwelling on my unhappy teenage years with my foster-mum, thinking of how much easier life became for both of us when I went into care. Maybe that was the answer. But could I actually bear to give Lucy up? For over a year she'd been the centre of my life and she was at least half the reason why I was working so hard and taking so many risks. Could I really just hand her over to someone else to look after? The thought was almost too painful to bear.

I knew I needed professional advice so one afternoon I plucked up my courage and rang my newly appointed social worker. Instead of being an intellectual sociology boffin who spoke in psychobabble, like most of the other social workers I'd met, she turned out to be a single mum of four who'd been educated, like me, mostly at the university of life. She visited me on the Monday and we sat to discuss my options. I tearfully explained how I felt and she offered me support. Despite her reassurances that she felt I could make a good mum, whatever my profession might be, I felt guilty about Lucy's bruise and the resulting investigation. I might have been cleared of abuse but by now I was starting to wonder if I really could make a good mother.

My unconditional love for Lucy meant that no matter what I wanted I had to put her first. I could see now that that might even include giving her away. History was about to repeat itself.

Despite having made the decision voluntarily, when the social worker actually came and took Lucy away I was devastated. It was as if someone had cut out my heart. I met the temporary foster-carers first: they were lovely people and had a large garden with a huge sandpit – something I'd always wanted to give my girl. I knew they would give her far more than I was able to, but could I actually bear to hand my daughter over to them? My mind was in shreds and my emotions in complete turmoil. Was I really doing the right thing? Was I doing it for the right reasons? I knew it would have been wrong to stay on the game and keep Lucy with me, because my situation and the environment I lived in were bound to be unstable. I've met many prostitute mothers since who successfully keep their work at arm's length, but I was now in it up to my middle. My work was becoming intertwined with my social life as I spent more time in the blues clubs. I knew it was affecting my judgement. I had no stable home life nor did I have a partner who could fill in for me when I wasn't around. I even had trouble keeping a good babysitter. And I was surrounded in the flats by jealous people who were living on benefits and were just looking for a chance to bring me down. Because I was earning a lot more money than most of them they began to notice that I had more nice things, like a new microwave or a fitted carpet, and they would start to gossip and bitch.

'You know how she can afford stuff like that, don't you . . .?'

By now I had even started to doubt myself. I didn't actually believe that Lucy was at risk living with me, but maybe, I thought with the benefit of hindsight, she was, although not in the way most other people imagined. There were a lot of people who thought that a woman who was willing to sell her own body must be willing to sell her child's as well. I reckoned this was completely unfair.

For six weeks after they took Lucy I kept away from her, hoping that the pain would fade. It was the most miserable time. Then, one sunny afternoon, I couldn't handle it a moment longer so I called my social worker. We went to the foster-carer's house, but we didn't knock on the door. We stood silently and watched Lucy playing happily with three other children in the garden. She was unaware that I was there. Her hair had been cut short. It didn't suit her and I didn't like it. As I watched, my heart tightened. I felt short of breath. She was toddling around with a face covered in mud and she was carrying a small plastic spade. My social worker put an arm around me, but I was starting to feel numb. In a split second Lucy turned and looked at me. Her face was blank. There was no spark of recognition. She walked off. Had she already forgotten who I was?

We got back into the car and silently drove off.

'Take me to my foster-mum's,' I said.

'Is that a good idea?' my social worker asked. 'I know you haven't spoken in months.'

'Does she know about this?'

'Yes, we informed her.'

That afternoon, my mother and I sat in her house and cried, comforting each other. So much had changed. Her long days of depression had gone and she seemed to be coping with life so much better. I could see that she needed to have someone in her life to look after almost as much as Lucy needed someone to look after her. Mum needed to have someone to fill the gap left by the departure of her husband and her own children. Having up till then taken the attitude that I had made my bed and would have to lie in it, she agreed to throw me a lifeline. Although she was not willing to do anything to support me personally while I was struggling to bring up Lucy on my own, she would take Lucy over and would bring her up, just as she had brought me up.

Two weeks later she took custody of Lucy. Instead of just the two choices – stay on benefits going nowhere or give my girl up for adoption – I could now work towards a better future for all of us. My foster-mum became Lucy's foster-mum too, as well as being her Nan, and I watched them both bond and blossom together. I hoped that Mum would be able to love Lucy unconditionally, even if she hadn't been able to do that for me.

12
MONA LISA

....

'Prostitution gives her an opportunity to meet people. It provides fresh air and wholesome exercise, and it keeps her out of trouble.'

Joseph Heller

I was nineteen when I opened my first escort agency. To start with, the business was nothing more than a telephone and a small ad in the local free paper; it was run from my council flat. For the first few weeks I went out myself to all the calls and put Helen's number on an answerphone. She took enquiries while I was out. She was such a good friend to me, always happy to support me in any way I asked. She would even come round and clean my house out of the goodness of her heart, because I was so bad at doing it myself. In the end I started paying her for the cleaning since she was doing it anyway.

Mine was the first agency of its kind in Sheffield and within months there was too much business for me to be able to handle it all myself. I was going to need to recruit other girls. At that time such ads weren't allowed in the evening paper. They carried sauna ads but not agency ones. It seemed ridiculous to me so I decided to see if I could change things.

I worked out the annual revenue that I estimated the paper would lose by not accepting my ad, and then rang them up to put it to them. I must have been pretty persuasive because they saw my point and agreed to accept my business. The ads had to appear in the 'personal services' section rather than in the 'recruitment' columns so that we could be sure everyone who answered them understood what was being asked. I had to be careful with the wording of the ads to make sure that I couldn't be accused of leading people into prostitution who hadn't already thought about it. Whenever I interviewed new girls I always made sure that they understood they could drop out at any time if they weren't comfortable. If they weren't completely sure that they wanted to do it they wouldn't have been any good at it anyway. Through the ads I recruited several lovely ladies who were in a different league to the other working girls I'd met: it wasn't long before I had established Sheffield's first escort service. A diploma in massage – genuine diploma, dodgy examiner – made it possible for me quickly to expand my services to Lincoln and its surrounding areas.

I also found myself a reliable driver, never having got round to learning to drive myself. Dennis was a taxi driver who also ran a white limousine for weddings. He was short, balding and wore glasses. He reminded me of Bob Hoskins in the film *Mona Lisa*.

We first met when he booked my services. When I asked for the address he wanted me to go to, I got a shock because he lived just around the corner from me. Providing professional services to anyone who lived too close always made me nervous. I didn't want to get a reputation with the neighbours and have to move on again. Luckily, when we did meet we discovered that we didn't already know each other. On the mantelpiece in his house was a picture of a young, slim, pretty redhead.

'Is this your daughter?' I asked.

'No.' He looked a little embarrassed. 'She's me wife. Do you know her?'

'No,' I said, examining the picture more closely. 'Should I?'

Dennis looked relieved.

'I only ask because you and her have summat in common.'

'What's that, then?'

'She's a working girl too. That's how I met her.'

It was obvious by the way he talked that he worshipped her. I wondered what could be going wrong between them that he needed to call on me.

We did it on his lounge floor, on a rug in front of the gas fire. Dennis said he felt less guilty than he would have done in his marital bed. He was gentle and tender and it was all over very quickly. I didn't know until after that his five-year-old child had been asleep upstairs all the time. It was the one and only time we 'did business' in that way. From then on he became my employee instead of the other way round.

One day Donna called me out of the blue.

'Charlie, I've got a favour to ask. I need a job. I've got

no nappies. I daren't go back on the beat. I'm already paying off fines from the last time . . .'

My heart sank. I was running a 'respectable' business now: I didn't want to use girls like her. I tried to turn her down gently. But she didn't want to listen.

'Look, you owe me!' She was angry and desperate.

'Okay, calm down. I'll see what I can do.'

I suppose in a way I still did feel I owed her for all she had taught me. Or maybe I just felt sorry for her, remembering how desperate it was to be out of nappies and having to beg for work. I rang one of the regular punters: Neil had always said he would try out all the new girls I found. He was a straightforward client and booked Donna immediately on my recommendation. I rang her back.

'Look, Donna, there's just one thing. Look after this one. Not only is he one of our best clients – he's in a wheelchair.'

I always warned girls when a client was disabled so that they wouldn't be taken by surprise and say something hurtful on the spur of the moment. Having set up the meeting I put it out of my mind.

Later that night I felt I was back where I'd started: I was sat in a grotty police cell, and Donna was in the shit up to her middle. The police told me what had happened. She'd gone in with two young Afro-Caribbean males and terrorised Neil, tipping the defenceless man out of his wheelchair and robbing him of the few measly quid he had.

The police had come to arrest me because my number was the only one Neil could give them. I felt sick about the whole thing. I didn't like the idea of being labelled a grass, but under the circumstances I had no hesitation in giving a statement, even though I was putting myself at risk of prosecution. I narrowly escaped charges of running a vice ring. This break was not because I gave evidence but because the sergeant involved agreed with me that it might cause further embarrassment for Neil should it come out in the papers.

The sergeant turned out to be a gem. He was very understanding. He also said that he thought mobile hookers were actually a great idea for disabled people, especially if they found dating difficult: why shouldn't they be able to have sex with an able-bodied woman if both parties were consenting?

Donna's barrister played on the fact that she was a single mother of two small children, one of whom was disabled. She was spared prison but that meant she was back out on the street and looking for revenge. After the trial the reprisals continued for some time. I was followed, mugged by a couple of guys who were strangers to our estate and hissed the word 'grass' at me as they robbed me on my way home. I was beaten and harassed for months. I had to move house for the second time in six months and had to start up my agency again, scared that otherwise I would be traced.

A friend, Gus, owned a house in Rotherham that he was renting out so I moved into it. Gus had a business that specialised in putting together business plans for new companies, a service which was relatively unheard of at that time. I'd met him when I went to him with an idea for a service company that would network businesses, which, had I launched it at that time, would have been unique. It was an idea I was very excited about. Through sharing ideas he taught me a great deal about general business practices and I have him to thank for encouraging my own business acumen. He also became one of my best friends.

Gus told me how surprised he was that I was a hooker. He became my mentor and commented flatteringly on things like my intellect and creativity – I couldn't believe that he was talking about me!

But Gus was no fool and he could see that there were other areas of my life that required more attention before I started launching a new business. In truth, I think he saw me as a daughter figure, which was very refreshing for me, since not even my parents seemed to see me in that light any more. His daughter from his first marriage was around my age and he'd had little contact with her for years. He was the only person I knew around that time who genuinely cared about me without trying to change me or screw me. Despite what everyone else thought, he wanted nothing from me except friendship.

Unable to find me once I'd moved to Rotherham, relatives of Donna's friends – the two black guys who had been sent away for what they did to Dwayne – came and smashed all my mother's windows. She and Lucy were terrified and eventually were also forced into moving to the other side of the city – something my mother never let me forget. It must have been her worst nightmare, reminding her of all the times she'd had to move as a child as Ethel had struggled to make ends meet. I hated the fact that I had caused trouble for her and Lucy, the two people I most wanted to protect.

My association with Donna was now well and truly over. She had crossed a dangerous line and had become my worst enemy.

Putting my troubles to one side as best I could, I concentrated on the new business, building up a nice base of regular clients, both for the agency and for myself, and recruiting new girls. As things got better financially I was able to hire a maid to answer my door and take bookings while I was working.

One of my most entertaining clients was an Irishman called Billy. He was a pub landlord in a small country village. Billy's family had come over from Ireland during the potato famine. As a young boy he delighted in stealing his father's whisky and graduated to chickens from a local farm, to fund his taste 'for a wee dram'. In truth, running a pub was a pastime for Billy to keep his soul afloat and his wife in shopping. One day when I was visiting him he came out with a new request.

'I feels I knows yer a bit better,' he said, 'an' I was wondering if you'd do something to make this old man happy!'

'Sorry, Billy, marriage is out of the question!' I joked.

'Now, b' God, if I could take ye for mi fine wife 'n' ditch mi own that would be grand,' he chuckled. 'But she'd surely sink me in mi own cellar! No, it's something else.'

'What's that, then?' I asked, forcing myself to listen seriously.

'The missus is going out Saturday morning, on a shopping trip with her sister . . . I don't have to open the pub up till lunchtime . . .'

I rang Dennis and asked him to collect me the following Saturday morning. One of the things I liked about hiring Dennis was that he would always open the car door for me like a perfect gentleman. I soon realised that he had developed a crush on me, despite the fact that he was still in love with his wife. He told me how he felt about me but I made it clear that it could only be a business relationship. I really didn't fancy him at all. It worked well, our little arrangement, and I was proud that I could put 'chauffeured limo on request' on my business cards.

We drove to Billy's pub, the radio playing 'You Win Again'. Dennis looked as if he was about to say something but then he looked away.

'You okay?' I asked softly. But he wasn't really listening, lost in his own thoughts.

'You know,' he said eventually, 'when you finish work, does it put you off sex?'

'Well, no – not unless I've been really busy,' I said, having a feeling that I knew where this was going. 'Sometimes it's loving rather than sex I want at the end of the day.'

Dennis smoothed his moustache, apparently plucking up the courage to say something painful.

'She's lost all interest,' he said eventually. 'I just can't seem to talk to her, I can't reach her . . .'

I was a bit surprised to hear that. I'd always thought they were a happy family, despite the fact that she'd been on the game.

'Sometimes,' he went on, 'I think she married me just because she wanted a stable family life, that maybe she never really loved me.'

117

He looked into his wing mirror. I could see that he was upset. I reached out to his left hand on the gearstick and squeezed it.

'I'm sure you're wrong,' I said. 'Maybe it's just a phase.'

'You were the only other one,' he said solemnly, making a left turn. 'Ever.'

'I know,' I said, 'and she'll never find out about it from me – I promise.'

10cc were singing 'I'm Not In Love'. Dennis turned the radio off.

'We're here now.'

The first time I'd met Billy, Dennis and I had stopped by his pub for a drink and a loo break. The pub looked like it was stuck in a time warp and didn't get many strangers. We'd stuck our heads in and were just about to make our escape when Billy shouted us in.

He had a round face and ruddy complexion and looked like the squire of the village. His charm, hospitality and loud, fast humour ensured that we felt welcome and pretty soon all the regulars followed his lead and were talking to us as well. Billy was what my gran would call a 'rum old bugger'. His rude, coarse laugh echoed all around the old beamed hostelry. He didn't miss a trick. As soon as he sussed Dennis wasn't my other half he instantly became more interested in me, eventually becoming one of my favourite clients.

Billy was from a strict Catholic background and his thirst for adventure was equalled only by his thirst for liquor. Now that I was working at the escort end of the

market, offering clients the complete 'girlfriend experience', I was finding I enjoyed the work a lot. I liked sex,
and I often liked the clients. When a client was paying for
my time, rather than just paying an itemised bill, it
changed everything. Rather than having to spend a full
hour or two hours having sex with them, I could make it
a lot easier on myself by using other forms of seduction
such as conversation, skills like eye contact, and tricks of
sexual charisma like crossing and uncrossing my legs in a
sensual manner. I would take great care over what I
wore, making sure that I had seams up the backs of my
stockings and that I wore suspenders. If a client said he
wanted me to take charge from the moment I arrived,
then that was what I would do. I had to know how to
listen sympathetically if he wanted to tell me his little
secrets. Sometimes I would have to listen to a completely
fantasised life story and pretend to believe him, and at
other times I had to pretend that the client was really
turning me on because he fancied himself as a real stud-
muffin who could put a girl on the ceiling. I had to know
how to massage a man's mind, a skill I came to think of
as cerebral masturbation, totally unlike the head-fuck I'd
been subjected to on the streets!

The roles of a class whore and the activities she performs
are a million miles from the clinical transactions on the
streets where girls are there to fuck or be fucked. It's more
like being a geisha or a courtesan. I had started to enjoy
learning the arts of sensuality in the saunas but the atmosphere in those places was never as nice as it was once it was
just me and a client together in a pleasant environment. As
an escort I could actually be myself and I could be in control.

It was a feeling of liberation, being free to experiment with more things and explore new fetishes. Although it was a much safer setting than the places where I had started out, it did make me vulnerable emotionally. I found I was exposing more of my inner self and I constantly ran the risk of becoming involved with my clients.

Billy and I had had a lot of fun in the past exploring all the general fantasy role-playing scenes like me being dressed as a copper and arresting him, mild domination and me playing the part of a nurse with a good bedside manner. Instead of feeling like a prostitute I felt more like an actress.

He'd told me what his fantasy was for that day and I'd come prepared.

Dennis pulled into the pub's empty rear car park and, as usual, Billy was waiting eagerly to sneak me in via the back door, straight up the stairs to his bedroom. Today was to be my introduction to *sensory deprivation*. Armed with a carpet-bag full of climbing ropes, silk scarves, cling film, bubble wrap, brown paper, pins, candles, duct tape – and a mystery container – I started on the assault course.

Billy had a large oak four-poster bed and I swiftly had his fat, hairy, naked body spreadeagled. I had climbing ropes securing his arms and silk stockings for his ankles. Then I blindfolded him with a silk scarf. Next I placed headphones over his ears. Now he was well and truly disconnected from the world, with only his beloved Herb Alpert's Tijuana Brass to keep him company. First part of the task now in hand, I set off downstairs for a nice little solitary drinking spree. Half a bottle of Jack

Daniel's and six small packets of peanuts later, it was time for the main event.

The mystery container was supposed to contain shit. In reality it was an old Tupperware dish filled with mud from my garden. This I was to smear over Billy's cock. Next I wrapped him from head to toe in bubble wrap and stuck pins in to burst the bubbles. He had duct tape around his mouth and was forced to lie on the bed like a frozen chicken, unable to move or speak.

During the next round I wrapped his entire body in brown paper and sealed it with wax, making him look like a huge brown-paper mummy. That was the moment when I heard a car pull up outside. Then I heard a loud banging on the front door. I looked out of the bedroom window to see a massive woman wearing a flowery headscarf and weighed down with shopping bags standing at the door. Fuck! His wife had come home early. I hesitated for a moment and glanced back at Billy. There was no time to free him. I knew it would be much worse if she saw me there. (Plus she looked pretty damn scary to me!) There was nothing else for it. I left him there, clattered back down the stairs and out of the back door, still dressed in my Luftwaffe uniform.

I ran into the rear car park, my PVC boots crunching on the gravel. Dennis realised that something was wrong and spun the car around to meet me. The tyres squealed loudly as we pulled out of the car park like something in a scene from *The Sweeney*.

The next day my maid told me that a client was ringing persistently, trying to get her to give him my address. I didn't like the sound of that. The next time he rang my curiosity got the better of me and I took the phone off her. I immediately recognised the Irish voice.

'Hi, Billy,' I said nervously. 'What's up?'

'I wants yer address, me dear.'

'What for?' I asked suspiciously.

'I wants to send yer sum flowers!'

I paused, waiting for the pay-off.

'I've been trying to get me wife to tie me up and batter me for thirty years – I got the biggest hard-on in me life when she took the blindfold off!'

I could imagine the sort of battering that formidable-looking woman would have given him. It was just as well he enjoyed that sort of thing as I very much doubted whether she would have been in the mood to do anything else for him.

Life is full of surprises. One Sunday in April the police turned up at my new home with news that I would never have expected.

'We've come to ask you some questions about the murder of . . .'

I was stunned. Dennis's wife had been found dead.

'Do you know her or her husband?' the policeman asked.

'Well, yes . . .'

'We have information that says you were his mistress.'

Where had that nugget of gossip appeared from? I should have laughed at that one but in all honesty I felt like I was deep-frozen. I couldn't breathe. Murder? That was a whole other ball game.

'We've found dried-blood handprints on the curtains where they'd been pulled closed after the murder,' he went on when I didn't say anything. I was just shaking my head in disbelief.

It all seemed so bizarre; surely this was a sick joke or a terrible mistake. Apparently satisfied that I didn't know anything else, the police left. I never heard another thing about the case, nor about Dennis, since we had no friends in common. It seems extraordinary that a murder would create so small a stir, but I suppose that in the eyes of the police and the press it was just another unsolved case.

13

STARS IN MY EYES . . .

....

'I awoke one morning and found myself famous.'
Byron

Mum and I had a very on/off relationship at that time. I would go round to see Lucy when I could, usually every fortnight or so, but Mum and I would always end up rowing about something. I was not a good mother: once or twice I even let Lucy down by saying that I would go and pick her up and then crying off at the last minute. I always had an excuse, which impressed no one except me. I was unreliable and all my priorities were the wrong way round, but I was convinced that I was doing the best thing for all of us by working hard and trying to get on in the world. I had become more interested in the business and in men than in my own child.

The sad fact was that my life was so exciting most of the time that motherhood seemed a pretty mundane thing – especially as I felt I had failed at being a mother in the first place by choosing to give Lucy away. Playing with children had been easy before I had one of my own. At college I had learned how important playing was for bonding but for some strange reason I didn't seem able to sit on the floor with my own child and actually play any games or make anything with her. I was okay when it came to the bedtime stories or taking her out, but it seemed that anything requiring any greater closeness was difficult for me and so I missed out on a lot.

I realised that one of the reasons Mum and I fell out so much was because I had disempowered her with my behaviour. I would swan in and out when I felt like it, appearing with wads of cash and making her feel like a charity case.

'I'm the one who gives out the discipline, as well as the love,' she kept telling me. 'And when you come along she idolises you, thinks the sun shines out of your backside!'

So I changed a few things. I started to send regular amounts so that Mum controlled how it was spent, and I tried to turn up when I said I would, generally appreciating them both in the way they deserved. It started to work wonders and things did get onto a better footing for a while. I felt I had finally started to grow up.

It wasn't long after I'd started the agency that I found myself catapulted into the national spotlight. Although I did accidentally set myself up for it, the speed with which everything happened still took me by surprise. It all started with the *Kilroy* show. I was watching it at home when some questions came up on the screen at the end: 'Are you a working mother? Do you find it hard to juggle work and family?'

Without really thinking what the outcome would be, I rang the number they gave and confessed that I had sacrificed my daughter for my career. Naively I thought people would be more interested in how difficult things had been as a single mum than in the exact nature of my career. I didn't even think about what I was admitting and didn't anticipate the sensation this revelation would cause. The researcher listened to what I had to say and then rang back and invited me down to London to appear on the next show that they were filming. It suddenly seemed like a very exciting thing to do; I guess most extrovert young people like the idea of appearing on the telly. I set off for London the next day, first class, all expenses paid, with no idea what lay in store.

A few hours later the studio lights were dazzling my eyes and my make-up had started to melt in the heat. There were rows of chairs, which the audience had begun to fill while chattering excitedly. The front row had names on the seats for all the celebrities who were busy being fitted with microphones somewhere out the back.

I was about to take a seat in the audience when a woman with headphones came over.

'Are you Charlie?' she asked.

'Yes.'

She took me out of the audience section and led me to the middle front-row seat. To my amazement it had my name on it! She tucked a cold black box into the back of my outfit and pinned a small microphone to my collar. The morning's caffeine fix kicked in and my head started to buzz. Why was I sat with the celebrities? Suddenly I felt important, yet I didn't know why. I became very excited.

On my left was Maeve Haran, a novelist, and on my right was Reneé Short MP. I couldn't believe I was really there, watching a TV crew running manically around the studio preparing for the cameras to roll.

A group of older ladies on the back rows started loudly comparing notes as the omnipotent host strode into the studio, his tan as golden as ever, the whites of his teeth and eyes giving him his characteristic 'George Hamilton smile'. He was captivating and assertive as he charmed his way around the audience, taking my hand and shaking it firmly. His sharply cut suit looked like it had come straight from Savile Row. There was the faintest aroma of expensive aftershave. He was every bit the smooth, debonair operator and grannies' favourite. I thought I wouldn't be star-struck, yet I truly was in awe of the former barrister and hot TV show host of the moment – Robert Kilroy-Silk.

It was now apparent why I was sat in the hot seat, since I became the central focus of the debate. The show opened with me admitting to sacrificing Lucy for my career.

The well-spoken Reneé Short MP asked me, 'Why couldn't you have considered a nanny?'

I remember thinking, what planet did you just drop off? I'd barely got off the streets when I gave Lucy up and prostitution is hardly a steady job: you might work for a couple of nights and then get your period for four days or get picked up by the police. Where would I have found the money to pay a nanny's wages? And what half-decent nanny would have wanted to work for me in my council flat? But I held on to all my thoughts and calmly replied

'I couldn't have afforded it.' Which was definitely true at the time.

The novelist had written a book entitled *Having It All* – I had about as much in common with her as I had with the MP and I couldn't relate to her or to her book title. I looked like the typical girl next door, having just turned twenty-one. I behaved as if my chosen profession was quite normal, because in my world it was. No one else mentioned it either and why should they? That wasn't the topic of the programme. Although I was nervous I managed to stay cool under pressure and delivered my comments in a pleasant, articulate manner. As I got control of my nerves I started to enjoy myself.

Kilroy-Silk steered the debate with a manipulative air, always the puppeteer with the velvet touch. All the women seemed to revel in his aura.

Not in a million years would I ever have expected celebrity treatment when I made the phone call to the programme, nor had I imagined that I would have my full name and the escort agency name flashing on the screen each time I spoke. And I certainly didn't expect to wake up on the following Sunday and find myself the subject of a *News of the World* investigation. I suppose, if I had ever given the matter any thought at all, I would have assumed that people who appeared in the Sunday papers knew that it was coming and would've had time to prepare themselves.

I bet one of my ladies was equally surprised to appear in the article alongside me. She wouldn't have realised that the last hotel escort I'd fixed her up with, in good faith, was actually a newspaper reporter. Luckily, the article only mentioned her stage name and they hadn't taken a photo, so she was spared any major embarrassment.

Neither did I expect the paper to print the name of the small street I lived on. I never dreamed that a reporter would dig through my bins, where he found out that I only paid thirty-four pounds a week for my council flat, comparing it with how much I charged by the hour, so making my comments about not being able to afford childcare look hypocritical. What he didn't explain when these details were printed was that I had only been earning good money for a very short time, and that it still wasn't a steady enough income for me to think about hiring a nanny for Lucy – even if I could have found one who would have been willing to be employed by a prostitute. I was hardly in a position to be able to offer a regular salary and job security to an experienced childcare worker.

At first I was mortified by the exposure. I felt violated, not sure what repercussions from my neighbours it would lead to, not to mention the consequences from the police and local authorities. But then my pal Gus calmed me down. 'How's the business line today?' he asked once I'd finished telling him my woes.

I had to admit that the phone had rung until the answerphone had overheated. But I had been too scared to answer any of the calls, fearing that it would be more reporters, or the police, or my mother.

He laughed: 'No publicity is bad publicity!'

By the time Gus had finished calming me down I could see that he was right. The skies had not fallen in. In fact, life seemed to be going on around me quite normally. I don't know what I had expected to happen, but I began to realise that my fears were irrational. Maybe this wasn't the end of the world. After all, the reporter had really only printed stuff that was largely true. In fact, the *News of the World* had provided me with an even more effective advertising platform than the television programme. Free of charge, too.

The following morning, I rang the *Kilroy* office to check that they didn't think I had set the whole thing up to cash in on their programme. I was reassured that Kilroy-Silk himself was not at all shocked and had enjoyed my mature and thought-provoking input in the studio – something that was validated later, when I was asked to appear on his show for a second time.

Once I realised that I wasn't in imminent danger of being arrested or lynched I decided to take Gus's advice and make the most of my sudden visibility in the public eye. I returned the messages on the answering machine and got on with building up the agency. Business was now going through the roof and I was suddenly earning thousands of pounds a month, exactly the situation I had been working to achieve for so long. The *News of the World* article had lifted me from being a small-town operator to being a nationally well-known madam overnight.

Now the truth was out I decided that I was going to exploit it. If I didn't want the story to die and my name to drift back out of the public's consciousness, I needed to add more fuel to the fire. I contacted a different paper, *The Sport* and the following week I appeared in the *Sunday Sport* under the heading 'Champagne Charlie's five star sex perks'. It was also my first topless photo.

'Take your top off, love!' the cockney photographer encouraged me, sounding slightly bored.

Click, click, click.

'Put your top back on, love – you've got tits like a spaniel's ears!'

His casual comment cut me deeply, bringing back all my old fears that I wasn't as attractive as other girls. I've got him to thank for inspiring my first boob job.

I was intoxicated at that time by what I perceived to be success, relating it completely to fame and money. I had no sense that my notoriety and the way in which I had earned it might be shallow. It felt wonderful. Suddenly people were recognising me in the street. I'd go into some shops and restaurants and be treated like a queen – and I loved it! The more attention I got, the more confident, flamboyant and extrovert both my outfits and my personality became. The more people made a fuss of me the more others whispered and wanted to know who I was. I felt that I had to live up to this persona that I had created – a loud, mad and bright character.

Now I can understand exactly how celebrities lose sight of reality and start to turn into the exaggerated projections everyone else has of them, because it is what everyone around you wants you to do. The image that I'd accidentally created was of a strong and powerful woman, which meant that I soon found myself in situations where I had to live up to my new reputation. I've heard how film stars who frequently play gangsters sometimes find themselves being challenged to fights by drunks in bars who want to prove their manhood. I suffered from a similar syndrome.

I felt like I'd hit the big time and in the good moments I was brimming with confidence. But underneath the new swagger I was still full of all the insecurities that had plagued me since I was a small child: can anyone love me? Am I attractive? Am I just a piece of clay for everyone else to model?

Once I had got used to the idea of being well known and had realised that it was actually very good for business, Gus and I started to look around for other publicity opportunities. Apart from anything else I was enjoying the attention now that I'd got over the initial shock.

Gus and I both supported Sheffield United so one Saturday we went to the match together. The stadium was a thronging, singing and chanting mass of 25,000 Sheffield United-ites and Aston Villa fans. Gus was wearing a big cheesy grin as if to say 'You lot don't know what I know!'

The whistle blew. The fans were shouting and jumping around. We were deafened by the 'Aahs' and 'Oohs'. The atmosphere was incredible and the tension was high – I was so excited.

I grabbed Gus's hand and we struggled through the mass of bodies together to get to the front. Once we got there I turned to face the crowd. My heart felt like a bass drum in my ears! Gus pulled the front of my coat together and held it while I wriggled my arms out of the sleeves and held onto the front lapels as if it were a cape: underneath I was wearing only a pair of knickers and a pair of high heels. I stepped out of my shoes. The fans next to us started to twig what was going on and began nudging each other. There was no going back now. Gus bent down and picked up my shoes.

'Good luck,' he shouted. 'Ring me when you get out!'

With that I threw my coat off, straddled an advertising hoarding and ran onto the pitch with only my knickers on! (Well, did you expect the Full Monty? It might have been Sheffield, but it was still a family match!)

As my feet felt the cold damp grass I heard the most deafening roar! The fans were going wild. I ran towards the ball. Paul McGrath (Aston Villa) was tackling Brian Deane. Deano, as us United fans used to call him, was concentrating on the ball – until he realised that the roar was not for him. He looked up at the naked vision running towards him and opened his mouth wide enough to fit the goal posts in. At that point I heard the fans chanting the same thing over and over

'She's got a lot o' bottle!'

It was an electrifying moment. I felt glorious and liberated. I ran for a few minutes more and then, when the cops decided that I'd held up the match for long enough, they sent one young red-faced bobby onto the pitch to chase me. I didn't resist for long and he wrapped his coat around me.

As I was escorted off the pitch I took one last look at the huge stands thronged with fans, all watching. It was breathtaking. We reached the edge of the pitch and a rapturous round of applause filled the stadium. Even the coppers were clapping.

They didn't even arrest me. I was simply let out of the office workers' entrance in full United kit and bare feet. I felt exhilarated and happy. It had been fun. Had Gus and

I planned it a bit more, of course, we would have chosen a match that was going to be televised. But at the time we were both simply reacting to the recent publicity and acting spontaneously.

Not everything about my new-found glory was positive. A lot of my old friends felt threatened by my new status. I was no longer the average working-class girl – I didn't fit in quite as I used to. I'd set out to make myself different from all the other people living in the tower blocks and council houses that I had come from, and I'd succeeded. But one of the results of being different was that not everyone was comfortable around me. I acquired a lot of new friends, many of whom turned out not to be genuine, but I lost a lot of good ones too. To some I was no more than a novelty, a token 'Meet my friend, she's a madam!' The publicity led people to expect that they'd meet a strong, extravagant, bold, dramatic character, so I was determined not to disappoint them. I always wore bright colours and animal prints, and sometimes I even added a little shock value by wearing classy outfits that were made of fetish materials like leather and rubber.

At the same time, however, I often felt lonely, even when I was surrounded by people. I found it difficult to trust anyone. I longed to have at least one decent man in my private life, but my newly gained reputation made that increasingly hard to achieve. How many well-balanced, decent men want to go out with a notorious hooker and madam? And where would I meet them, anyway? I only really mixed in rough circles like blues clubs.

*   *   *

One guy I met was John, an insurance salesman with a flash car. I even took him home to meet Mum. Mum spotted a hole in the bottom of John's shoe and warned me off, though at the time I thought she was being ridiculous.

'That one's all fur coat and no knickers,' she counselled, but I knew better, didn't I? I assumed she just didn't like him because he was black.

'This one's different, Mum,' I insisted. 'He's a hard-working guy.'

Not long after that we were sitting in John's flash car, which it turned out he didn't own anyway, and we got into an argument about something stupid, I can't even remember what it was. By this time I had learned to spot some of the danger signs of a man with the potential for violence, but I really had no idea that John was about to explode. Next thing I knew, he was chasing me up the street. I could hardly breathe and I certainly couldn't run any faster – but he was already catching me up. What had I said that had made him snap like that? The usual sexy look on his handsome black face had changed, making it look contorted, and his eyes were bulging with fury.

I saw the mini-tower on the estate where I was living and I ran for the stairs with every ounce of strength I possessed. My feet pounded up the concrete steps two at a time and my heart felt like it was going to burst. I'd got my key ready in my hand and I was almost at my door. I could hear John getting closer and I felt his heavy breath on my back. Suddenly my feet went from under me and I hit the deck face down as he grabbed my ankles and pulled my entire body weight down onto the grey stone steps. Thud, thud, thud – my chin bounced off each one and the pain in my head was terrible, throbbing and pulsating. Chink. The key dropped over the banister. My high-pitched screams echoed around the concrete walls. As John dragged me down to the landing I felt the concrete grazing my face.

A neighbour came out to see what the noise was all about. The monster looked annoyed at the interruption.

'Get back in your flat and mind your own fucking business!' he snarled.

The door slammed shut and I heard a chain slide on.

I was sat cowering, covered in blood, and one of my teeth had come loose. John grabbed a handful of my hair and tried to pull me up by it. I was trying to resist but it was no use.

'Get up, you stupid fucking bitch, or I'll smash your head into the floor!'

I jumped up and half thought about trying to escape, but as I looked around he anticipated it. Grabbing my arm this time, he made me find the key and escort him back to the flat. I tried to take my time, hoping that the police would come, summoned by the neighbour, but they never did.

As soon as my door had slammed shut, John started with his fists. First a flattening blow to the stomach and then one to the chest. One of the punches winded me and I was on the floor. He must have kicked the back of my head next – I don't remember feeling it but I do re-member passing out briefly and seeing stars as I came round. He pulled my arm up behind my back, twisting my little finger. I pleaded with him to stop but he was somewhere and someone else. He was still pulling on my finger and he started to yell again.

'You stupid whore – look what you made me do!'

I screamed as I heard the snap.

For the last time John pulled me up, grabbed my hair and smashed my head through the window.

After he'd gone I crawled to the phone and rang Gus. I couldn't talk properly but he knew it was me and came around to pick up the pieces. Before he took me to the hospital he held me, cradling me like a baby, but I couldn't even cry. I was still shaking.

Was there something wrong with me? How could I have been so ecstatically happy for three months with this gorgeous man, an apparently hard-working and professional guy? John wasn't even the ghetto type that a working girl might attract. When he'd been punching my face I'd looked deep into his eyes as I'd pleaded with him but I'd hardly recognised him.

When I got to the hospital the sister said I was lucky: the top of my head had taken the impact of the window. We joked about me having a hard head. I *was* lucky – only one small splinter of glass had become lodged under my purple right eye. The sister looked into my eyes as she bandaged my hand. I looked away, embarrassed to imagine what sort of a woman she was seeing.

14

SUFFER LITTLE CHILDREN

....

Let me slumber in the hollow where the blossoms
*   wave*
With never stone or rail to fence my bed
Should be the sturdy station children pull the blush
*   flowers on my grave –*
I may chance to hear them romping overhead.

Adam Lindsay Gordon

I was dreaming that the phone was ringing, until I woke up and realised that it actually was. I looked out of the window, hoping for some sunshine, but it was just a dull grey, ordinary day. The phone continued – must be important.

One arm fell out from under the quilt as I clumsily manoeuvred the handset.

'Do you do hotel visits, please?' enquired the well-spoken male voice on the other end. My trained ear told me that he was in his fifties.

'Certainly, sir. Where are you staying?'

'I'm at the Grand, on Main Street. Do you know it?'

Of course I knew it. It was the finest, most expensive hotel in town. I was glad that I hadn't already given him a quote! 'I can have someone there in an hour.'

I opened one eye, pushed back the quilt and looked at my alarm clock. Damn, no lie-in this morning.

'Could you give me some details first, please?' The slight trace of a soft Scottish accent was present.

'Well, she would be a sexy busty brunette.' Sitting up in the large bed, I checked my reflection in the ceiling mirror. 'Aged twenty-one, slim and attractive.'

I certainly wasn't feeling very sexy as I smoothed down the crow's-nest that had appeared on my head. After the heavy excesses of the previous evening I had a mouth that felt like a camel's in the Gobi Desert. Still, I thought, life must go on.

'Haven't you anyone younger?' the voice persisted.

Here we go again, I thought – I'm definitely getting too old for this; I'll have to send one of the others out. Feeling a small fib coming on, I bit my lip. 'Well, er, um, I have an eighteen-year-old, a petite blonde called Jane . . .'

My eyes closed. Okay, so Jane was twenty but she *did* look younger. This sort of thing was all in the mind, anyway. If the customer believed that she was the age of his fantasies then he would be happy.

'Actually, I was wondering about someone, well . . . younger.'

Whether I liked it or not I knew a lot of guys fantasised about the nubile bodies of teenagers. 'Younger than eighteen?' I replied, my sexy phone manner disappearing as the first traces of suspicion appeared.

'Well, I've never done this sort of thing before, I was just wondering . . .'

'What did you have in mind?' I asked cautiously.

'About eight, actually . . .' He waited for my response.

My heart jumped into my mouth and my brain went on strike.

'Pardon?' I spluttered, my stomach churning.

He started to get flustered. 'Sorry, sorry.'

My brain was now working overtime: he's going to hang up. Don't blow it; keep him on the line – must be some way to deal with this sick bastard.

'Look, let me be straight with you,' I said, trying to regain my composure and keep my voice even, like a true professional. I wanted to swear at him, call him a foul name, slam the phone down, but something held me back. 'You just caught me off guard, you know, maybe I can help you . . .' By now the room had started to spin.

'You think so?' His tone brightened up. I guess maybe he hadn't been feeling too optimistic that he was going to find what he wanted.

'Yes, definitely. But let me make sure I've got this right – tell me exactly what you're looking for.'

My knees were trembling. This can't be right, I thought. He must be a reporter. But whatever is going on, something is wrong. I'm going to have to play this one thinking on my feet.

'Well, I want a young girl, no more than eight.' His voice was still nervous – maybe he suspected a trap – and he hesitated slightly. 'With curly blonde hair and rosy cheeks.'

My body became hot, flushed, paralysed by this stunning statement. By now I realised he was deadly serious; this was no reporter.

'Okay. Look – I need to make some enquiries and get back to you. I'll need your details first.'

'My name is James . . . I *can* trust you, can't I?'

'Of course you can!' I said, hoping that I didn't sound sarcastic.

I was screaming inside. The truth was, no matter how hard I tried to remove it he had now imprinted a strong vision in my mind of the young girl of his fantasies playing naked in the sunshine, unaware of her vulnerability. I felt contaminated by him, guilty of being privy to his fantasy.

Something about the relish with which he'd described the girl he wanted struck me as chillingly evocative, as if recalled from a memory of someone he once knew . . .

A few minutes later I was sitting with a coffee, reflecting on the situation that I had suddenly found myself in. Making room for other people's differences and deviations was a necessary tool of the trade. Right from the start I'd experienced my fair share of weirdness. I'd been part of a world soaked in fetishist imagery, exposed to every pervert's peccadillo.

Like most people working in the industry I had my own small unspoken code of ethics that was never to be broken, wherever I worked. Never anything without a condom, never animals and, most importantly, *definitely* never – ever – kids.

I looked over at a beautiful photograph of Lucy watching me with trusting eyes. I felt the anger prickle every nerve of my body and I held the picture against my chest.

How could this man want to place his adult-sized

penis into a human less than three feet tall, whose vagina had not yet been opened? A girl who sideways on would have none of the curves of a woman, a body not yet in mature proportions, tummy sticking out and no trace of puberty? I was now completely certain that I had to do something to put a stop to this James creep.

One hour later there was a loud knock at the door. As I opened it, a familiar rugged face, framed in blond wavy hair, smiled at me.

'Come in, John,' I said. 'Thanks for getting round so soon.'

The tall thirty-something blue-eyed man leaned against my porch. 'Nothing beats having a cuppa with you!' He winked cheekily.

I'd first met John on the night when Donna had robbed Dwayne. He had been the investigating officer and we had clicked immediately. There had been a spark between us from the first moment but it had never gone anywhere. He was a married man and neither of us was foolish enough to risk his home life or his career through him having an affair with me.

'You sounded upset on the phone – is everything all right?'

'Not really,' I said. 'In fact, I want to talk to you about something serious.'

He laughed; he'd heard that one before. But this time I didn't need him to check out another car registration number of some dodgy client.

John cocked his head to one side when he saw my expression.

'After all this time,' he sighed, 'I still put up with you manipulating me.'

I managed a half-smile, poured the coffees and we both walked into the lounge. We sat on the settee. 'For once I do want to help you. Think of today as the big payback day.'

I gave John a word-for-word account of the telephone conversation with James at the Grand, or as much of it as I could remember. All the flippancy left his manner immediately. Once he'd heard what I had to say he made one quick call and within minutes a special unit of plain-clothes officers had invaded my lounge. John wasn't part of the team and he left them after briefing one of the suits.

I spent almost an hour making endless coffees and repeating myself over and over. I was starting to wonder what I'd got myself into. This wasn't a situation I was comfortable in on any level. Normally I went out of my way to avoid the police. In any dealings I'd ever had with them all of them, except John, had treated me with something between contempt and lechery. I was used to receiving the tart treatment from most coppers and one officer in particular seemed intent on winding me up that day. His name was Jack and he had a long beaky nose and a rather unattractive case of dandruff snowing around his shoulders.

'So this is where you bring your clients, then?' He twitched his nose like a rat as he spoke, looking round the room and sneering. He obviously thought he was being clever. His clothes hung limply on his skinny frame. His shirt looked as if it had been slept in. I reminded myself that I must try and stay polite. The last thing I wanted was to make an enemy on the force; there were so many ways they could make my life uncomfortable if they chose.

'I've already explained,' I said. 'This is my home – I'm mobile.'

Jack tried his best to extract from me how I knew John, but I simply referred back to the robbery.

A pleasant-looking guy with ginger hair sensed the brewing animosity. Walking over briskly, he placed his stocky frame between us, aiming an aggressive glance in Jack's direction. Dandruff Man left silently. Ginger seemed to be more senior, even though he was much younger.

'I'm Detective Inspector Fowler,' he said, introducing himself to me. 'But you can call me Jim.'

So Ginger had a name and a personality. Perhaps things were looking up.

'I've met his type before. Divorced grumpy old bastard who's not getting any!' I said.

Jim raised an eyebrow. 'Some of us are human, you know!'

I knew what he meant. I shouldn't judge all policemen, any more than they should judge all prostitutes.

The phone rang and the previously buzzing room fell silent. It seemed as though the whole world by now was staring at me, expecting me to handle this right.

Ginger spoke: 'Keep calm, think, talk slowly and tell him you'll call him back. Wait for David on recording to give you a nod before you start talking.'

I moved towards the phone in slow motion. I carefully

lifted the receiver from its cradle. My hand was shaking. I looked at David who gave me the nod.

'Hello, can I help you?' I said, trying to keep the tremor from my voice.

'Hello, love, it's Mum. I couldn't get you on your personal line – the answerphone was on.' My mother's voice boomed in my ear as she started rattling away at high speed. The officer who was hooked up to some kind of recording device cursed, pulling an ear-piece away, feedback screeching around his head.

I let out my breath, feeling relieved. 'Hi, Mum.'

The buzz in the room started again as the plain-clothes unit went back into waiting mode. I guess coppers must spend half their lives hanging around waiting for things to happen.

As I put the phone down I realised that Ginger was laughing. I was glad *he* thought it was funny. I couldn't stop shaking. I stormed into the kitchen, slamming the door behind me. The room fell silent. Ginger opened the kitchen door tentatively and poked his head round. 'I'm not enjoying this much either, you know. It's just that after a while in this job you learn to distance yourself.'

Ironic. Wasn't that supposed to be *my* line?

I stood with my back to him, motionless, staring at my garden through the window.

Ginger didn't see the tears that were by now flowing freely from my eyes. The phone rang again and I flew back into the lounge.

By the time James rang back that afternoon I'd decided that I needed to think one step ahead of the coppers. Unlike them, I couldn't risk reprisals. I had to be sure that I would be safe if anything went wrong and most of all I didn't want there to be any risk of finding myself stranded alone with James if there was even a chance he could suss that I'd stitched him up. I knew my cover would be blown if I arrived at the hotel without the girl, having promised to bring her with me.

So, with that in my mind, I told him there had been a change of plan. I would now collect him from the hotel and take him to the girl, instead of bringing the girl to him.

Of course, it would never get as far as actually having to take James anywhere. With any luck he'd be arrested in the hotel, but only if I could win his trust *and* skilfully get him to repeat his requests for the benefit of a wire *and* hand over the money. The police needed to have concrete proof of his intentions, not just the word of a madam.

I'd decided that the money was to be one thousand pounds, up front. At first James had been taken aback by the amount but then, sensing his dream slip away, he'd asked for extra time to go to the bank.

Ginger challenged my plan. He thought I was running a risk of losing James if he couldn't afford the price. I wanted to make sure that the jury would convict him and the way I saw it the greater the sum of money, the greater the intention. After all, the last thing I wanted was for him to walk away from court, free to reoffend or to come looking for me. I had to demonstrate just how serious he was in his plans.

Once in the hotel lift I pressed the button marked six to take me to the top floor. I watched the numbers climb steadily, secretly hoping for once that the lift might get stuck and the evil moment would be delayed for at least a few minutes. The doors opened suddenly, making me jump. I stepped into the corridor and glanced back into the lift. I bit my lip and hesitated, tempted to jump straight back in and head for the street. The transmitter strapped against my chest might have been concealed from view but it only served to increase the weight against my heart. I forced myself to turn and walk away as the lift's doors closed behind me.

The corridor seemed to go on for ever. Unnecessarily, I checked the slip of paper – the room number was now branded in my mind: 650. It was the end room. Other than the wind whistling, like in a cheap horror movie, there was an eerie silence.

I walked past many doors. All the rooms behind them seemed quiet and lifeless. I couldn't hear the usual muffled TV and people noises. But then, the hotel had been undergoing a recent refurbishment so maybe the rooms were unoccupied.

Finally, standing in front of the door to number 650 I could hear movement in the room. The TV was barely audible. Taking a deep breath, I tapped lightly. No reply. I tapped again, louder. I heard someone shuffle to the door. It opened slowly. I stood back, preparing myself to take in a full view of this hideous monster.

In front of me stood a weaselly little man who stood no higher than my chest. A few strands of chestnut and silver hair were combed across the top of his head and on his face was a beard of matching colours. His suit was old-fashioned tweed and on his feet were mustard-coloured socks and Jesus sandals. The monster had a kindly face, which was wearing a genuine smile of welcome. I looked into his eyes, searching for some clue, but they were not at all scary. He reminded me of one of my favourite old teachers. I must have the wrong guy surely.

'Hi, is it James?' I asked.

We stood for a moment in awkward silence, and then both of us went to speak at the same time. This embarrassing moment was followed by nervous laughter.

'Aye, lass! Well, last time I looked, anyway.'

He slid sideways and ushered me into the room politely. The blood was pumping round my heart like a river about to burst its banks. God, I hoped I didn't mess this up. I must try to keep my head clear.

'Would you like to join me in a wee dram of whisky to warm your cockles?' James enquired, like the perfect host.

I nodded politely. I noticed his hand was shaking as he poured me a more than generous measure. He handed me the glass. I hate whisky.

'Would you care to sit down?'

'No, no, I . . .' I was lost for words.

'Aye, well, I guess time is ticking along.'

I knocked back the drink far too quickly and my head started to thump.

'Would you like another?'

'No, thank you – purely for medicinal purposes.'

The exchanging of pleasantries was becoming tedious. I wanted to ask James to confirm the arrangements. My mind went blank. My whole body was frozen. I'd rehearsed the part in my mind a thousand times, but it was all lost somewhere in space – somewhere I would rather have been.

He gently tapped me on the shoulder, making me jump.

'Shall we go, then?' he asked.

'Yes, of course – have you got the money?'

'Oh yes – hang on a minute.'

James reached into his inside pocket and pulled out a tatty brown envelope.

'You might like to check it first.'

I took the envelope from his hand. It was damp with the sweat from his palm. I counted it carefully as I planned what to say next.

'How much is here?' I asked, wanting him to say it out loud for the microphone.

James looked at me, agitated, and dabbed his forehead with a neatly pressed handkerchief that he had produced from another pocket.

'A thousand pounds – that was right, wasn't it? I haven't got any more!'

His manner was stern and accusing: he was starting to panic, worrying that he might be being ripped off.

'No, yes, I mean yes, that's right, I was just checking.' I still hadn't got James to say the magic words that would confirm what he believed he was purchasing with the money. 'Are you sure this is what you want?'

'Yes, I'm sure, but I have a couple of questions to ask first. I didn't like talking on the phone.'

Gratefully, I let him take the lead. Maybe he would incriminate himself without my help. 'Fire away.'

'Well, has she done this sort of thing before? Because I don't want that.'

I felt the whisky returning to my throat, mixed with bile. I swallowed and caught my breath. 'No, she hasn't.'

I'd found it so difficult to be angry with James up until now. This all seemed so unreal. It seemed impossible that he was the man I'd spoken to on the phone but as I looked at the money I finally accepted that he was. I felt my fury rise. How could he? I closed my eyes.

I could see the girl again. Now I would have to bring her to life for him. 'Julie is an eight-year-old virgin and she is exactly as you described.'

The lights in the room seemed to be getting brighter and I started to sway.

'Are you all right?' he asked, with genuine concern.

But I wasn't and I was starting to lose my patience with him. I still needed to get him to confirm his perverted intentions. 'I'm fine! Now, I just want to make sure . . .'

James interrupted me again. 'Oh, and another thing: will she be drugged?'

I glanced at my empty glass. I didn't know how to answer. 'Erm, well, not yet.'

He was rubbing his hands together. 'No!' His voice changed and became frustrated. 'I don't want that either!'

I had to strike now. 'Are you actually going to have sex with her?'

'What's going on?'

I felt myself colour up. If he'd smelled a rat, he would never confess now.

'Of course I am, you stupid woman,' James blundered on, showing his true colours. 'Did you think I wanted her for adoption?'

My whole body went stiff. He started fumbling around in a drawer, looking desperately for something. What was he trying to find? Was I in danger? I took a quick step back towards the door. I opened it and shouted down the deserted corridor.

'The rat's in the trap!'

I heard a dozen doors slam, followed by the heavy thud of running feet. The room was instantly filled with action and confusion.

I was pushed sharply to one side and fell over a briefcase. I crumpled onto the floor in the corner. No one even knew I was there. James was floored instantly under a pile of officers, landing face up. The police had left nothing to chance and by now they were combing the room for anything suspicious.

It all seemed too much – like an overplayed melodrama. I almost felt sorry for James but then I saw the vision of the little girl again. Would even this much drama stop him pursuing his sick adventures?

I rose from the floor, sliding my back up against the wall. My mouth went dry. 'Look what that dirty bastard's left over there!'

For a split second I diverted the attention of everyone in the room. They turned to where I was pointing. Then I was on him! A knife I'd smuggled into the hotel in my boot was now pressed against his neck. From the base of my soul I bellowed into his ear, 'Think of little girls again and remember how I nearly slit your fucking throat . . .'

Now it was my turn. I was disarmed, face down and crying. Now I was the one in cuffs. It was no consolation that a warm trickle of golden liquid had seeped through James's trousers, covering both of us.

Someone shouted from the other side of the room. 'You dumb whore! What makes you think you're any better than him? We didn't need the amateur dramatics.'

'Jack – get out!' Ginger screamed. Dandruff Man stormed out of the room.

After a few more moments of confusion Ginger came over to me, holding his head in his hands. At the other end of the room some of the other officers were escorting a shaken James out. Ginger undid my cuffs silently. Only the two of us were left in the room. I rubbed my wrists.

'Where on earth did you all come from?' I asked.

'We had the whole floor evacuated room by room this afternoon.'

'Talk about overkill. Was that really necessary?'

'Not my idea – orders from above. Look, don't you think *we* were angry? But we just can't mark him, or the whole thing falls apart. The best deal we get is the arrest.'

'Did I blow it?'

'No, you've done a sterling job. But he *could* try to press charges against you.'

But it would be months before I would know the true consequences of my actions . . .

15
THE BODYGUARD
....

'Of one so young,
So rich in nature's store,
Who could not say,
'Tis pity she's a whore?'
John Ford

Soon after the arrest of James at the Grand, I rented a building right in the middle of Hanover Square, Sheffield to turn into a massage parlour. It was the red-light district – formerly known as Havelock Square – where the infamous Peter Sutcliffe, the 'Yorkshire Ripper', had been arrested. I thought it was an ideal location: a stone's throw away from the city centre, it had been developed quite recently and rents were still pretty cheap there.

My business was booming. As well as working myself and running the agency, I had also rented several private flats and I'd collected a great base of international girls through the ads in the papers. Many of them were students, including Russians, Brazilians and virtually every other nationality. One of the national papers ran a story about the five-star treatment that I was offering the ladies who worked for me, giving me a nickname that was to stick for years – *Champagne Charlie*. The women I now worked with were not the usual jaded sauna girls like Cheryl, or cokeheads like Tania; they were mostly reliable and had no other commitments. More importantly, they were beautiful and intelligent.

One of the key elements in becoming a successful madam is matching the two sides – the working girl and the client – together. The business had grown from nothing to being seriously substantial in just a few months. Basically the girls rented rooms off me and I would drum up the business for them. What they got up to with the clients in those rooms was between them.

The place in Hanover Square was an ordinary small shop unit that I fitted out, fronted to look like a beauty salon. Each room had a handmade wooden massage couch with a coloured leather top that coordinated with the room's decor. It was clean and tastefully furnished – a million miles from the usual dirt and squalor of downmarket massage parlours. Because of the calibre of ladies I hired, it was totally different to anything else in Sheffield at that time.

I'd also made a good friend in one of my ladies, Amanda. She'd been working for me for so long that I no longer charged her room-rent. She'd helped me set up and run the place and was good all round for business. Amanda was a very pretty middle-class girl, a buxom size 16 with long auburn hair. She always looked immaculate and mostly wore snappy business suits, stockings and high heels.

The police knew we were there but they didn't bother us. One of the local bobbies, Ben, was a real down-to-earth character. Occasionally he would drop by for a cuppa, something to eat or a game of cards. Having learned my lesson from the incident with Donna I was always careful not to give him any information about the business. I didn't want to be classed as a grass again, but I did want to remain on his right side. He was a funny, likeable man who said that he openly supported girls who worked behind closed doors as distinct from, as he put it, 'the dregs that crawled along the local gutter'.

The entrance to the parlour was discreetly placed at the rear of the building, as was the car park. Unfortunately the local street girls found out we were there, having seen the constant stream of luxury vehicles arriving and leaving, and moved their beat so that they were directly on the street at the entrance to my car park, hoping to tempt our clients with their cheap pick-up lines and catcalls. All they did attract, however, was trouble.

The nearby residents had been battling for many years to clean their area up. They had to keep calling the police to move the street girls back. As you can imagine, a constant police presence was not conducive to the successful management of a busy brothel. There was no way of knowing how many potential clients had driven straight past when they saw the police cars there.

Some of the street girls got frustrated that the new wave of clients visiting us were obviously not interested in them. I guess they were jealous of our success and felt that we were making them look like second-class citizens. They organised a group of ghetto guys (some of whom were their boyfriends) to damage or steal from the clients' cars while they were parked up. A couple of clients were even mugged as they left the premises.

It soon became obvious that if I couldn't get the girls to move back to their usual location myself I would either have to close down or find someone who could persuade them for me.

To start with, I hired a security guard who claimed to be ex-SAS but turned out to be more like a Girl Guide. The street girls ate him for breakfast! It was almost funny, especially when I got an anonymous tip-off saying that he was outside the pub, tied to a lamp-post, and I should go and fetch him. When I got there I found him with his trousers down round his ankles. They'd dressed him in suspenders and put a sign around his neck that said 'I am a pervert'. Of course, I had no other option but to add to his humiliation by sacking him.

In a weird twist of fate it turned out that my hairdresser, Carrie, had been a working girl many years before. She was not happy in her current profession and so came to work with me as a receptionist. Unfortunately, she ended up being tempted by the money the other girls were making, something I was not happy about because I knew her husband, who never realised she'd switched sides.

More problems arose inside the parlour when our close-knit circle of ladies started expanding. Carrie knew a lot of the local street girls and had originally tried to smooth things over with them on my behalf. She also recommended one of her pals to me as a receptionist. This woman turned out to be a rude, aggressive former street girl who, when sacked, became very bitter and added to the bad feeling about me on the street. I don't think Carrie had any bad intentions; she just seemed to attract problems.

Wanting to live near to the job, I had moved around the corner from the brothel into a soulless basic converted-warehouse apartment. I was miserable and lonely there and it never felt safe. Unknown to me, I'd been clocked going home by a couple of the troublemakers and twice I came back to find the door hanging off and the place totally trashed. Then I found myself being followed by a couple of black guys in flash cars, and they didn't look like clients or police to me. It was beginning to seem like I might be in personal danger. I was living constantly on edge, determined not to give in and allow them to drive me out of the business I'd worked so hard to build.

Amanda recommended a new security guard but he tried to muscle in, fancying himself as protection. He also turned out to be a cokehead. So then I had to hire more security – *to get rid of security*. I was in it up to my neck.

Things were tough around that time and I was getting used to hearing bad news, but one bulletin came as a specially big shock. Ben, the policeman, came round to the parlour on one of his regular visits. As always, he came to the back door after hours for what I would call his 'cuppa and occasional supper', bringing with him a Chinese takeaway.

'He's out,' he told me.

'Who?'

But before he could say any more it clicked with me that we were talking about James the paedophile.

'He got community service . . .'

'Oh, great irony – I bet they'll put him to work in a nursery!'

'Problem was, it was only attempted,' Ben went on as he opened up the takeaway.

'He *was* going to go through with it! What about the huge sum of money he had handed over? The way he was going to follow me? The whole thing?'

I simply couldn't understand it.

'How did the jury judge him?'

'They didn't. He pleaded guilty – it went in his favour.'

'I don't believe I'm hearing this!'

'I'm sorry I had to tell you but there are limits to what a judge can do on that charge . . . and, well, the guy had no previous.'

'You mean he hadn't been caught before! Bastard!' I paced around the room. I had a strange feeling that I hadn't heard the last of this one. The idea that the creep was out there and angry with me added to my paranoia. But, as it turned out, it wasn't James the paedophile who I needed to worry about.

16

MOTH TO A FLAME

....

'Mad, bad, and dangerous to know.'
Lady Caroline Lamb

The new man in my life was a guy I'll refer to as Hector. He was mixed-race and unlike many of my previous fellas he was strong and loving. He was the first man other than Don who could stand up to me and I found that irresistible. Hector offered the one thing Don had never been able to – commitment. Like a moth to a flame, I saw his strength as an asset.

Hector adored me. His actions clearly showed that he worshipped the ground I walked on and, again, this was all new territory to me. So it was hardly surprising that when I started to reciprocate the feeling we entered into a highly charged and passionate relationship.

Strangely enough, he also lived on the same estate as my birth mother. For six months everything went well. I'd never met a man, other than a client, who wanted to do so much for me and I even stopped working myself while we were together. He was intelligent, deep and thoughtful and I believed that I'd finally met my soulmate. We'd both had a past – but what did that matter? To me all that counted was the future.

Don wasn't so sure about the union. I'd actually met Hector through Don, who'd known him for years. He'd taken me with him while they were doing some business together.

Right from that first moment I'd been enchanted by Hector's charm.

Don, who had sensed the attraction, warned me off immediately. But surely he must have realised that when he told me Hector was 'mad, bad, and dangerous to know' it would be a red rag to this silly bullette. I simply passed it off as Don being jealous since this was the first time I wasn't going to be available at his convenience. At last I had found a man who wanted all of me instead of just the parts that suited him.

One day I was sat in Hector's lounge playing a computer game. It wasn't even a very good game, but I was hooked. I'd been playing for over two hours and had just got myself onto the next level. Hector was trying to put together some kind of a business plan. He wasn't good with reading and writing and asked for my help. I paused the game. Hector was trying to think of the right words and so, while he was doing that, I switched the game back on – much to his annoyance. He was right: it was inconsiderate of me not to pay more attention – he was always very good about paying attention to me. But of course I never had much patience and we ended up having a small verbal disagreement. Suddenly Hector landed me a crushing blow to the side of my skull and sent me reeling into the TV.

I was taken by surprise, unable to understand how he could have fallen so far and so fast from loving me so gently and completely. Did he mean to hit me so hard that he cracked my jaw? Did something snap inside him? Could he not control it?

'Get upstairs!' he bellowed.

I climbed the stairs, shaking. I knew I was in for it. Something had flipped in Hector's brain and he was beyond reasoning with. He had turned into someone else, someone I didn't recognise, the guy that Don had warned me about. I heard him locking the front door and knew there was no other way out of the house.

'Get undressed, you fucking whore!' Hector flicked back his shoulder-length braids. I'd never noticed before how small and beady his eyes were. I didn't want another beating – I'd had enough of those in my life – so I undressed slowly and got into the bed. He picked up my clothes and shoes and disappeared downstairs with them.

Hector was gone for some time and I lay in the bed, locked inside the house, waiting for whatever would come next. Eventually he returned without the clothes and got into bed with me. He was no longer my loving, tender Hector. He stuck it into me violently and slapped me about a bit, getting off on it. He fucked me hard and seemed to enjoy hurting me. Why did he think I was such a tough nut to crack? Then he came back for more. The violence went on and on for hours. I began to doubt that I was ever going to leave that house alive.

I later discovered that he'd buried my clothes in the back garden, but he didn't tell me – he just left me a prisoner in the house. I was terrified and confused. How had my bad manners suddenly turned me so evil in his eyes?

After Hector had kept me in there for two days without any food I was begging for mercy, but he showed me none. My chance to escape finally came when he had to go out to the bank. He carefully locked me in as he left. He had already locked away all the telephones in the house. I knew this might be my last chance to get out alive. The moment he was gone I searched frantically until I found a spare key for the back door, the pounding of my heart booming in my ears as I listened out for the sound of Hector's return, knowing how angry he would be if he even suspected that I'd tried to get away. At that moment I had no idea what he'd done with my clothes, so I ran from the house dressed in whatever I could grab from his wardrobe. The only person I could think to turn to was Don, who I trusted to protect me.

The next day Don went to see Hector and they had a big fight. Hector was an ex-boxer and Don was into martial arts. It must have been like *Clash of the Titans*. It all ended in a stand – off, but somehow Hector managed to take Don's Filofax/diary from him – a theft which would seal my fate.

Six weeks later I was getting over Hector in my own way, which meant I was in a blues club in the Pitsmoor area of Sheffield, coincidentally about a hundred yards from the spot where my birth father had been murdered.

I knew everyone there and everyone knew me. Of course, I was notorious for all the wrong reasons and there were several of my former ladies milling around in there with their men of the moment. It was always interesting watching the young men who hung out in those places: one moment they looked like kids and the next moment they were fighting the big men of the time, trying to take over their 'runnings', which was the street way of saying their dodgy dealings. I was seeing a couple of guys at the same time, but nothing serious. One of them came in and bought me a drink, then went off somewhere, I didn't ask where. Another arrived and had a dance with me – that was all he was going to get from me that night. I'd decided that from then on I was going to be calling the shots.

The club's owner was a big one-eyed black guy. He had an awesome reputation with the ladies and more kids dotted around the city than he had customers for his den. He called his club 'Donkeyman's' – but I won't speculate about why! I liked his club the best of all of them. He poured me a drink as I smiled at someone I knew. He handed me the plastic cup and touched my arm.

'Watcha dat woman who 'ave more man than man 'ave woman!' he growled.

I looked at him and laughed. Why not? I thought. It was about time that the balance changed a bit. Blues clubs were always intimidating but in truth I loved the adrenalin rush they gave me. Rightly or wrongly, I enjoyed the fact I was always shown respect for being what they called 'dat big woman who runs t'ings'.

Two of Hector's henchmen came up to me. I knew them both pretty well and didn't think to question it when one of them asked me to come outside. I felt happy and confident and the peach drink I'd just had was warming my insides. But once outside the cold air hit me and I was in for a shock.

Hector was waiting for me in the back of the car that they were now bundling me into. The next thing I knew I was sat next to him and as I watched the other two walk away one of them turned and pointed the key fob at the car. The central locking clicked down.

I stared at the car's leather interior and tinted windows.

'Raped you, did I?' Hector sneered.

'No! I never told anyone that!'

Hector had read what I'd told Don – in Don's diary. I hadn't told Don that Hector had raped me, but Don had listened to my saga and had written that he did. Was it really rape? I was so scared at the time; I didn't put up a fight, did I?

Now Hector was furious to think that I would talk about him to someone else. He was out for revenge. Gone were his neat braids. His hair was now in a new lank wet-look shoulder-length style – I hardly recognised him as the same man I had been so in love with just a short time before.

I must have looked desperate, pushing at the car-door handle, but it was no use – I was trapped, helpless and in Hector's power once more. I had no idea what he had planned for me next.

A few minutes later the other two returned. As the central locking clicked off, Hector got out and left me in the car. His two henchmen now got into the front of the vehicle. I thought for a split second about fleeing but as soon as the notion entered my head they'd locked the doors again.

I tried to reason with them and even offered them money – but it was no good, they were too scared to go against Hector. One of them tried to reassure me that everything was going to be fine but my stomach told me different. Hector returned and climbed back in next to me. I had one more desperate try at escaping but he grabbed my hair, forcing my head down onto his lap. I knew by then that my attempts to escape were not just futile, they were actually making things worse.

We drove silently for a few minutes to a dimly lit area full of flats. All three men seemed to know where they were heading. From what I could see through the darkened windows as we pulled up and Hector jerked me upright, the place looked rough. Gripping me hard, Hector dragged me out of the car, forcing my arm painfully up my back. He escorted me – I was stumbling awkwardly – towards a building. The entrance he was heading for was down some stairs – it must have been a basement flat but I wasn't taking in many details, too fearful of what was to come. I do remember that the front door was behind a padlocked iron gate. Hector took a key from one of the others and I was forced inside.

The stench that greeted me was foul. Now I had time to take in the details of my surroundings. There was a kitchenette attached to a living area and there were mouldy plates and green-slimed milk bottles everywhere. The sink was crammed full of nasty pots and pans that looked as if they were breeding bacteria.

Hector was grinning. He sent the others out, coming up close to my face, cold and angry, impossible to reason with.

'I treated you like a fucking queen,' he hissed, 'and look how you respect me – spreading shit around about me!'

'I, but, I . . .' It was no good: he didn't want to listen. I doubted that he could even hear my voice. I was petrified and I begged and pleaded until I was on my knees. I knew I had no other option – maybe this was all he wanted of me, to see me grovel.

'Well, it's about time you got your hands dirty for me,' Hector said.

I had no idea whose flat it was, or how long he had been saving those putrid pots for me to wash up. The idea of it seemed to really excite him. He'd always known that washing-up was something I disliked doing and he used to say that he would do the dishes for me ' 'cos you are my queen'.

I could see that there was no escape. I stood slowly and started to wash those pots in boiling water; I scrubbed and cleaned until my fingers were raw and red. The hideous look on Hector's face, as an erection and a damp patch appeared in his jogging bottoms, will be for ever burned into my mind.

I have no idea how long this had been his sick fantasy. He made me kneel down to please him, and made me choke. And when he told me to lie down and open my legs he seemed to enjoy making me beg and plead and sob like a child. When he was on top of me with his greasy wet-look hair on my face, his look was so evil that I still see it in my nightmares.

When Hector finally felt that he had punished me enough and allowed me to stumble away, it took me three days to talk to the police. A doctor had to open me up and scrape inside me – my vagina, my mouth and my arse. It felt as if he was violating me all over again, just like Hector had.

There are some things in life that make us all angry, creating a simmering anger that boils up over years and will not evaporate. I still fantasise every day about my revenge: I never knew that my thoughts could be so evil.

The Crown Prosecution Service decided not to go ahead with prosecuting Hector for raping me. They also didn't bother with kidnapping charges, despite the fact that his two co-accused turned Queen's Evidence against him and actually admitted to their part in the events.

One reason I was given for letting him off was that he had made me put a condom on him, which suggested I'd been cooperating! Another reason was undoubtedly because of my background. They didn't think they would be able to get a conviction and they didn't want to waste taxpayers' money. I heard two very different off-the-record stories from the police. The first was that they were after him for heroin smuggling and that it wasn't in the public interest to prosecute him as it would blow thousands of pounds they'd spent on observation. They said I should be patient as he was looking at a much bigger sentence for that. But I later heard a more likely reason: Hector was a simply a local small-time informer.

I wanted to kill Hector. One night I went looking for him in the blues clubs, carrying a baseball bat. One of the guys who had helped him to abduct me took the bat off me, saying he would do the job for me. The guy had just finished doing a stretch for armed robbery and the next day I had to go and explain to his wife why he was now lying in a coma after Hector took the bat off him and stoved his skull in. She naturally assumed that her husband had gone after Hector because he and I had something going between us. It was hard to convince her that he simply felt he owed me.

Suddenly stories about Hector's violence were doing the rounds. I heard how he had once inserted a bottle into one of his baby mothers and then kicked it up inside her. On another occasion he made a girl suck on some heated curling tongs when he discovered she'd given another guy a blow job. I felt lucky to have survived at all. I'd somehow convinced myself that if I couldn't feel pain I wasn't in love. What a fool I was. It seemed as though I had 'shit-magnet' tattooed on my forehead – because that was all I ever attracted! But it was hardly surprising when I still limited my choices to guys I'd find in the murky depths of the ghetto blues clubs.

Why was I always attracted to violent, dangerous men? Was the excitement all part of wanting to be different? Was 'violence' merely the flip side of 'glamorous'? Maybe there were some nice, kind, ordinary guys out there who would have suited me well, but I just never noticed them because they didn't draw attention to themselves, weren't 'different' enough. Pain and suffering certainly seemed to add to the intensity of my love affairs. But my tastes were gradually dragging me lower.

17

TRIALS AND TRIBULATIONS

....

'The woman's a whore, and there's an end on't.'
Samuel Johnson

The tensions around the parlour in Hanover Square were building all the time. I knew that all the street girls outside hated me with a simmering resentment, but I still didn't appreciate just how much danger I was in. Then one evening the situation boiled over. We'd been closed for several hours and I was busy sorting out some paperwork when I heard a gentle tapping at the back door. Cautiously, I looked through the spy-hole and could only just make out a woman (who had previously worked for me), standing smiling in the dark. As I opened the door to ask her in, I got the shock of my life when she was ambushed by a group of street girls who had been waiting round the corner. My immediate thought was that she was being attacked but I soon realised that she was part of a trap – for me. I was pushed to the floor with such force my skull felt as if it had burst. There was a lot of screaming and shouting and someone produced what I think was a baseball bat, but I'm not sure, because it all happened so fast. I felt crushing blows and violent kicks as I curled helplessly into a tiny ball.

There was nothing I could do, I was completely outnumbered. One of them shouted at me, apparently on a high after inflicting their own version of rough justice, that they were going to be in the pub celebrating and I should meet them in there if I fancied my chances. Then as fast as they had come they were gone, with only the echoes of their laughter resounding around the empty car park.

I laid there for the longest time turning everything over in my mind: this latest attack, Hector and the way my life was heading. Bloodied, bruised and broken I pulled myself to my feet and stared at my reflection in the mirror. I had had enough. I couldn't live like this, in fear, for the rest of my life. Something inside me had snapped.

I staggered from the parlour in a daze, moving like a zombie, and found my way into the pub on automatic pilot. I must have looked a terrifying sight, walking into the bar covered in my own blood and carrying the screwdriver that I'd taken from the top of the fish tank. I don't remember clearly what happened next: I had to read later in my depositions that I stopped and lifted the heavy wooden security plank across the door to stop anyone leaving the premises.

I was not shouting or showing any visible signs of anger as I walked into the room. The group who had attacked me were all sat laughing, talking and drinking their pints, oblivious to my arrival. Suddenly I felt my arm move. It was now beyond my control. Someone else had possessed my body, someone who had nothing to lose anymore, someone who was numb. I brought my arm down suddenly in a frenzy of jerky movements and lashed out wildly. At first I couldn't hear any noise. I was in a world of my own and then suddenly there was one piercing scream, followed by the landlady yelling, 'Charlie – get out!' I looked at the girl in front of me clutching her face – it was all like something from a horror movie, blood was spurting from her eye socket.

I have no memory of how I got back to the parlour. I just remember hearing another knock at the back door and finding one of the local beat officers standing there.

'I've been called out on an argument between tarts over t'road, but I thought I would check in with you first,' he announced as I opened the door, still covered in blood.

'Oh God!' he said when he saw me and realised what had happened. 'Okay. Stay here.' He turned to leave, then did a double take. 'You won't go anywhere – will you?'

I waited obediently. Where could I have gone?

When he came back, accompanied now by another copper, he said very little, obviously moved by the state I was in. He knew all the participants in the drama and had also watched, over the previous weeks, as the tensions escalated.

He wouldn't even let his fellow officer cuff me. He could see that he didn't need to worry: I was broken and listless and would never have resisted arrest in any case. From the police station I put in a call to the only solicitor I knew, Robert, who had been my Sunday-school teacher when I was a child.

I was stunned and appalled to think that I was capable of such a dreadful act. I had terrified myself. I knew the girls had been asking for retaliation by beating me up, but no one could have anticipated that they would unleash such a terrible reaction – least of all me. Events moved fast after that, leaving me little time to reflect. I was put into a holding cell, charged and moved out of the area the following day to a bail hostel in Birmingham. As I had more time to think and my mind began to clear, bits of memory returned from that evening and I kept having to relive the moment when I had brought the screwdriver down. I was so, so sorry for what I had done, and frightened that if I was ever pushed like that again the same thing might happen. I was also afraid that my victim might come looking for me, wanting to avenge her lost eye.

A few weeks later my taxi pulled up in front of the courthouse. Crowds of onlookers, photographers and journalists pushed up against a line of policemen, all straining for a better view. I was still only twenty-one years old.

As soon as my high-heeled leg emerged from the door, journalists started to shout questions, cameras clicked away furiously and the volume of the crowd's voices grew louder.

Determined to make an impact, I had chosen my clothes carefully. I was wearing a well-tailored electric-blue suit: a double-breasted jacket (with padded shoulders), and a knee-length skirt that revealed silky stocking-covered legs. I got out of the taxi with a purposeful expression on my face, determined that no one would be able to guess how scared I was.

'Miss Daniels, are you expecting to go to prison today?'

'Charlie, tell us about the brothel!'

On the way over, Robert, my solicitor, had directed me not to smile or comment. He might as well not have bothered because my only concern was to get inside the building quickly and with as much dignity as possible.

He ushered me through the thronging crowd, aided by one of the policemen.

As soon as we were inside the building we managed to push our way out of the busy corridor and into one of the side rooms. A policeman stood outside the door to ensure we wouldn't be disturbed. Once inside the sanctuary of the room I let out a huge sigh of relief, even though I knew that the worst was yet to come.

Karen Stockton QC was already seated in the room. I could tell that she didn't like to be kept waiting. As my solicitor and I entered she stood up and smoothed down her black gown.

Her dark hair was severely scraped back underneath her white wig, making her chiselled cheekbones seem even more prominent. She looked about thirty, but her manner and the seniority of her position made it difficult to accurately assess her age. She extended her hand towards me sharply, only just connecting. She squeezed my fingers briefly and released them swiftly, indicating with a nod of her head that I should sit down. Looking down at the paperwork, she turned the pages of the file quickly as if giving them one last scan.

I found Karen's formality and manner intimidating (and I don't say that about many people). She certainly had an awesome presence and maybe, I told myself, this was a good start. If she could intimidate me, maybe she could impress a courtroom with her arguments.

The room, square and sparsely furnished, not much bigger than a prison cell, had one small window. The sun briefly appeared, its rays catching a gold crucifix on Karen's neck and momentarily filling the room with a glittering light. Although I didn't feel like it, I tried to thaw her frosty manner with a warm smile. It had no visible effect on her. How did she see me? I wondered. I waited patiently for her to speak, determined not to show my nerves by starting to babble.

'It seems to me quite straightforward, Miss Daniels,' she said eventually.

'Please, call me Charlie,' I said, trying my smile once more.

Karen raised her head solemnly. She looked directly at me, her annoying client.

'Obviously the charges relating to the running of the brothel *et al* are just icing on the cake. The prosecution will merely use them as a tool. But of course the other matter is a little more grave . . .'

I looked down at my bitten nails and started to pick at them nervously. She sternly advised me to plead guilty to the manslaughter charge. Her tone was sharp and it startled me. It was as if she was telling me off for what I'd done. I opened my eyes and stared into her calm face, searching. I leaned towards her. She knew that the women involved had attacked me moments before, that I had been provoked, but because of the circumstances I was battling against major prejudice. Robert had already warned me that it was going to be tougher for me to win the sympathy of the court because of the nature of the business I was involved in.

'I know what I've done,' I told Karen coldly. 'I don't need a lecture on feeling guilty.'

A day hadn't gone by when I hadn't reeled from the memory of what I'd done. Squalid police cells and manic

174

bail hostels in Birmingham and then Liverpool had given me plenty of time to think about it. From the day it happened the night terrors had arrived to haunt me. I would wake up in the morning, never knowing what I would find I had done in my sleep.

'Things simply weren't that black and white,' I said.

'Perhaps,' she snapped. 'But then, I doubt whether the jury will see it that way.'

'Why? Because I'm a madam? Because I'm a prostitute? If I'd been you, wouldn't I have been up on nothing more than a charge of excessive self-defence – instead of attempted murder?'

Her somewhat grey pallor turned crimson. 'Miss Daniels – *I am not you!*'

Tears welled up in my eyes. I could sense the hopelessness of my situation. If my own defence counsel held me in such contempt what chance did I have with a judge and jury? I looked towards my solicitor.

'Robert, is this really what I can expect?'

His small round bespectacled face twitched. He looked towards the window. 'I'm afraid the jury could well go against you – and yes, their decision may seem unfairly based on *what* you are, rather than *who*.'

Karen triumphantly snapped shut the file.

'Well,' she said, 'time's ticking on. Any questions, Miss Daniels?'

I watched, too choked to speak as the cloaked black crow silently left the room, the door slamming behind her.

I stared hard at Robert. 'Where did you get *her* from?'

He shuffled awkwardly in his seat. 'We originally met on the church circuit,' he almost whispered.

I rolled my eyes back in my head. It seemed ironic somehow. Robert had left a lasting impression on me years ago as my Sunday-school teacher. He was the only person I could think of to go to when the shit hit the fan.

'Look,' he said, 'she may be tough. But trust me, she knows her stuff.'

He cocked his head to one side, trying to smile. What had happened to make me surround myself in such a prickly shell? It was clear that he couldn't believe the freckled naive little girl he'd once taught was now hidden behind the mask of the young woman sitting in front of him.

'Did you mind me calling you?' I asked, suddenly aware that it must be as weird for him as it was for me.

'No, but it *was* a bit of a shock. Strangely enough, about a week before your call my wife asked if I'd heard anything from you – you've been in her prayers.'

Now it was my turn to shuffle. I looked away, trying to fight back the tears. Robert picked up his briefcase and led me silently out of the room.

The oversized courtroom had all the grand splendour of the Victorian age: tall Gothic arched windows and high vaulted ceilings plastered with wedding-cake trimmings. The public galleries were reminiscent of old school-rooms. Huge expanses of dark highly polished wood panelling surrounded an enormous organ-shaped pulpit, raised up like a stage, elevating the judge nearer to God. The Crown's crest boldly shone in gold above the pulpit.

'All rise.'

The room that had been buzzing with conversation fell into silence as the judge appeared. The formalities were well under way when I glanced to the back and recognised a few unwelcome faces in the galleries, plus several of the journalists who had been outside earlier and were now sat scribbling furiously.

The clerk rose. 'Charlie Daniels, you are brought here before this court charged with attempted murder. How do you plead – guilty or not guilty?'

I could hear the words *not guilty* in my head, which were the ones I was supposed to be saying. But then I remembered Karen's words: in a clear crisp voice I replied, 'Guilty, Your Honour.'

A murmur spread round the courtroom and the journalists stopped scribbling.

'And to the charges of exercising control over prostitutes, how do you plead?'

'Guilty.'

'And to the further charge of running a brothel, how do you plead?'

'Guilty as charged, Your Honour.'

Loud conversations broke out between the surprised observers as they forgot where they were in their excitement. An usher called out furiously for silence.

A guilty plea was completely unexpected, and the dramatic impact of my about-turn was obvious to everyone in the room.

The judge, who had been leaning over his paperwork, sat up suddenly and pulled his half-rimmed spectacles further down his nose, peering over the top of them. He looked for the first time at my bold blue-clad form and our gazes made contact.

'Do you wish to say anything to the court?'

My knees began trembling and my voice had become unsteady. I cleared my throat. 'I know no one believes me, but I am sorry for what I've done . . .'

Out of the corner of my eye I saw one of the journalists lean forward, staring intently.

'I know it's a terrible thing. I wasn't even angry when I did it, sort of out of my mind . . . like on the outside looking in, like in a movie . . . I wasn't even shouting or anything . . . it was just after they'd beaten me – I just totally lost it!'

But right now I was breaking down. My usually strong emotional shield was melting and tears started to cascade down my cheeks – the one thing I hadn't wanted to happen. I thought the witnesses might wrongly assume that I was putting on an Oscar-winning performance.

I saw the many staring faces and the room was now spinning. I felt isolated and vulnerable. 'I know I have to go to prison for what I've done – I don't deserve anything else . . .'

I stood, rendered silent as the noise in the room drowned out my speech.

'Silence!' The judge's cheeks were flushed. He looked back over to me but I was in another world.

The noise in the courtroom died down to a respectful whisper.

'Am I hearing you right?' the judge exclaimed loudly, bringing me back. 'Are you saying you meant to *kill* your victim?' He scratched his brow.

I tried to regain composure. 'Well, no – not exactly.'

'Miss Daniels, I ask you one last time! Did you or did you not mean to *kill* your victim?'

His impatience was starting to upset me. 'No! I didn't

even mean to hurt her. I know that I was wrong . . . I know it doesn't make it all right . . . I'll never forgive myself, I was a monster!'

I saw coloured flashes in front of my eyes and felt my feet go from under me. A female security guard rushed behind to keep me upright.

'Let her sit,' the judge told her.

That's it now, I'm done for – they'll throw away the key . . .

Actually, I couldn't have been more wrong. In a highly unusual move, the judge refused to accept my plea, clearly stating that I had what he called substantial mitigating circumstances.

When he said that, the noise in the gallery erupted; it sounded more like a football match. By now I was holding firmly on to the box to ensure that I didn't fall over and my knuckles were turning white.

'I *will* have silence!' the judge roared. 'If those of you in the court cannot conduct yourselves in a reasonable manner you will be removed from the court *immediately*!'

Security guards entered the gallery and I wiped my eyes on a tissue that the female guard had given me. For the first time the room fell into a deadly silence.

The judge turned to me again, lowering his head a little. He looked at me kindly as he told me, 'You are to be given full credit for your plea, one that could have saved the courts time and money, but that would surely do you an injustice.'

There would be another hearing. For the time being, at least, I was free to go. And I knew one thing for sure: I was going to change my counsel.

18

BAND OF GOLD

....

'Hanging and marriage, you know, go by Destiny.'
George Farquhar

The final bail hostel I was moved to was in Leeds, where I landed a job in a small family-run publishing company, selling advertising on commission. It was a revelation to me to discover that I could hold down a normal job and actually be useful. Not only did the experience teach me a great deal but I also formed some solid friendships with people I could trust. The company produced a local 'what's on' type of magazine.

The family who owned the company were very strait-laced compared to people I'd previously met. But as they got to know me they showed themselves to be immensely broad-minded and warm-hearted. I responded well to their encouragement and actually started to dream up special features of my own in order to sell more advertising for them. One such feature, 'Living with a disability', was particularly successful. It started as just a one-page article and ended up being a regular pull-out supplement after I persuaded Sir Jimmy Savile to give me an interview on the subject.

It felt so good to discover that I could contribute something positive to society, and also the job restored some sense of normality to set against the bizarre world I'd been a part of. Was there finally a chance for me outside the sex industry? Might I actually be able to turn my life around and win back the right to see Lucy regularly and be part of her life?

Not every part of my life, however, was going as well. I still didn't seem to be able to get the hang of personal relationships. I met Joe in a bail hostel and we'd become mates. He was a deep, interesting guy but he had serious problems and was a former heroin addict. He was always a Dracula shade of pale and was covered in self-made tattoos.

Mavis and Donald also lived in the hostel. They were both alcoholics who fought endlessly and then declared their undying love for one another. A month after they'd met they'd decided to get married. After their bizarre marriage, Joe and I started talking about ours – it started out as a joke. We laughed about how much better off we would both be in our respective court cases as a 're-spectable' married couple. We chatted about the wedding party and how many criminals from the hostel we would invite.

Then our relationship suddenly went from platonic to physical and became very intense. I'm still not sure if it happened because deep down we both so desperately wanted to meet our soulmates, or whether we both just needed someone to care for us. But whatever the reason it was intoxicating. Joe moved into a different hostel, where the staff only worked part-time and he had more independence. Everyone thought we would fizzle out once we were separated but we didn't: we missed being around one another immensely.

Desperate to cling on to something that seemed as if it might be real, I threw myself into the idea of getting married, although ours was a far from traditional wedding. I wore the one decent dress I'd managed to salvage from my days in Sheffield, a stunning navy-blue full-length ball gown with a beaded bodice.

The groom wore a black bolero jacket, grey trousers, brown crocodile shoes and a red kipper tie – different and interesting. Our witnesses included hostel staff and residents. Instead of having a 'proper' photographer, someone brought a pocket camera and took half a dozen snaps.

The wedding breakfast was a nosh-up in a greasy spoon. There was definitely no honeymoon – but at that particular moment we were blissfully happy.

A few days before the ceremony, Joe's best man, Gary, shocked us by perming his hair and dyeing it blonde. Then he asked us to call him Janine. Now, both Joe and I prided ourselves on being open-minded but this was still a surprise. Anyway, we decided to fully support our friend on his 'coming out' and, although I drew the line at him attending the ceremony in a formal bridesmaid's dress, I let him borrow one of my skirt suits and gave *him* a pre-wedding make-over.

After the wedding we went back to Joe's new hostel. Not long after, he disappeared off to the shops and I was left chatting to 'Janine'. A little later I went upstairs to the bathroom and that was when I heard the banging and screaming. My adoring new hubby had been out and stolen (yes, while on bail *and* on our wedding day) a large bottle of vodka and had been drinking it neat. He'd failed to tell me that he had exchanged his heroin addiction for alcohol, or that it made him violent when he used it. Yet again I had attracted someone dangerous. I came downstairs cautiously to find him pinning Janine to the kitchen door with various kitchen knives, like a circus show. Luckily, none of the knives had caught more than clothing but it was all too much for the unwilling victim who was flapping his arms around and squealing when it might have been wiser for him to stay very still indeed.

Realising that I might be the next target, I ran back up to the bathroom and locked the door, my head spinning. Was this really happening? Seconds later I heard Joe crashing up the stairs. Then he started to bang on the door and shout abuse. There was no reason for his anger – seemingly it had come from nowhere other than the bottom of a bottle. *Crunch!* I heard the door splinter as he kicked it off its hinges. Then he lurched drunkenly into the room, barely focusing. I didn't recognise him – he sounded like a film soundtrack on slow motion. I knew then that one of us was going to get hurt.

Between the bath and the toilet was a solid old wooden chair. As Joe came lunging towards me I instinctively picked it up and waved it in front of him.

'Stop!' I shrieked. 'What's the matter with you, for God's sake?'

But nothing he said was comprehensible – he just swayed and slavered and kept on coming towards me. It was then that I saw the knife he was still holding.

I felt the chair in my hands as my fingers started to

tingle. With all my strength I jabbed Joe several times with one of the chair's legs. It tore part of the roof of his mouth and removed several teeth. I refused to be ashamed of what I'd done: it was purely survival – him or me.

Janine, having unpinned herself from the kitchen door, called the police. His bail breached, Joe went straight back to prison. We wrote to one another for a little while. At first I told him that he'd had a fall and hurt himself, since he had no recollection of the event in the bathroom. In the end I had to tell him the truth because he couldn't understand how he'd got locked up and why I'd left him. Because I had acted in self-defence and because my new husband wouldn't be pressing charges, I was advised that the whole incident wouldn't affect my forthcoming trial.

So that was the end of our beautiful marriage. It lasted the sum total of four hours and was never even consummated. It had started out as a joke and I wasn't that surprised it had all ended in disaster, just disappointed; especially as most things seemed to end the same way for me at that time. I haven't seen Joe since that day.

Meanwhile Mavis and Donald's respective cases came to court. The original cases were dropped, but then it turned out that both of them were already married to other people. So they each did time for bigamy instead.

A few months after I'd left court for the first time I arrived at the office of Robert, my solicitor. He was sitting behind his desk. The office was a lot smaller than he needed or deserved. But he never complained – it wasn't his way. He'd told me how he'd put in many late nights over the years, including missing the birth of his first-born through spending the night at some police station as duty solicitor, something he said he would never forgive himself for.

I opened the door slowly and peeked round it like a child. I looked around at the organised chaos. There might have been piles of paper and files scattered everywhere, but I suspected Robert knew exactly where everything was.

'Nice and tidy as usual!' I teased.

He blushed and smiled. 'Come in – how are you feeling?'

I wanted to ask the same question. He hadn't changed over the years since he'd been my Sunday-school teacher – still the dedicated family man and workaholic. Photos of his children adorned every wall. I was willing to bet that he was an excellent father.

'I haven't seen my daughter since it all happened,' I told him, 'and my mother's already told me that she doesn't feel it's right to bring her to visit me inside. Whatever happens today, that's the highest price I'll ever have to pay.'

Robert's head sank. As a family man himself, I was sure he could imagine just how I was feeling. The phone rang to announce the arrival of the man I'd come to meet and I felt a twinge of nerves.

Robert ended his call with, 'Send him in.'

The door opened and a striking man entered the room. I felt a wave of relief. Robert rose from his chair and shook the stranger's hand vigorously. He seemed genuinely pleased to see him.

'Charlie, may I introduce you to Greg Bamford.'

I stared at the tall man in awe. He was Italian-looking and very charismatic.

'*Enchanté*, madam!' He took my hand and kissed it slowly, looking cheesily into my eyes with his own big brown sparklers. He followed this up with an exaggerated bow – I couldn't help but laugh loudly. A long ponytail trailed over his shoulder. Just his appearance had done the trick of releasing the tension of the situation.

Robert grinned: he knew how Greg would handle me because he'd already warned him of my strong personality. Greg seemed like a character from a Dickens novel, a bohemian dandy in a fitted jacket with rows of buttons and high lapels, and a big white collar and floppy white cuffs. I liked his style. I wanted to make him like me and see that I wasn't as terrible a person as my previous barrister had thought.

He pulled up a chair and spun it back to front before sitting astride it. He folded his arms and leaned over towards me, raising his eyebrows quizzically. 'Well,' he said, 'haven't *you* had a ride?'

I giggled, deliberately misconstruing the comment, wanting to inject a bit of humour into the situation. When it came to flirting and bantering with sexy men I knew I was on home territory.

Robert cleared his throat, looking flustered.

'You could lose that ponytail,' I quipped.

Greg looked at my own outfit but held on to his thoughts. 'And you can lose the cheek, lady, or suffer my hand across your backside!'

'You do – and I'll send you a bloody invoice!'

Judging by Robert's expression I don't think he'd ever heard Greg talk like this before. But whatever he was doing he'd got my full attention and that was okay with Robert.

As serious as this day was, all three of us fell about laughing. I could see that Robert was hoping he wasn't going to regret this introduction.

'Well, firstly, Charlie, let me explain something to you . . .' Greg's expression grew serious.

I listened intently.

'What happened at your first trial was most unusual. I've certainly never heard of anything like it!' Robert nodded his agreement. 'In fact, coming from that *particular* judge it can only serve to add greater weight to your case. The prosecution have already reduced the charges.'

'What do you mean?' I couldn't believe what I was hearing.

'Well, at today's trial the choice for a jury will be either Section 18, Section 20 or an acquittal – and they're not even interested in prosecuting you for the brothel.'

I was confused, but I didn't want to ask him too much. At the same time I didn't want to get it wrong this time but Greg carried on anyway.

'Basically, in English – wounding with intent or straightforward wounding. An acquittal would mean that you'd walk away scot-free. By the way, though, you won't get *that* result.'

I nodded. I'd accepted that much, anyway.

Greg continued, 'And you're certainly going to get less time than you would have done for attempted murder.

Now, as for the procedure. First, all the evidence and witnesses will be heard. Then the prosecutor will sum up why the jury should find you guilty of the more serious charge. And then it's my turn to counteract that and try to do some damage limitation. After that the judge will instruct the jury on any points of law and do his summing-up. The jury then goes out and comes back with a verdict. Effectively, regardless of whether that verdict opts for wounding with intent or the straightforward type, the judge has it in his power to inflict a sentence at either end of either scale. So his view is still important.'

Robert cut in, seeing that I was still confused. 'The judge will form an opinion of you based on things like your conduct in court, reports from hostels and the probation service, that sort of thing. So it could be that you're found guilty of a lesser charge by the jury and the judge could still give you the maximum sentence for that charge, or if you were found guilty of the worst charge and the judge was impressed by you he could give you the minimum for it.'

Greg smiled and delivered his parting shot.

'Oh, and one last suggestion.'

'Yes?' I said, keen for any tips I could get.

'Lose the power dressing, Joan Collins.'

One all! I smiled at him, showing my teeth. 'Oh, you mean try the virgin-teacher look! I think I still have that outfit somewhere!'

Greg's face took on a different expression. 'No, seriously – you might just lose it on appearance; the jury are expecting a powerful, all-controlling madam. Go more for softer lines, subtle colours and a more conservative feminine look. Show them the Charlie that Robert used to know.'

He looked over to Robert who blushed yet again. Greg obviously enjoyed winding him up, as if it were a sport. Greg liked to win. The game wasn't about right versus wrong or moral judgements, just about getting the best result.

'Well, I look forward to representing you,' he said, standing up to go. 'You seem like a really interesting character.'

Likewise, I thought, feeling encouraged.

The day of my trial finally arrived. The horror of the crime I'd committed had not faded with the year that had passed while the wheels of the system ground their inevitable course. Okay, so there were, as the judge had said, 'mitigating circumstances', but I knew I could do nothing to repair what I'd done, short of turning back time. I was guilty of something, even if it wasn't attempted murder.

The same crowd were sat once again in the Crown Court's gallery. They hadn't changed, but I had. I was a lot calmer than at the first trial: I was just as apprehensive but not as emotionally upset. As unlikely as it was, a year on bail had restored some routine and normality to my life, despite my sudden descent into an unsuitable marriage; drama had been replaced by hope. I felt a new balance that I hadn't experienced before, even with the insecurity of living in crazy hostels.

Greg set the scene for the jury. I watched closely, impressed by his flair but hoping his debonair showmanship wouldn't count against me. He explained how I had become caught up in events beyond my control. And he went on to describe 'the menacing outside influences of people driven by greed and malice.'

I was worried when the sour-faced prosecutor asked, 'But wasn't Miss Daniels herself guilty of the same sins?'

But I needn't have worried for, as Greg pointed out, I'd always viewed running the brothel just as if it were any other business. I'd never denied what it was, but I had run a place that had provided a safe and secure environment for those consenting adults who chose to work for me behind closed doors. The act of running the place itself could be viewed as no more than a victimless crime; it did not demonstrate that I was the sort of person who would deliberately set out to hurt anyone.

The year that had elapsed since the event I was being tried for had given the witnesses plenty of time to talk over their stories and think of new angles, and they all contradicted each other. A new witness who I'd never heard of before was also introduced. He claimed that he'd seen the whole incident from where he'd been drinking in the pub. Under cross-examination Greg showed that not only was he a close friend of the victim but he couldn't possibly have seen the incident from his self-confessed position in the bar. It was easy to spot what Greg called 'collusion'. The new witness had spent twelve months talking to the others and they had tried to synchronise their stories, but the lies unravelled under Greg's suspicious eye. He was definitely no fool and I was starting to feel very glad that my fate was in his hands and not those of Karen the Crow.

The prosecutor's argument for what he said was my

'deliberate intention to wound' was based upon the fact that a few minutes had elapsed between the girls attacking me and my retaliation. So, in his estimation, I must have intentionally harmed them, which showed that I was cold, evil and calculating.

He claimed that what I had done was not the same as lashing out in the heat of the moment or in self-defence. I had, he said, deliberately tracked my victims down, locked the doors so they couldn't escape, and taken my revenge in cold blood.

Fortunately the local bobby's statement contradicted that. He told how I had fully cooperated with him on my arrest, confessed and demonstrated my remorse immediately. He also said that I was in a trancelike state and badly traumatised when he found me.

However, one thing time could never change. It was a solid fact – I *was* guilty of stabbing the girl. Whether I'd intended to kill her or not, whether I was fully in my right mind or not at the time, I knew I had to pay for the crime that I'd committed.

Eventually the jury went away to decide and we waited. The minute hand on the court clock seemed to stand still under my stare and I could hear my own breathing in the quietness of the surroundings.

The trial was on the verge of collapse. The jury were hung and for a moment I thought we'd have to start the whole process all over again. I didn't know if I could stand the sword of justice hanging over me any longer. Just when I thought I couldn't bear another moment of it we were asked to go into the judge's chambers by the prosecution – who proposed an unexpected deal.

They offered to reduce the charges further still, to a straightforward wounding charge. I knew it was the best offer I was going to get and I so badly wanted it all to be over so I could go home, even though I knew 'going home' would mean going to a prison cell. My few belongings were already in storage. I had the clothes I stood up in and a toothbrush, nothing else.

Then the judge astounded both Greg and me. An unusual development had taken place. I'd been given what really amounted to a commendation for bravery. The judge had received a fax from the police regarding the paedophile I'd helped arrest, an event that seemed a long time ago now. They had made me out to be some kind of heroine, talking about how I'd gone to them voluntarily and put myself in considerable danger in order to make sure that the operation was a success. I'd never thought about it in those terms.

The surprises kept coming. The family who ran the publishing company had also written a glowing reference about the highly successful charity feature I'd pulled off. But the biggest surprise of all was the opening of an envelope that contained the written confirmation of the judge's credit from the original trial. It looked like I might end up with a much-reduced sentence.

I was very emotional. Not just because of how I felt about what I'd done but also from a sense of relief. Finally, I was going to be able to get on with serving my time. It was almost as if I was glad that I'd just been sentenced to two years in prison.

19
POND LIFE

....

'*My God, I never saw so many whores in all my life.*'
Duke of Wellington

The Group Four bus got stuck in heavy snow on the way
to prison and had to turn around. We had no alternative
but to spend the night in the holding cells of an abandoned wing of an old police station. The cell was small
and filthy. The walls were covered in mindless, illiterate
graffiti – 'Tracey loves Ian', pictures of genitals, and tea
stains decorating the room like a sick artist's joke of a
modern mural. At least, I *hoped* it was tea.

There was a wooden bench about seven feet long and
a foot wide. It had a slim piece of foam covered in blue
plastic to serve as a mattress. There was also a grey wiry
wool blanket that felt as if it was full of fleas, although I
was assured that it was the only thing in the cell that
was clean. There was a toilet, which was in a bad state,
at one end.

My skin felt grubby but there was no shower area.
When I eventually did get to a bathroom it was for a
strip-wash with a female officer standing on guard
behind me. I had to stand on paper towels because

the floor was so dirty. I dried myself completely with more paper towels, which was as unpleasant as it was difficult.

After reading all the graffiti and feeling sad for doing so, I wiped down my mattress with a leftover paper towel, which turned black and disintegrated. As I picked up my book a packet of cigarettes fell to the floor – I'd forgotten about them. I don't smoke but Robert had given them to me in the belief that they might be useful to trade for essentials like toiletries once I was in prison.

Some time later I heard two sets of footsteps pounding the stone corridor. The door opened to reveal a friendly auxiliary or 'civvie', as they're known to the police, who introduced me to my new cell-mate. There was only one bench so the new recruit was issued with her own plastic mattress, which she placed on the floor.

She was not a pretty sight, dressed in layer upon layer of filthy-smelling clothes. She was a big girl and smelled of body odour. Her worn-out trainers had holes in them. She wasn't wearing any socks, so the air became even harder to breathe when she removed the offending articles. She seemed frightened and miserable and I wanted to comfort her, but it didn't take long for me to realise that she wasn't quite the full shilling.

She sat rolling one cigarette after another using sheets of toilet paper, the tracing-paper kind – mumbling to herself in a quiet, annoying, gibberish voice. She smoked the home-made cigarettes one by one, lighting each one from the last, until they'd all gone. I decided to do the right thing: I would open the cigarette packet and let her have one. But when I went to open them the seal had been broken and there were some missing. Robert must have given me his own packet instead of the unopened one by mistake. I gave her one and she grabbed it without saying a word.

'Boss! Boss!' she shouted loudly at the hatch, trying to obtain a light. Eventually, and in his own time, a not very friendly officer gave her one. Twenty minutes later, when she shouted for another, it finally dawned on me that it was *her* who had opened the packet and stolen them from me earlier.

By the next morning the snow had all but disappeared. As we waited for the bus to take us to prison the civvie had a better idea: she put three different women in with me – and the other woman in a cell on her own.

Tina, Susan and Karen had been introduced to me as 'major drugs barons' but since I had been introduced to them as a 'top madam and lady gangster' I realised this was meant to be a humorous exaggeration. Like myself the girls had never been in any real trouble before. We all got on instantly. It turned out that the three were co-accused: they'd never met before but had been thrown into this hell-hole because of their boyfriends, who were being charged with trafficking and supply offences. The women had been remanded as accessories.

Susan was in her forties. She had grey hair and was a staff nurse at a local hospital. She appeared abrupt at first but was merely putting on a brave front. The other two were a little more subdued. Tina was much younger; she had long black hair and was nervous but bubbly. She was coping very well considering that she'd been separated from her small child suddenly and dramatically.

Karen had big brown eyes: she was very sheepish and spent the whole time crying and panicking.

Finally, after some discussion, Susan let her barriers down and sobbed. Fate had put us together for a reason: I kept them going by making them all laugh with my stories. They were emotionally and physically worn out after enduring days of questioning.

When the bus eventually arrived we were all put into our little individual metal cases. I started to sing 'Spread a Little Happiness' and the others joined in.

Newhall Prison was a stark old Victorian building in Wakefield, with high ceilings and large expanses of brick and metal. As the cell door clanged shut, the walls looked as if they were closing in. I lay on green and grey blankets on a tiny steel bed, staring at the ceiling.

The reality of my arrival in the cell gave me a physical jolt so severe that it struck me like lightning. As I closed my eyes my body and soul seemed to separate at high speed, leaving me breathless. Sounds, smells and movements seemed spookily familiar, as if I was in a déjà-vu state, and my heart reacted with palpitations. A feeling of total powerlessness and fear gripped my entire body. I thought I'd either had some great psychic experience or a heart attack.

It wasn't until many tests later that I would have to accept the reality of what had hit me. According to the specialists it wasn't a brain tumour or heart condition. Apparently this had been my first embarrassingly termed panic/anxiety attack.

*   *   *

That day I lost my identity and was stuck in yet another system. I was no longer Charlie Daniels; I became Prisoner Number FWO 911 – commonly referred to by the screws as 'Daniels'. As part of this new cattle market we were paraded unceremoniously in front of the prison governor for a few seconds. I had to find a way out of this nightmare and immediately suggested to him that I would make a most suitable candidate for open conditions. To him I must have appeared as brazen as an airline passenger trying to get a free upgrade. The accompanying screw glared at me and was about to quell my mini-rebellion when the amused governor spoke up.

'If and *when* I decide to move you, I promise you I'll let you know!'

Whether it was because Newhall was full or the governor thought he would rather let someone else manage me I don't know, but somehow my wish was granted. I was 'shipped out' to open conditions a week later.

Askham Grange was a paradox. Situated in an idyllic country community just outside York, with a pond, ducks and all the usual village life, it was an extremely imposing blot on the landscape, a huge former mansion built in the ugliest mock Tudor. How the villagers felt about the building or its use I'm unsure. The only drama they were ever exposed to was the loud clanging of the 'abscond bells' as someone else set off into the sunset on a bid for freedom. Every time I heard those bells I would look out of one of the huge leaded windows to the gardens and imagine what it would feel like to be heading for freedom.

It was very difficult at times to resist the temptation, knowing that you were in open conditions and could just walk away. But absconding proved to be a fruitless exercise. If you were caught you did extra time anyway, and would go straight back to a normal security prison, (or 'bang-up', as we called it).

But girls *would* run. Some couldn't hack the temptation; family dramas occurred that took priority over doing the sensible thing, and others found themselves under too much pressure one way or another within the prison.

When we arrived at Askham, we were immediately searched and taken to a booking-in area where our few allowed belongings – clothes, toiletries and precious letters – were emptied out of transparent plastic bags that bore the navy-blue prison logo. Each item was carefully logged, with paperwork in duplicate and triplicate and all manner of pastel colours being ticked and signed. Then, as it was lunchtime, we were escorted straight to the dining hall. We joined a queue on a raised platform, suspended above the seated dining area. It felt like we were on stage. A couple of hundred eyes surveyed us as if we were aliens. The women were sat at tables in the centre of the room and the screws were lined up around the walls. I would rather have arrived at any other time so that we could have mingled a little less conspicuously. But, to the apparent pleasure of the others, we were lined up like Miss Sarajevo contestants for all to judge.

That morning I'd decided to make a special effort. I might be in prison, I told myself, but I wasn't going to let myself go, so I'd put on a pair of old leather trousers and a bodysuit. I wore a full face of make-up and held my head high, smiling and trying to look confident. I don't know why, but some of the women who were staring seemed to find this objectionable. One girl in particular looked up in disgust. I was to learn a lot of lessons while I was inside, the most important of which was going to be humility.

Later I was shown to a huge dorm. I was stunned: when the house had been in its heyday this would have been a large master bedroom but now it contained about a dozen single beds. I quickly realised that I was going to miss that about Newhall if nothing else: it might only have been a cell but it had been my own space and sanctuary.

I started to unpack my possessions and the same girl who'd been staring at me earlier in the dining room walked in. Her bed was right next to mine.

Tracey was a Geordie lass, loud and abrupt. Her dark hair was short on top and long at the back. She had a masculine face and various girls' names tattooed on her arms.

Word had already got out that I was in for a violent offence and that's never a good thing. You spend half your time standing your ground with those determined to push you over the line and the rest being avoided by others who are wary. Once an audience had assembled Tracey started shouting and pushing me around.

'Who d'ya think you are, you stuck-up fucking bitch?'

I had only just opened my mouth to defend myself verbally when I felt the first blow. It had incredible impact as it connected with my cheek, sending me reeling. Egged on by her friends, Tracey started kicking me in the ribs while I lay curled up on the floor in agony.

'You think you're something else, don't you? Well, I've got news for you, *madam* – you're shit like the rest of us!'

It was then that I heard another noise that was soon to become familiar. First there was a shrill, piercing alarm, followed by the sound of pounding feet and jangling keys. Walkie-talkies squawked as screws flew into the room. Two young women wearing trousers and matching crew-cuts stormed to my rescue – or so I thought. But Tracey had a back-up plan. A couple of the others in the room had already rehearsed a new version of events. She whipped up a convincing chorus of false witnesses who swore that I'd started the whole thing. I was to spend my first twenty-four hours in solitary confinement, in a small room with only a tiny window in the ceiling. In the enforced period of loneliness I sat and thought of what I had left behind and the precious moments I was missing.

The next morning, while still in the solitary-confinement compound, I received an unexpected visitor. I heard footsteps outside in the corridor and a key turned in the lock. I looked up to see a gnomelike lady with a wrinkled face wearing an old-fashioned A-line skirted uniform. She was the first officer I had seen wearing a skirt – most of the other female officers were butch-looking. She introduced herself as Gladys Booker and told me that she was one of the prison's senior officers. I was assigned two of what they called 'personal officers'. One was Gladys and the other was Miss Bullfinch who, as it turned out, had been one of the arresting officers during the fracas with Tracey. As she spoke, deliberately and slowly and in well-modulated tones, I noticed Gladys's head nodding constantly. She reminded me of a mini-Mrs Thatcher. This odd-bod woman had a very imposing presence. She also had a huge mole on her face that sprouted wiry hair and I couldn't take my stare off it.

Gladys sat with me as I slowly recounted the incident. I soon found myself nodding in time with her and I also noticed her perfectly set hair move, or should I say *slip* – she was wearing a wig.

'I really didn't do anything,' I explained when she asked me about the incident with Tracey.

'Well, I'm not that surprised,' she sighed. 'That girl is a real troublemaker, and I can see why she chose you as her target!'

I was confused. 'Why? What have I ever done to her?'

'Well, let me see. You speak nicely, and you communicate an intelligence that she'll never have and you're probably just as physically capable. I'm sure you neither anticipated nor deserved such a deliberate and malicious assault.'

I could feel my face colour up.

'She's throwing her weight around and wants to intimidate you. Let me guess: did the others back her up?'

I nodded tearfully. My face was still sore and swollen from Tracey's blow. I must have touched it unconsciously because Gladys cocked her head to one side in concern.

'Hmm, they're all scared of her, you see – and they're probably wary of you. Don't forget, a lot of the women are only here for lightweight offences, shoplifting and so on. Mostly they'll keep their heads down and blend into the background. Unfortunately for you, you seem to have made quite an impression!'

She was the unlikeliest looking angel, but she was all I had to guide me through this alien environment. Our chat continued for over an hour.

'Right,' Gladys said when she'd finished hearing my story. 'I have a plan. Come with me.'

She led me up the grand main staircase, where a huge arch-shaped window lit the beautiful stairwell; it was hard to remember this had once been a family home. The speed she was now moving at made it clear that she was on a mission. We arrived at a small room, which she unlocked. There were only four beds in it.

'Go and fetch your things and move in here!' she instructed me sharply. 'Look, that bed's vacant.'

Then she surprised me by giving me a key to the door, explaining that everyone in this room had one.

This room was not at all like the dorm; it was homely and cosy. There was an open, empty locker next to the bed. I looked at Gladys gratefully and thanked her. She waved away my words and left me to move my things.

I sat reading in my new room while the other women, who'd been working, were having a tea break downstairs. A short time later I heard a key rattling around in the door and two girls fell in, laughing loudly. They were both quite young and had long straight hair. One was only about nineteen and was a blonde with a very formal way about her. The other had jet-black hair and brown eyes. You could tell that both of them were different from most of the other women. For a start, neither of them were on drugs. Judging by their reaction, which made me aware that I was an unwelcome intruder, they obviously weren't expecting to see *me*. The dark-haired one in particular seemed very perturbed. She stormed out of the room (once she'd realised that glaring at me was not going to make me disappear). The blonde girl went silently over to her bed and ignored my pleasant attempts to chat. I felt alone and depressed: somehow a cold shoulder seemed worse than an empty room.

A few minutes later the other girl returned. She promptly informed me that I was to go to Jim Swaine's office. He was a six-foot senior officer with an imposing face, which looked like it had been carved out of granite. His Irish voice boomed around his small dark office, and his glasses kept slipping off the end of his nose as he became more and more animated. As he stood up from his desk and moved around he didn't walk so much as lollop like a big wolfhound, trying his best to intimidate me. There must have been something in my manner that he found deeply offensive.

'That room you've put yourself into is a privilege room!' he bellowed. 'The ladies in there have earned respect – they *deserve* to be in there!'

I tried to explain that Gladys had put me there – that I hadn't just decided to move in on my own – but I didn't get many words in. To Swaine my remarks were protests of deliberate obstinacy, making him even angrier.

'I don't care who put you in there! Get out of my office

and out of that room. I've no time for mouthy trouble-makers.'

I knew I couldn't win this one. The only option was to give in and move my stuff back into the dorm, right under Tracey and all her cronies' noses. I was completely humiliated. No sooner had I arrived back than a huffing and puffing Gladys appeared in the room, her face a beetroot red. News obviously travelled fast in this place.

'Get your things and move back now!'

This really was more than I could cope with. I sat on the bed with my head in my hands, unable to move, as Gladys silently picked up my bags and carried them back to the small room for me. Still my legs wouldn't move. By the time she came back into the dorm to fetch me the others had scattered.

'Follow your things,' she told me. 'I'll sort that bloody Jim Swaine out.'

That was the first and last time I ever heard Gladys swear. And sort Jim Swaine out she did! This amazing woman, who was small in stature only, walked into his office without knocking, the legend goes . . . and I'm told you could hear the argument from the other side of the prison. Did she win? Well, I never moved back to the dormitory . . .

Askham time dragged slowly compared with the rest of the world: breakfast, work, break, work, lunch, work, another break, work, and then teatime, all marked by the sound of school-style bells. After tea we were free for the rest of the evening. This was called 'recreation', when we had limited choices – like a hundred women fighting over one television, reading in the library, or getting up to mischief elsewhere. This was usually the time when all the druggies would disappear off together to escape the monotony in their own private ways.

The small room I was in became somewhat of a sanctuary. Once she'd accepted that she was not going to be able to get me out of her room again, Heather, my new dark-haired room-mate, actually spoke to me for the first time.

'You need to go and see the nurse about that eye – it looks serious, it's going a lovely shade of purple.'

The other girl, who was sat reading on her bed with her head down, muttered, 'You need a steak on it.'

Heather shrieked with laughter.

'Where on *earth* would we get steak from? And what a bloody waste!'

We all fell about laughing. The ice-like tension in the room had begun to thaw.

Heather was an interesting, mysterious character, with only a trace of her original northern accent. I started to look forward to lights-out, the time when we would exchange confidences like schoolgirls.

In one all-night talking session I told them my whole story. From that moment on we started to bond. Initially Heather was very sparing in the details she gave about herself. She'd entered the prison system as a youth offender and was serving life. In the beginning that was almost all I knew about her. I could tell that despite her attempts at putting up a hard façade she was a lovely girl, clever, ambitious and very private about her past, which I respected.

One thing Heather did like talking about – she would elaborate her stories with every minute detail – was her 'town visits'. Once you'd been at Askham long enough to be 'risk-assessed' you could be considered for the occasional trip into York with designated family or friends. It was like being a kid taken for a day out from boarding school.

Heather's town visits all had a common theme: great food. This was one thing she seriously looked forward to all week. It didn't matter whether it was Chinese, English or Indian: she knew all the best places in York. It was hardly surprising that it was such a main event – prison food was even worse than my old school dinners. Nobody ever wanted seconds.

One afternoon, while we were on tea break, receiving orange-coloured stewed tea from a large urn, Heather told us in great detail about her many visits to Betty's famous tearooms, where the staff still wore the traditional black and whites, where there were more types of tea than you could ever imagine, where mini-sandwiches had their crusts removed and huge scones with smiling faces, called Fat Rascals, begged you to eat them.

In Askham everyone started as a cleaner, a job that I had always hated and had been happy to delegate to Helen as soon as I could afford to pay her. Jobs in the prison created a kind of social pecking order: cleaners were seen as the bottom of the ranks and were the lowest-paid party, getting around three pounds per week. At the end of my first week I queued for the canteen. I had already discovered that queuing was a regular prison pastime. The staff checked a file to make sure that I hadn't had my privileges removed; they also had a record of my earnings over the previous seven days. For sale were smokes, chocolates, toiletries and phone-cards, all of which Heather had warned me to guard with my life. I didn't smoke or bother with chocolate so the phonecards were to become my one major luxury. Phones were our main link to the outside world but they were also a major factor in women absconding: this was when prisoners found out about their partners' or kids' domestic problems. Conversations were rarely private; they were recorded or listened in on and there were always women stood ready to report back any gossip. Phone calls could be bitter-sweet experiences.

One day I joined the queue of noisy women who were all waiting desperately for their turn at the phone. The first time I called my mum from Askham I rehearsed in my mind what I would say to her and to Lucy. As I picked up the receiver, I felt as if many pairs of eyes and ears were focused on me and wished I could have been sat in a phone booth instead of a crowded corridor. The number rang for ages but finally my mum answered.

'Oh, it's you,' she said in a disappointed tone.

'You had a bad day, Mum?'

'No, but I'm just about to watch the TV. What did you want?'

'To talk to Lucy, if that's okay.'

'She's gone out with next door but you can ring back later if you like.'

I looked at the clock and knew that would be impossible. We chatted for a few minutes and then the pips started.

'I have to go now, my card's running out. Will you bring Lucy to see me?'

My mum's irritation now turned to full-blown anger. 'Are you joking? You know I don't drive, and besides I don't think it's a good idea to bring a small child to the prison, do you?'

And with that she hung up. In some of the letters that she had sent me previously she had stated that the reason for not visiting was financial, so I wasn't even sure why she wouldn't bring Lucy to see me. One thing I did know was that I hadn't been a good enough mother to judge or complain.

Most of my outside contact was done via mail. Mum and Lucy wrote to me without fail every week, which I appreciated more than they could ever know. I treasured every card, every photograph and every letter. Being locked up, away from the material compensations of the life I had chosen, gave me plenty of time to reflect on the choices I had made and how much I had given up when I'd decided that I couldn't face the responsibilities of motherhood. I had no way of distracting myself from my thoughts or from the pain they caused me.

Missing Lucy's first day at school was the worst punishment of all, something I cannot forgive myself for. I was beginning to see just how distorted my priorities had been over the previous four or five years, and I felt nothing but regret for all the time with Lucy that I had missed and would never be able to get back.

Each time I entered the dining room for visits from my friends, mixed in with the pleasure of seeing them would be the pain I felt as I saw the other women being emotionally reunited and then separated again from their families.

It seemed as if there were constant cruel reminders of family life. Askham boasted one the of country's special mother-and-baby units. A few women, whose sleeping quarters were in a separate wing of the prison, were allowed to keep babies with them for the first few months of the infants' lives. Imagine that: babies in prison. And imagine the moment when they had to be taken away. You'd also occasionally get a pregnant woman in the main unit who'd have her baby at York's hospital, and would then be transferred to the mother-and-baby unit. Most of the time they were in their own wing, but at mealtimes we were all integrated: it served as just another painful reminder of what we were all missing. All the inmates would behave surprisingly well when the children were around, curbing their language and showing a lot of respect.

A few weeks into my sentence I was given the chance to leave the cleaning team. I opted to go for part-time education and part-time work as a librarian, which I had to do by way of a formal interview. It suited me just fine. For one thing, I love books. It also meant I could keep my head down and stay out of trouble because I would be working when the others were socialising. More importantly, however, was the fact that it allowed me plenty of privacy – the library was hardly the throbbing epicentre of the prison. Privacy in prison is a much-needed luxury. I craved as much 'head-space time' as possible. As well as missing seeing Lucy growing up, I was also missing being able to snuggle up to someone, which wasn't going to happen unless I suddenly became 'prison bent' like some of the others did. Sleep wasn't easy at night because of all the screaming and crying that went on, as well as on account of my own nightmares. My library work and studying also meant I could get a shower while everyone else was working, without having to keep my back against the wall.

Being a librarian meant working on weekends and during evenings but, considering that all my time was now taken up at Her Majesty's pleasure, working weekends didn't really make much difference to my newly structured social life. In charge of the library team was my guardian angel, Gladys, who mostly left us alone in quiet seclusion. Gladys and I had formed the unlikeliest of alliances. We were both art lovers. Even more amazingly we shared a passion for a specific period: the Pre-Raphaelites.

One day Gladys popped her head around the library door.

'Halloo, Charlie, and how are we today?'

This was her signature opening and I loved the way her sing-song voice brightened up my otherwise boring days. She breezed through the door with a large briefcase in her hand, looking carefully around the library.

'Is everything tidy enough, Miss Booker?'

'Quite so – quite so,' she said, quickly opening the case. Winking in a conspiratorial manner, she revealed its contents.

'For your eyes only!' she said, her eyes twinkling.

I looked through the old leather case in amazement as

the door clicked softly shut behind her. Over the coming weeks this strict, strait-laced woman, who had all the hallmarks of a bygone headmistress, brought me dozens of books from her own personal collection. In an unprecedented act of selfless and unconditional generosity, and without the need for words, my new mentor encouraged me to study.

Time was one thing always on my hands in prison and so, having developed a thirst for further education, I attended extra English and office-skills tuition. Encouraged by my enthusiasm, June, the education coordinator, came to me with a file full of leaflets that she thought might interest me. I went through them and found a book of poetry and short stories written by prisoners who had won Koestler Awards. They were all moving, funny and well written. There was also a competition application for that year. It explained how Arthur Koestler, this twentieth-century author and intellectual, had believed that prisoners could be rehabilitated through the development of their talents in sculpture, painting, writing or other media and that they might be prevented from slipping into recidivism by harnessing their creativity. Sometimes when I hear theories like that I think 'Bullshit.' But, as I read on, I realised there had been a few cases, other than just the 'Bird Man of Alcatraz', where prisoners really had re-invented themselves through a new-found passion. With my growing sense of self-confidence, I wondered if I could go in for the award. Over the next few lessons I asked for time and a PC to construct my entries, and eventually produced two poems and a short story.

One day Gladys suggested that I should apply for

funding for an art course and a couple of weeks later I'd started 'Understanding Western Art'. I sailed through the course in half the expected time, working on it during my hours in the library and my recreational periods. My thirst for more knowledge had begun and Gladys was watching my progress carefully. One day, apparently convinced that I was genuine in my desire to learn, she broached a new subject.

'Charlie,' she said, 'have you thought of doing a degree course when you come out?'

'Not really,' I replied, completely taken by surprise. 'I mean, I don't think I'm university material. I'm not as clever as my foster-brother and sister.' There was no false modesty in the statement – it was just a fact, as far as I could see.

'Ah well, maybe it has taken you a little longer than them to reach this point.' Gladys was choosing her words carefully. 'But I think you're underestimating yourself greatly.'

To have someone like her praise me like this meant a great deal to me. I had always wondered if I was capable of achieving more in life but it was wonderful to hear that someone else had faith in me. I'd already made the decision that when I was released I was not going back on the game, not just because of all the heartbreak and drama that I'd encountered but also because I badly needed a new start. I would have a clean slate and also perhaps a chance to stretch and challenge my own intellectual boundaries for once.

I also knew that I couldn't stick with a menial job, so I'd been puzzling over what my path forward should be. I don't know if I would ever have had the nerve to consider going to university on my own, but if Gladys thought I could do it then maybe it was a possibility. I'd accepted that Lucy was settled with her Nan and that it would be too disruptive for me to even think of taking her back until my life was going better. But at least now I could start to think about building a more stable future for all of us. Although it was painful to admit it, I knew that Mum offered her the most secure home and loving Lucy meant wanting the best for her. I was beginning to see that I had responsibilities towards both of them that I hadn't been shouldering in the way I should have been. Even though I wanted Lucy back, in my heart I knew that this probably wouldn't be the best thing for her.

So, after a lot of thought, I approached June in the education department. I'd already decided that Leeds was the place I most wanted to go to when I came out, so we got the prospectuses from both Leeds University and the Leeds Metropolitan. June rang the Met, my preferred option, regarding a mature students' course and they asked me to write a letter explaining what I loved about art.

While working on my arts course, I found my life had some strange parallels with that of the artist J. M. W. Turner. Firstly, I was astounded to read that there was evidence he had owned a brothel in Wapping and had made drawings of his various trysts, all of which were subsequently destroyed to protect his reputation. Then, in a strange parallel to my birth mother's own life, his mother went mad after losing a child. Turner also described his mum as having an 'unquenchable anger'.

I know that anger.

I found one of his pictures in a book. It was called *The Snow-Storm*. Legend has it that Turner had himself strapped to the mast of a ship during a storm. The wind tossed him around violently and rain lashed at his flesh. I was like all the narrow-minded critics of his time because I couldn't understand the viewpoint or the experience so I dismissed the picture at first as a wash-out. But slowly, with the benefit of the greater knowledge and understanding that I was gaining from my studies, I was able to look at it and actually *see* the storm encircling the ship. The more I thought about this picture, the more I thought about my own life.

The storm sweeps up everything in its path – innocent or otherwise. It lashes out violently, without fear, abandoning reality and perspective, a huge mass of energy, all-consuming, all-passionate. It was the same after my father left home. It was as if an emotional storm had engulfed us all.

I still wonder if Dad ever understood the emotional twisting of my soul that happened that day. Love and betrayal in equal doses. Like all abandoned kids I missed him for the key moments but even now there remains a desert of broken dreams and truths.

I missed sitting on his knee, peeling the paint speckles off his smiling face. I even missed the daily counting-up of his coppers. I missed his strong opinions on everything, even the ones I didn't agree with. I missed our long country walks.

From the moment Dad left our entire family collapsed. Everyone went – leaving me with the hollow shell of what was once my happy mum. We went through cold and lonely days in her dark depths of depression, an endless abyss; where sunshine shone only in glimpses and then was covered quickly by the dark clouds, thunder always on the horizon.

He wasn't there to see the pain, the anger, the devastation, the bitterness and the rejection. Was his new life worth all that?

In the coming years I couldn't connect with anyone properly and I needed him to show me the way. I rested my head on many a man's pillow and discovered no sanctuary, I searched in a thousand eyes for Dad and his wisdom but never found it. In the arms of any man I have ever loved I never found the warmth that he showed me so briefly. I cannot forget but I learned to forgive.

As time went on my childish anger passed as if it never was – there came a peaceful calm until all that remained was the wreckage gently bobbing around once the storm had rolled over. Now was the time to let go of the painful memories and stop them holding me back, to use the experiences in a positive way and move forward.

20
AMAZING GRACE
....

'Prisons are built with stones of law,
Brothels with bricks of religion.'
William Blake

I was surprised to see Gladys in the library – she rarely visited me while I was working. The room was empty and so our chat was private. She pulled up a chair beside my desk.

'Hello, Charlie, and how are we today?'

God, she even sounded like Maggie Thatcher.

'Fine, thanks, Mrs Booker – and yourself?'

She smiled and started nodding. I could feel my head beginning to mimic hers already.

'I've got some good news for you – but it has to remain between us.' She tapped her nose. I could sense that this was going to be interesting and I beamed, feeling proud that she could take me into her confidence. I drew my chair in closer and leaned forward to be sure I didn't miss a single word.

'There was a staff meeting today . . .'

Apparently all the 'heads of state', as she called them, had met for their monthly review. Lenny Masters, the governor, had sat at one end of the very long committee table. Richard Potts, the vicar, had sat at the other end and everyone else had taken their places down the sides.

'"So," Lenny Masters said to Richard, "have you any candidates for confirmation or baptism this year?" And Richard replied, "Only one, and for both, actually." And then Lenny asked, "Who?"'

I smiled back at Gladys and then she used a phrase I shall never forget.

'"*Charlie Daniels*" – and silence ensued!'

I looked at her and laughed. I knew that to the governor I was the most unlikely candidate imaginable, and I loved the idea that I had stunned him and the other doubters into silence. She continued. 'But right then Miss Summers championed you! She said, "Well, I'm not so surprised."' I didn't know Miss Summers (one of the senior officers) that well; but apparently she'd voiced the opinion that she'd seen a change in me.

Gladys touched her wig, subconsciously checking that it was still in place. 'Lenny Masters topped it all off with "What's she up to?"'

We both fell about laughing. In my mind's eye I had the perfect picture of the meeting and could just imagine Lenny Masters's face as he tried to make sense of it all.

So what was so unbelievable? Hadn't they heard of Mary Magdalene? Didn't they know about the famous whores in the Bible? I did, thanks to Richard Potts, the chaplain. He was an amazing man who I had a lot of respect and admiration for, and who had been watching me and helping me to grow spiritually. Heather had introduced us, assuring me that he would never judge me, whatever I told him. She was right.

I wasn't totally alien to the Church. I'd always gone to Sunday school and had been to several different churches as a girl. I'd been part of the Evangelical Church for a long time and then the Methodist Church for two years. Even though we weren't a religious family we did accept that God existed. I was never sure quite what it was I believed in and would describe myself as 'spiritual' rather than 'religious'. I'd shut out all my beliefs when I went on the game – I never wanted to be a hypocrite.

My room-mate Heather always referred humorously to her church recruits as her 'victims'. I found the chapel to be another sanctuary, a place where I could escape the manic hell of prison life and find real peace. Heather might have dragged me there the first time, but as the weeks went by I found myself gradually rekindling my childhood faith. I could see that the chaplaincy team had a much more peaceful life than I did and had an air about them that I wanted to share. It didn't irritate me to know that the governor thought I had ulterior motives – it just seemed predictable and amusing.

One day I was in the chapel with Richard, having a confirmation lesson. Sister Janine, a nun who attended services, had called in briefly and had just left. In front of us on the table were the Bible, several books, and pens and paper. Lenny Masters, the prison governor, burst in, making us both jump. Lenny rarely checked the chapel. Now, when anyone's in a place of worship people usually creep in, maintaining a respectful quietness, so this was an unusual entrance by any standards. When he saw us behaving innocently I swear Lenny looked almost disappointed. He pretended to be interested in what I was learning and we all exchanged awkward pleasantries for a few minutes. When Lenny left, Richard and I paused for a second before simultaneously bursting out laughing.

After that, at the end of one Sunday service, Richard gave me some incredible news. 'You know we usually hold confirmations here, in the chapel?'

I looked at him quizzically, waiting for him to go on.

'Well, we've got special permission . . .'

I held my breath.

'To use a very special location.'

'Bilbury?'

Women who had been 'risk-assessed' were sometimes escorted out to church. Bilbury was a beautiful country church nearby.

'Well, no, Miss Daniels,' Richard teased. 'He who is above aims higher.'

'No way!' I almost shouted.

He nodded. For me, and for the first time in Askham's history, the service was to be held at York Minster. Sister Janine had been in the chapel office and came through when she heard my yell of excitement.

'Well, Charlie, you never cease to amaze me – you seem to do everything in style.' She winked.

I was so happy; I couldn't wait to tell Heather. That night, back in our room the night duty officer had to come in twice to tell us to keep the noise down. Heather, in her exaggerated posh voice, kept announcing:

'Charlie's getting confirmed at York Minster, darlings, and the Pope and the Queen are bound to be there!'

We giggled uncontrollably, especially when Heather wondered aloud if we would be able to sneak out after the service and visit Betty's Tearooms for a cup of Darjeeling and a couple of Fat Rascals. It may appear as if our comments trivialise the whole experience – but in all honesty, when you're in prison the only way to stay sane is to keep a sense of humour about everything, especially the serious things.

One week Richard asked Heather and me to have a chat with him after the service. He told us all about the Sleights Retreat in Whitby. A few carefully selected prisoners would be allowed to stay with the chaplaincy team at the retreat, a time for soul-searching and reflection, a rare opportunity to break free from the daily routines and restraints of prison life. We had been lucky enough to be among the chosen few and it was exciting to think that we would be near both the seaside and the legendary place where Dracula's ship had arrived in England.

The house itself was peaceful and had an old-world charm. The furniture was simple and possibly antique. Even the garden had a captivating mystery about it. One afternoon I sat down with Richard and we drank tea like people used to, with a proper pot and bone-china cups and saucers. He looked at me with his kind eyes and smiled softly.

'There's something you need to talk about,' he said, 'something that's deeply troubling you, I can tell.'

And so that afternoon I opened up my heart to this wise old man whose facial lines told many tales, whose hands had joined couples and held many babies before God, who seemed to be able to read me like an open Bible, telling him a secret that I had not discussed with another living soul.

'Yes,' I said. 'I have to make a decision and it's not going to be easy.'

The day of my confirmation ceremony was 21 June. The sun streamed through York Minster's beautiful stained-glass windows and I was showered in an array of rainbow colours. It was a magical midsummer's dream. There were twenty other candidates from all around Yorkshire and I was glad they didn't know where I was from.

I walked slowly forward towards the altar and looked around at a few familiar faces. Heather stood with a couple of the other girls from the prison, beaming at me proudly. Sister Janine nodded sweetly as I took the last step up to the altar.

I looked back to see Richard dabbing his eyes with his cotton handkerchief, his glasses in one hand, the other holding on to the pew. I felt very emotional and moved as I turned towards the bishop and knelt before God.

I prayed with all my heart that God would forgive me for going to His altar knowing that in one week I would be destroying the life I'd just discovered was growing inside me. This was the secret that Richard had seen hiding in my eyes.

I hated myself for getting pregnant. I'd decided that it served me right. The news had got out quickly on the jungle drums; although the news wasn't from Richard's lips, my condition was fairly obvious as morning sickness had set in and I looked like death. Most of the prison was busy taking bets on whose baby it was. The vicar was the favourite at 3 to 1 (with the running joke that, despite his being eighty, it hadn't been an immaculate conception). At 4 to 1 was one of the senior officers, and way down the list at 25 to 1 was the prison governor.

Joking aside, the truth was less exciting and really too awful to contemplate. It had actually happened when I'd gone out on a town visit with an ex-client, in exchange for toiletries. He was a sales rep for one of the big beauty-products firms, and his products were like gold dust to a girl in prison. I'd always used condoms while working – every time, no exceptions – until this occasion, and I could make no excuses for such a stupid lapse. When I first rang him to arrange the visit, I asked him to bring a packet with him and he agreed. We were out in the middle of the countryside when I asked for them, and he said he'd forgotten. I suspect that like most clients he preferred not to use them. I should have just said no – but I didn't. I confided in Gladys, who was very kind: she organised the practical details from the test onwards.

I hadn't seen Lucy for some time and I rang her on a couple of nights to see how she was doing. In a way, my pregnancy seemed like it had something to do with her; after all, it was her little brother or sister that I was trying to decide about, even if she didn't know anything about it. Time was running out and I needed to make the final decision. I really thought through whether I could have this baby. I knew that if I did it would probably be another fatherless mite – I was pretty sure the client in question wouldn't want anything to do with it. I'd be right back where I'd been when I was seventeen, starting my new life on the outside with nothing and a huge new load of responsibility. I also hated the prospect of the baby being born in prison. I'd seen what it did to the mothers; what a legacy to leave any child. It was a lonely time and I had few people I could talk to.

Eventually, I decided to let the prospective father know. I was certain he wouldn't want to play happy families, but nevertheless I was distressed when he became angry. He justified this by ranting about his fear of losing his wife, kids, home and job, all the usual stuff. At first he accused me of lying and pulling a stunt, until I got the doctor to call him and confirm it. Even though I'd pinned no hopes on him being supportive, his attitude wounded me deeply and I could see that he was going to be worse than useless. Once he'd calmed down, he did offer to pay for the abortion, even though he'd told me that he wasn't even sure the baby was his, which rather cancelled out any generosity in the gesture. Unable to see any hope of being able to offer the new baby a decent life, I made my decision to have a termination.

While I was in hospital I received a couple of visitors; the chaplain came, but there was also a surprise visitor. Gayle and I had only met a couple of times. She was the Quaker representative in the chaplaincy team, a woman who was only ten years older than me and yet was herself a single mum of two young boys and a girl. I'd been asleep when she'd arrived and she'd sat quietly in prayer medita-tion, which she later told me was the Quaker way of worship. As I came round from the anaesthetic she was organising me a cuppa, and her voice gently soothed me.

'Hello, Charlie. How are you doing?' I tried a faint smile but she could see through me. She reached out and held my hand. 'Silly question, I know.'

'Do you think God hates me?' My body started to tremble as I fought back the tears that were now making a bid for freedom down my cheeks.

Gayle sat back in her chair and thought for a moment. 'I think he loves you unconditionally, and you should learn to love yourself again.'

I sat in silence as Gayle comforted me quietly.

21
INSIDE OUT

....

'. . . The family, with its narrow privacy and tawdry
secrets, is the source of all our discontents.'
                                        Sir Edmund Leach

At last my time inside had almost passed. For the final
few weeks of my sentence I was transferred to the pre-
release hostel, a small outbuilding in the prison grounds.
Here, long-term prisoners got a taste of working and
being 'out', a sort of dry run for 'normal' life. It was also
an opportunity to save cash for my release, a kind of
quasi-existence. We had to return to the hostel after
work and were not allowed to mix with the prisoners on
the main site. I had my own small bedroom and a little
more freedom, but technically I was still a prisoner.

The many hours I'd spent over the previous year
reading and rereading the notes and pictures that Lucy
had sent me had made me realise how much I was
missing by separating my life from hers. Even the simple
things like the first time she rode a bike had come and
gone and now I would only ever read about them. When
she'd been a baby, Lucy had been the most important
thing in my life – everything had revolved around her.

How had I managed to let that all slip away? I knew that I was going to have to change my ways once I was out if I wasn't going to waste even more opportunities.

By day I worked as a tour guide on York's open-top tourist buses, and by evening I served in a pub. I was lucky because most of the other women in the hostel worked in the packing factory. It was great to get out into the *real* world but it was always a head-f*ck coming home at night, so I decided to do something about it. I got on very well with the landlord of the pub and managed to get my own room above the bar. He would occasionally cover for me and tell the prison that I was working when in fact I wasn't. I knew that if the prison found out I would be in big trouble but I needed to taste more freedom. I had also fallen in love with one of the tour-bus drivers who unfortunately was married. I needed someone so badly at that time I didn't really weigh up the consequences. All I knew was, it was an addictive, passionate affair and the fact that it should never have happened at all just made it even more intoxicating. Once I was back in the hostel I had a genuine intention to get my life together, but I found it hard to resist the temptation to be naughty.

The hostel was a long narrow building with lots of rooms coming off it – a bit like a cheap motel. I rarely saw any of the other inmates as we all worked at different times, so mostly the place resembled a deserted rabbit warren. One of the nicest screws on the hostel was having an affair with one of the officers from the main prison. I was the only prisoner who knew about it and, despite knowing that this was the biggest, juiciest piece of gossip, I kept the secret well. I discovered their liaison by accident when I found them cosy in the office one night. I didn't make a fuss or say anything. Later that night the female officer involved poured her heart out to me and even had a little weep as we shared our experiences. Soon I was able to trust her to know about my affair on the outside, which was *my* secret. It was not just a polite stand-off: rightly or wrongly, we actually carved out a friendship based on mutual trust and respect.

One day another officer rang the pub when I was supposed to be working and found that I wasn't there. Next thing I knew, I was thrown off the hostel and back on the main unit. I didn't miss much about the hostel itself – it was a soulless place – but I did miss the freedom and the late-night confidences. Another of the hostel screws was an alcoholic, who was permanently pissed but dead funny. She'd worked for the prison for over twenty years. Sometimes I think the prison deliberately farmed out specific officers to the hostel for a reason.

Going back to the main unit from the hostel was a head-twister, but it was nice to see Heather again. We sat in the library chatting.

'Do you think you're going to set up again when you get out?' she asked

'Nah, I've done with all that,' I assured her. 'I'm looking forward to a new start.'

'But won't you miss the cash?'

'Maybe. It's going to be hard. I've got nothing and no one. Just a few quid from the hostel, not much else.'

'Will you keep in contact?'

'Sure I will.'

Heather bent towards my ear and whispered, 'If you set up again, I'd work for you!'

'*Pardon?*' I couldn't believe what I was hearing. Heather didn't seem the type at all. Her family were working-class and had built up a successful business from scratch, but because of that Heather had always acted as if she were middle-class.

'Look,' she said, 'I'm going to trust you with something that none of the other girls know – the bloke I killed, well, it was a guy I fell for at fifteen. I'd always loved money. For a couple of years he showered me with it, bought me wonderful presents and clothes. Then one day he told me the money had run out but that I owed him and that was when he got me working for him.'

My head was spinning. I couldn't believe what Heather was saying and I was in complete shock. She'd always been so private. All those nights she'd listened to my tales and never even hinted that she knew nothing about the life I was describing. I realised then that although I'd spent a full year with her I didn't know anything about my friend at all.

She took off her jacket and showed me scar after scar on her body. I'd always assumed she was shy when she'd turned her back as she got undressed. Slowly I began to understand, but it appeared that the courts hadn't.

To them Heather was an unbalanced teenage prostitute who had plotted to kill her lover. To me she'd been a naive young girl who'd got way out of her depth and, having been exposed to the man's style of life, could only see one way out. She was to serve at least eight years.

'I was trapped. I couldn't take any more – and I, yes, did plan it. I'm not going to deny that – but I knew it was him or me.' Her eyes started to fill with tears.

I reached out and squeezed her arm. 'It's over now.' The words seemed so hollow.

Heather was an amazing girl, kind and intelligent. While in prison she'd made the most of every minute and had trained and qualified in teaching aerobics. She then organised classes for the other prisoners. I couldn't believe that she hadn't decided to turn her back on the game like I had.

'Do you *really* want to go back to that life?'

She looked at me, raising her arms in a gesture of resignation. 'No one else is going to feed us out there!'

'But why can't you put your trust in God?'

Heather smiled sadly. 'Charlie, for someone so bloody intelligent, I reckon it's *you* that's still naive . . .'

For reasons of security, all mail at the prison was opened and read before we got it. So the day I received an invitation for an interview at the university Gladys handed me the news personally.

'Something here you might be interested in, Miss Daniels . . .'

I couldn't believe my luck. 'Wow! That's fantastic news . . .'

Gladys smiled a knowing smile.

Then, with horror, I realised the date for the interview. 'But I'll still be inside – how am I going to attend before I get out? I'll need to if I'm going to start in January after my release.' Suddenly I felt despondent and frustrated as if my bubble had burst. But the new mood didn't last long because Gladys had already been to see the governor.

'Here, I think you'll need this.' She passed me an envelope containing a special day-release pass and a travel warrant. Before I could thank her properly she walked off.

On the day of the interview Gladys even gave me five pounds out of my 'spends' to buy a coffee while I was out. The idea of being able to go into a coffee shop and get a *real* cup of coffee and have an outside life again felt amazing. The interview went well, but I had no way of telling immediately if I would be offered a place.

I rarely got letters, so when a small package arrived a few weeks later I was very excited. I couldn't wait to hear from the university. So at first I was disappointed when I opened the packet of find a booklet of Koestler Award stories and poems with that year's date on it. They must have put me on their mailing list after the competition, which by now I'd forgotten all about. It was then that I discovered a letter in the bundle, advising me which two pages of the booklet to read. I'd won an award in two categories: for one of my short stories and, to my delight, for one of my poems as well. I held in my hands my first published writings.

A suspenseful month after the interview, I heard back from the university: I'd been accepted to start in January. It really did look as if I was going to be offered a chance to turn my life around once and for all.

*　　*　　*

In the end I served a year inside. On my last night there, as you can well imagine, Heather and I were on a high. Heather kept singing to me from an old song, 'Tie a Yellow Ribbon' – 'I'm going home I've done my time!' But the reality was that I was going out to another hostel, and I knew I was still a long way from 'home'. But at least I could leave behind the monotony of prison, even if I felt guilty that I was leaving my friend behind.

I couldn't contain my excitement and, despite the fact that she was saying goodbye to yet another close friend who was leaving her behind, Heather was pleased for me.

That night we went out of the prison together on a minibus, on a trip to Rock Church. For several reasons it was by far the most popular church among the women. Not only did it mean a trip outside, you could really dance and sing and let your hair down without looking ridiculous. But the number of prisoners who could go to Rock Church had to be limited. Some women had abused the privilege, secretly meeting relatives during the service, and others had even picked up drugs that had been dropped there. So we were very lucky to be going at all.

When we arrived the church was throbbing with life. There was an electrifying atmosphere. Towards the end the vicar's son got up and sang an amazing solo. It was the latest pop ballad but with Christian words – everyone had tears in their eyes. He had the sweetest voice and sounded just like Jimmy Osmond.

One of the church leaders approached me and asked if I would be a part of the service. There I was, now stood at the front of the church with the church elders, Bible in hand. I was really scared: half of York seemed to be in front of me, with a big gang of Askham girls at the back. Another pop hymn was sung while the vicar spoke via the microphone, asking people to open their minds and hearts and come forward to any of us stood at the front. Many people came forward to the other elders around me – and then something amazing happened. Just as I thought I wouldn't be needed, one of the girls who had bullied me throughout my entire sentence came forward – to me. I was never sure if, inspired by my own faith, she had seized that moment to discover her own, or whether she was simply acknowledging the pain that she'd inflicted on me during my sentence. But in truth it didn't matter: it was an overwhelmingly emotional moment. We embraced and cried.

When we got back to the prison everything seemed unusually quiet. There was no one downstairs as we came in. The TV room was empty and I thought everyone must have gone to bed early. I should have known better. As Heather and I climbed the grand staircase to the circular landing, a huge cheer went up. I stood in amazement as fifty or so women sang their goodbye overture. Just as I was about to say something my arms and legs were pulled from under me and – in the usual send-off style – I was thrown into a freezing cold bath. Apart from this usual ritual, they also covered me in a bucketful of slops that they'd been saving in the kitchen for *over a week*. Not knowing what to say, I thanked them! Another song was sung and then I spent my last night sat talking to Heather in our room until the first light of dawn broke.

The next day I was 'checked-out' at the main office. Reams of colourful paperwork were yet again signed and countersigned. I was handed the few quid I'd managed to save and a travel warrant. I walked out of the main door and looked back with mixed feelings at the monstrous building. Behind every one of the huge leaded windows stood smiling females, all waving frantically. I stood for a moment taking it all in, clutching three black bags and a picture of Lucy. It was then that I noticed Gladys peering through the library window. I grinned and saluted before turning away.

22

PHOENIX FROM THE ASHES

....

'Freedom's just another word for nothin' left to lose,
Nothin' ain't worth nothin', but it's free.'
Kris Kristofferson and Fred Foster

The high wooden couch was torn and filthy and none of
the tatty grey towels were clean. I'd noticed rat droppings in the corner of the room. I couldn't believe I was
actually going to have to pay money to get shifts in this
soul-destroying hole!

The owner of this place had been the only person I
could find who would give me what's called a 'working
interview'. Basically it meant he interviewed me and I
worked straight after. The 'interview' was a joke. He
looked me up and down, smiled and showed me where to
get changed. I suppose it could have been worse. At least
I wasn't back on the streets.

I'd settled into uni upon my release much more easily
than I'd thought I would. My head of department
believed that I deserved encouragement and made sure
I got benefits while I studied part-time until September,
when I could go full-time and get a grant. I started off

with good intentions and a positive attitude, determined to make a go of it. Everything had been going well. Until, that was, I attended the social-security appointment.

'Miss Daniels?' A bespectacled woman with dark hair sat in front of me shuffling papers around. 'Date of birth, please.'

Then she gave it to me, straight to the gut. 'We're suspending your benefit pending adjudication.'

I almost choked. 'Can you say that again in English?' I'd heard the words but I couldn't comprehend them.

'Basically, it's like this. We suspect that you are not doing less than fifteen hours of study per week. We know lecturers lie on behalf of the students – we're suspending your benefits.'

'Suspending?' I couldn't believe what I was hearing!

'Pending adjudication.' She saw the look on my face and continued: 'That means we do an investigation, have a meeting, make a decision and get back to you.'

'How long?' I spluttered.

'The process takes around six weeks.'

'Six weeks!' I squealed as all glimmer of hope was extinguished.

How could they do this to me? Why? I hadn't cheated anybody! After the initial shock my practical head took over.

'What about my housing benefit?'

The look on her face and lack of eye contact gave me the answer.

'Please don't get angry, Miss Daniels, or I will be forced to get security to remove you from the building.'

She walked off, leaving me at the desk, trembling.

'And what am I supposed to live on?' I shouted.

But that was that. No more dialogue. Case closed. The door that Gladys and June and the others in the prison had opened for me had been slammed in my face. I had no choice but to go back to work. I might have learned all sorts of new things in prison and during my short stay at the university, but I still only knew one reliable way to put food on the table. And after several weeks without benefits my choices were becoming somewhat limited.

I'd got backache from sleeping on different friends' sofas. The hostel I was in hadn't wasted any time kicking me out once the housing benefit stopped. I'd borrowed from just about everyone I knew – and from a few people I didn't know very well. I never thought I would become a scrounger. I tried to get a straight job but the odds were stacked too high against me: last known address, HMP. Being homeless didn't help, either. In most people's eyes I was the worst kind: a destitute prostitute.

I stood staring around at my new reality. I'd been sitting in this depressing sauna for hours without seeing a soul; no wonder they called it 'the graveyard shift'. Where was my God now and why had he forsaken me? It seemed that taking the spiritual path wasn't going to work for me, so it was best to close that door and not think about it any more. If God wasn't going to watch over me, I would have to do it myself.

I pulled to one side a grey threadbare net and stared out of a filthy window in a miserable sort of trance. God, tell me that's not snow in the middle of April. It was coming down in one solid drift. I turned on the small paint-splattered radio but reception was poor and I had to strain to make out what they were saying.

'Leeds is now totally gridlocked due to freak weather conditions. If you don't have to go out – stay in!'

Could this dire situation get any worse?

I picked up a magazine and read my stars. *You'll meet a tall dark handsome stranger who will change your life* . . . I looked at the front: thought so – two years out of date. Just my luck! I flicked through the rest of the magazine half-heartedly. Tomorrow I would have to find a better place.

The radio interrupted another song. 'The snow has now reached severe heights. All roads are blocked. Around four feet has landed in the last half-hour.'

I shivered and turned up the tiny electric heater. It sparked, made an odd popping noise, gave off a funny burning smell and died.

At last the door buzzer went, bringing me back to my grim reality and away from staring out the window. I smoothed down the horrible ill-fitting overall I had to wear and fixed my lipstick in a plastic-framed mirror. I pressed the door button and it opened. A man had battled through the drifts in search of his holy grail. He was wearing a hooded parka and a scarf halfway around his face to protect him from the freak cold; he looked like something out of *Nanook of the North*. I turned to him and smiled warmly as he removed his outer layers. It was only then that our eyes met. In front of me, shaking from more than just cold, was – one of my university lecturers.

* * *

While I'd been inside, my foster-mum had done a great job of bringing up Lucy – but she'd struggled financially, making a lot of sacrifices. I wanted us all to have an easier life and I could see no other choice but to continue in prostitution full-time. This time I meant business. I had learned so much over the years. I would do things differently; avoid some of the mistakes. No more itchy-scratchy saunas.

I got myself into a couple of half-decent parlours, worked some long shifts and got some cash together. Finally I was able to rent a small shabby Victorian terrace house, close to the centre of Leeds. It was the only time I ever lived and worked in the same premises. The house belonged to the Church of England, which was a constant reminder of what I was doing with my life, as distinct from what I *should* have been doing.

The house hadn't been properly maintained for years and was literally falling down around me. The rooms all had high ceilings and cornices and the lounge walls were freshly painted in cream. There was a tatty stripy brown three-piece suite, its crummy upholstery carefully concealed under new silk throws.

The kitchen, painted a horrible dark mustard colour, was a relic. If you hunted in the original 1940s cupboards you'd find cooking utensils that would have looked more at home in a post-war museum. An old square-legged dark wood table with matching carved chairs squatted on the dark green linoleum.

The telephone on the table rang constantly.

The cellar door was next to the table – I hated going down there to the only toilet. Not only was it spooky, it was a real hike when I had to make the journey from upstairs.

I came out of the kitchen and climbed the steep narrow stairs to the first floor. There was another floor to the house but I'd only been up there once: it was like a set from a Hammer Horror movie. In one room the window had a broken sash and there were cobwebs everywhere. Damp seeped through the wallpaper, which hung off the walls. The paint on the ceiling was yellowed and flaking. There were boxes filled with someone's junk from years ago. It smelled horrendous up there, so I avoided that part of the house. Sometimes, when I was downstairs in bed, I heard scratching noises above my head.

The first floor was very different. My bedroom was clean and comfortable. As humble as it was, it was one hundred times better than sharing a room in prison. It had been freshly painted in white. There was the aroma of vanilla that I'd just sprayed – I was once told that it's the natural scent closest to a woman's fundamental odour, hence its use as an aphrodisiac. My bed had a clean bedspread on it – not the one I slept under, which I'd removed when I got up that morning, carefully folding it and storing it away. I would be putting it back later that day.

Next to the bed was a small chipped Formica bedside table covered in a piece of silk. On it were my oils, talc and, under a box of tissues, my hidden condoms. An old dresser with a triptych mirror sat under the window. One of the small side panels was cracked. I looked into it and saw my fragmented face staring back. Taking out my warpaint from one of the drawers, I set about applying my work mask.

I changed out of my comfy fleecy pyjamas and donned cream stockings, suspenders and a garter. I carefully put on a beautiful satin bridal negligee and gown with hand-sewn beads and sequins – even the slippers and knickers matched. I looked over the dresser, out of a dusty window, and saw my first of the day scuttling across the cobbled street.

I left the room and, looking back, scanned it one last time to check that everything was in place. I glanced at my reflection in the dresser from across the room and closed the door, behind which a French maid's outfit, a variety of whips and a set of handcuffs hung.

He came into the house and looked nervously around. I assured him it was clean and he relaxed a little more. He told me how attractive I looked as I took him by the hand up the stairs, leading him into my boudoir. As instructed, he slid a small bundle of used notes under the pot on my dresser.

I discreetly checked the cash while he went off to shower. I didn't need to. My customers always left me the right amount, and some even left tips. We wouldn't need to mention the money thing again. He knew it would stay there the whole time and if he was unhappy at the end of his time he would be able to take it back. Like many others he could recount endless tales of coldly clinical transactions and being robbed by someone with the face of an angel. But no one ever took the cash back.

He came out of the bathroom, wrapped in a towel. I gently dried his back with another. He looked around for the toilet. I smiled apologetically and sent him down two flights to the cellar, hoping it wouldn't put him off. He returned to the bedroom a few minutes later.

For the next hour I would be his girlfriend.

As he lay on the bed his excitement was already visible. I put on some music to strip to; they all like that bit. I carefully maintained lots of eye contact to make him feel special.

Julie London sang, 'Who would like to pay the price for a trip to paradise? Love for sale.'

I got down to my lingerie. He wanted me to keep it on, but I couldn't because it was too delicate, so I coaxed him into having a body-on-body massage instead. He lay face up on the towel, audibly panting in anticipation. I carefully removed the last of the lingerie – the silk knickers – and straddled his left leg, deliberately placing my moist velvety flesh against his skin just long enough to elicit a small moan. As I said, he had only been wearing a towel: I removed it to see his growing erection and smiled knowingly, giving him the full eye-contact treatment.

Moving towards his thighs, I softly tickled the inside of his legs, just avoiding the most sensitive area, and then gently massaged his back for a few minutes – this was only a warm-up and not the main event.

I poured sweet almond oil seductively over my boobs and started to massage them, taking his hands from by his sides and placing them on my breasts, gently encouraging his participation. (I never used baby oil as it not only smells offensive, it also erodes the latex of condoms.) Then I started with gentle downward strokes of his shoulders and ran my hands down his arms until I reached his hands, placing my palms on his and at the same time gently spreading out his fingers and massaging each one individually. I could feel him starting to relax and unwind. Then I placed the whole length of my naked body on his and writhed against him slowly.

His skin felt leathery and the palms of his hands grabbed at my obvious bits clumsily. They felt like sandpaper gloves. I got closer and cuddled him, putting my cheek against his. He turned his head and tried to French-kiss me. I would have but for his stale-tobacco breath. I closed my eyes and let my body go onto autopilot.

He would never know that I was somewhere else, with someone else, because I could hide it so well.

When he left, I followed where he'd been, using a spray-gun of bleach and water. I knew that for the sake of my own sanity I couldn't go on living and working in the same house much longer.

At first I worked at the house on my own. Then I decided to get someone to answer the phone and the door: in private places such a woman is always referred to as 'the maid'. At that time I had a mate called Jenny who'd been very kind to me when I was homeless. I asked her if she fancied a job with me and she jumped at the chance.

Jenny sounded very sexy on the phone. She was a funny lady who joked with the clients and quickly put the apprehensive ones at ease. But as lovely as Jenny was she was no looker. She was twice as wide as me and wore large framed glasses with milk-bottle-bottom lenses. She had a poodle haircut, short and curly on the top and long at the back. She also had a bad case of dandruff and psoriasis, so her skin was flaking all over. Luckily she was thick-skinned and had a great sense of humour: she used to open the door and say to clients, 'Don't worry, love, it's not me!' Sometimes they wouldn't be able to hide their huge sighs of relief, but she never seemed bothered. She always called me 'Classy Chrissie', and I would try to live up to the reputation by wearing tasteful, expensive underwear and speaking about my love of music and art.

Eventually I was so busy that I couldn't cope with working all the clients and all the hours. So I decided to find another girl to work with me.

Earlier I'd answered an advert in the paper for glamour models. The place I was directed to was like a camera club in a studio over a shop. Fifteen or twenty guys would come with their cameras, most of which I suspect had no film in them, and they would tell us what to do and pretend to take pictures. Sometimes one or two of them would ask afterwards for extras, which meant we could make a bit more money on the side. It was all an illusion to allow the clients to kid themselves they weren't using prostitutes; to them they were merely artists who were shagging their models. Sometimes a guy would book me and the studio for a private session, having picked me from a portfolio of pictures. That nearly always meant more money because we would spend about ten minutes taking pictures and the rest of the time having sex.

At the studio I met a smashing blonde girl who had never worked before but wanted to try it. She was a single mum and had thought about it for over a year. We complemented each other nicely – on the telephone I was billed as a 'busty green-eyed brunette' and she as a 'slim blue-eyed blonde'. First we became friends; then she asked me to introduce her to a few clients. For the first month we doubled up and I showed her how to be a good hooker, including how to seduce clients, as well as all the safe ways of working.

I also shared my secrets with her: how to keep eye contact, how to use body language and how to make clients feel special. Keeping eye contact makes a girl seem confident, which men find attractive. It also makes the man believe that the girl is attracted to him, an impression she will not give if she keeps her eyes averted all the time. I trained her in my speciality, which was an erotic body-on-body massage and striptease. In some ways we were the perfect combination: if customers requested it I could be dominant and she submissive, but never the other way around.

We'd both decided that if we were going to do this we would do it to the very best of our abilities. Where it was not physically repulsive we kissed clients and gave them what I called 'the girlfriend experience'. Within a few weeks, we were both amazed to find we were so busy that we had no alternative but to put the price up.

Then a funny thing happened. Work started to become enjoyable. There was no hostile stale environment and no bitching. We had fun together. My visitors were all smart, executive-type clients who were polite and respectful. I started to go out on escorts with them to the opera and the theatre. If I couldn't go to university then I didn't want to think about it, or about the chances that I might be missing. I wanted to concentrate on what I could do to improve my situation and not dwell on what had gone wrong.

Gradually I became a little more cultured and refined myself, just through experience. I continued to study the art that I had discovered in prison, and shared it with the clients, who talked to me about things they liked in return, building my knowledge all the time. I found I'd moved into a different league and started earning more than some of my fat-cat clientele. My clients were also becoming more like friends and would shower me with gifts and jewellery. I loved it; I'd made my bed and now I was going to enjoy lying (and other activities) in it. It was one of the most enjoyable working periods I'd ever had. I got on really well with my colleague and all the clients were nice to us. Eventually I gave up working from home and moved to other premises but, luxurious as some of them were, it was never quite the same as that short golden period.

I returned to Sheffield most weekends to visit Lucy, who was now six and starting to seem very grown-up. Once I bumped into Doreen. She hadn't changed much since I'd last seen her. I almost didn't stop when I first spotted her: she was still smelly and tatty, with one eye going to the shop and the other coming back with the change.

She took me into a flat where I saw my natural gran for the first time in years. My gran had moved (despite the fact the house was actually in her name), probably to get some peace from my strange mother. I enquired about my little sister, Amanda, and was told she was still doing fine – with her own partner and children now.

My gran looked much older and thinner and was so overwhelmed to see me that she bawled her eyes out. I could hardly tell what she was saying between her heartbreaking sobs and her ever-strong Belfast accent. I said I'd try and bring Lucy to see her and at the time I meant it. But, regretfully, I never did. It was awkward, as

I had no intention of introducing Doreen to her grand-child. I'm only sorry I didn't get to know my Gran and my half-sister better. Sadly, as hard as I tried, I could never find any room in my heart for Doreen and I would never grow to see her as my 'real' mother.

Once I stopped working from home I started having Lucy over for weekends. The regular maintenance had started again so that things were easier for Mum, and I began to feel as if I was on the road to becoming a proper mum myself at last. I knew I could never have Lucy back with me full-time as long as I was working, but at least we had a relationship. My mum was doing a brilliant job on bringing her up and I was so proud of them. I knew that if I'd tried to bring her up myself it would have been a disaster for both of us, but I couldn't help wishing I had been a different person when I had her, and I couldn't help thinking about how much of her childhood I had missed. She still didn't have any idea what I did for a living. My mother and I agreed that I'd lost my innocence early enough and we both wanted Lucy to be able to hang on to hers for as long as possible.

I'd gone back to work out of desperation but suddenly it didn't seem so bad. I was earning more money than I'd ever seen in my life and I was starting to enjoy a fabulous lifestyle, something I could never even have imagined when I was that tower-block Rapunzel. If only I could have found some other way of earning the same kind of money and having Lucy back full-time, my happiness would have been complete.

23

RAT RACE

....

'*We don't sell our bodies. Housewives do that. What we do is rent our bodies for sexual services.*'

Valerie Scott

'Sauna for sale' . . . I read the ad again, several times, before picking up the phone to ring the number. A softly-spoken woman answered.

'I'm looking for around two thousand pounds for the lease,' she told me.

'Why so cheap?' I was immediately suspicious.

'The place has run into the ground,' she confessed. 'I'm a working girl, I know how to handle clients, but I don't know about running a business or managing other girls.'

Cheap or not, where was I going to find that kind of cash? I'd only been out of prison a few months and although I'd now built up a nice home and indulged myself in a few luxuries, I hadn't got to the stage where I could save anything yet. But I also knew I didn't want to work hands-on for ever. In order to move on and manage other girls I had to get larger premises.

Why, I don't know, probably curiosity more than

anything, I said I'd meet her and take a look around. She told me that she was called Yvette and would be waiting for me inside when I got there.

Yvette was in her thirties; she was slim with curly dark hair and blue eyes. I couldn't take my stare off them, or the hideous blue eyeshadow that she had lathered up to her eyebrows. But she seemed a very gentle and pleasant lady nevertheless – more like a housewife than a hooker – and I guess that was her particular charm.

She'd said the place needed a tidy-up – that was an understatement. There was a lingering odour that reminded me of old ladies and the walls were a gruesome cerise-and-lime-coloured Artex. The massage benches had ripped plastic covers masked up with duct tape, and there were red bulbs in all the rooms, probably so that you couldn't see how filthy the cubicles were.

The building itself was a zoo: it was an old converted industrial unit with rodent houseguests and dogs for workers. It felt as if it was crawling and there were tell-tale mouse droppings everywhere. What was supposed to be the 'sauna' was actually a heap of broken pine and an old rusty stove. It all needed ripping out and rebuilding. Yvette saw the look of disgust on my face as she followed me around from one revolting room to another. It was certainly not an environment conducive to lust and eroticism!

I rang Gus, my old friend and business adviser, that night. 'It's in a right state, mate. Beside that, it's off the main road on a bloody industrial estate! The outside isn't exactly inviting.'

'So what? I don't suppose your punters come to

admire the outside. The insides you can fix up! Surely you're not scared of a challenge? As for its location, if I was a punter – which I never would be – surely discretion is everything! If you're worried they won't find it, just give good directions. Was it a sauna before? You could say it was "formerly known as" . . . whatever it was called.'

' "Riviera".' I suppressed the urge to giggle since it was more like Leeds Canal than the French Riviera. 'And it's got a terrible reputation.'

'New name, management, interior and girls – a fresh start.' Gus had an upbeat answer to everything. 'Give the first few punters through the door some kind of reward: if they have a great time and an incentive to come again, you've got them hooked!'

I'd certainly never heard of any brothel I'd ever worked in giving out incentives, but my guru had spoken. He'd been right before about all the publicity and I trusted his judgement completely.

There was one other small issue that I'd failed to mention in discussing my big-time plans for my future business empire.

'Truth is, Gus, I haven't got the cash.'

He was silent for a minute, deep in thought.

'I've seen you move mountains, Charlie,' he said eventually. 'You can do this – I can't imagine a little thing like insufficient money stopping you.'

Yvette rang me again the day after. I didn't really know what to say. I'd thought about what Gus had said over and over. But unless I borrowed the money I wasn't in a position to move in on what I knew was a great deal, and I really didn't want to get myself into debt, having just started to lead a comfortable life again. I had to be honest with Yvette.

'I'm sorry,' I told her. 'I don't have the cash – I didn't mean to waste your time.'

'You didn't,' she said softly. 'Look, let me lay this on the line: I can't go on losing money on the place – the rent was due last week and I haven't got it. Take the lease off my hands: you can give me the cash when you make it, and, believe me, I think you will.'

I was speechless. (Another of those rare moments.) I signed the lease that afternoon.

Yvette seemed over the moon at having the responsibility lifted from her shoulders. 'By the way, can I have a job?'

Of course I said yes and initially it worked well – because she really was a great hooker.

The first job I had to do was not very pleasant. I cleared the building of all the rubbish and then had it fumigated. The 'death squad' in gas masks carried away sacks full of dead mice. The stench was horrendous.

Building work started almost immediately, with the help of one or two clients who were in various trades. We filled two large skips with the crap we threw away. The pile of rubbish that was supposed to be a sauna was slung and we made another room of the space instead. We even painted and tidied the outside and put hanging baskets up to try and make it look a little less bleak.

Finally the sign went up. We were almost ready. I looked around proudly on the opening day and it took my breath away – it was a totally different place.

We were busy straight away and, just like in an episode of *Challenge Anneka*, the paint was still drying and we were still stripping the plastic off the new mattresses as the first clients arrived. On the theme of Gus's incentive advice, we handed out free lifetime entry passes for the first twenty customers. When we scrapped charging an entry fee three years later we worked out that an incredible sixteen of the original passes were still in circulation.

Now I was really on my way: this was to be the first in a successful chain of parlours that I would own. Gus had convinced me that learning some basic general business rules would assist in my quest and he gave me all manner of business books on how to be a commercial success. I lapped them up, hungry for any hints they could give me, and immediately started applying my newly learned principles, most of which were unheard of in parlours at that time. To me it wasn't just a knocking shop, it was my passion and right then I was very proud of it.

I was enjoying my new status of 'madam' and started living up to it well. I employed a driver and wore the finest outfits. I was proud of my reputation for being a firm but fair boss. I was generous to all my management staff and felt as if I'd found my ideal role in life.

Recruitment of good girls was always a major problem; you can hardly ask for references, after all. In one bar where I was a regular I met a gorgeous barmaid. She was stunning: she had straight shiny waist-length hair, big eyes and an olive complexion. She was as dainty and supple as a ballerina, with a real ethereal beauty.

When I first met her she was genuinely not aware of quite how breathtaking she was. However, for all her looks, she hadn't got a clue about how to be sexy. She was fascinated by my business and to some degree by the lifestyle I'd achieved. We quickly struck up a friendship, went shopping and enjoyed some coffees together. The more time I spent in her company the more I liked her – she was a very bubbly and intelligent lady. She watched how I would manipulate her manager, flirt with waiters and generally how I used sex appeal, and she was a fast learner.

Then somehow we lost contact. I didn't see or hear from her for several months. When I went into the bar where she'd worked I was told that she'd moved on. But just when I'd started to think she'd disappeared from my life for ever she called me out of the blue: to thank me. Apparently my encouragement had given her great confidence and so instead of earning two hundred pounds a week behind a bar she was now earning three times as much working shorter hours – as a stripper. In place of the shy, pretty girl I'd once been able to make blush quite easily had emerged a captivating snake-charmer. She started to enjoy the money and the finer things in life but it wasn't enough for her. Somehow we ended up having a conversation about what she could earn as a class hooker, which at that time in Leeds was around a thousand pounds a week – even stripping money didn't compare to that. She asked me for a job and I didn't hesitate. I knew she was going to be a winner. During her regular Sunday-afternoon pub stints there had often been a whip-round and then basically a gang-bang, resulting in a nice little couple of hundred pounds for her for two hours' work.

To start with she was a great hooker. She told me, and the clients, straight out that kissing was out of the question. However, she did offer an alluring striptease to any 'willing victim' and maintained eye contact to a degree that was later described to me as 'smouldering'. She was bringing in so much business that I thought it would be a good idea to promote her so I gave her a chance to work in a beautiful riverside cottage: just her, a maid and lots of upmarket business-type clients. She was set to make a fortune, but somehow as time went on she became colder and colder and the clients started to become disenchanted.

In the end I had no alternative but to send her back to the sauna. She had even complained that she was missing the camaraderie of the other girls. Most of the women who worked for me were a little bit special but she, a lady who had once been my star turn, was now described to me by clients as 'just like any other sauna girl, clinical and unavailable.' I knew that she'd changed. I'd started to notice that instead of her running over the time with the clients she was now short-changing them. Her general attitude had altered and instead of being the life and soul of our team she had become a bitchy, malicious gossip.

I should have heard the warning bells sooner but eventually I realised there was nothing for it but to gently confront her and see what her problem was. By now I hardly saw her: sadly, she was no longer a friend, just an employee. As soon as I started talking she exploded. Screaming and shouting, she swept up her belongings and stormed out, leaving us all feeling completely bemused. Several days later she called and it became apparent to me that she'd suffered some kind of a nervous breakdown. She'd become so greedy, bitter and twisted that I hardly recognised her – and all because she'd hated the job from the start.

The truth was that no matter how beautiful, intelligent or talented she was she'd known from the beginning that she wouldn't earn this kind of fast cash (I would never call it 'easy money') anywhere else – but she'd hated every moment of it. She'd given in to the material temptations dangled in front of her and regretted it.

I never encouraged anyone into prostitution again. Back then I was building a business: I needed good people to work in it. Based on my own experiences, I'd always thought the act of prostitution itself a harmless one and had seen the dangers of the game as external, not internal. Certainly, I was aware that women were at risk from pimps, dodgy clients and all the obvious unsavoury elements. But because at that time I thought I had escaped without any mental damage from the act itself I had simply assumed that everyone else was the same. If a woman could enter into the game for a short space of time of her own free will, if she protected herself, worked in a safe and secure environment and ensured that she remained physically and mentally unscarred – then I believed it could be done without too much damage and without creating too much emotional baggage. What I didn't realise was that the more complex issues it creates do not always surface immediately.

*   *   *

A couple of years into the business and we were looking for new ideas. That was when Jada joined us. Jada modelled herself on Marlene Dietrich. She was uncommonly tall for a woman but frequently tottered in ridiculously high heels that increased her height still more. She was not young, although none of us were actually sure how old she was – maybe in her thirties, or possibly a young-looking forty-something. Experience in this case won out over youth, which rarely happens when men are confronted with the visual choice between young slender beauties and more mature ladies. But Jada was a real woman, complete with curves, warm banter and a worrying array of unusual toys and implements.

Jada's trademark uniform consisted of leather, rubber or PVC – she took 'kinky' to the extreme. She was always immaculately turned out and, unlike with quite a few of the other girls, I never needed to remind her to wax, manicure or tan anything. In that and many other respects she made the others look like amateurs. What God didn't bless her with she added: dramatic fake eyelashes, long curved scarlet nails and permanently tattooed eyebrows and lips, which contributed to the idle speculation about her original gender. Peter, one of the security guys who worked nights, was convinced that she was a sex-change artist. He not only whispered this to the other girls but, more worryingly, announced it to the occasional regular who, bizarrely enough, seemed to become even more intoxicated, as if in the presence of a freaky legend.

Jada had a distincitve way of speaking. 'Come with me now, baby,' she would drawl as she took customers by the hand and drew them behind closed doors.

She had spent a long time working in Berlin and spoke fluent German. She would also sing in it, frequently belting out numbers from musicals like *Cabaret* and *Chicago*. Her energy, personality and enthusiasm were electric. Even those clients who did not choose to take her through to the room would love to sit in the lounge chatting with her.

Jada told me all about the swingers parties in Berlin where married couples, bisexuals and transvestites came together. I was fascinated and with her input we started to run our own versions. We started with ticket parties where we charged a set fee and laid on a small buffet, booze and a group of willing girls. Then clients would exchange vouchers for time with the girls, but instead of everything happening behind closed doors all the rooms were left open for the others to watch. Jada was a master ticket-taker. She moved through the parties so swiftly that she always made more than the other girls – she was also always the party starter, taking the most confident client she could find under her wing and getting the action rolling.

Then we tried couples parties with Yvette, who had also been active on the swinging scene. Most of the guests would be aged somewhere between their late twenties and early forties – so when a much more mature couple turned up we joked about them being in their 'swinging sixties'. The woman was wearing a lurex top and a pink rinse and as a couple they looked like *Coronation Street*'s Jack and Vera Duckworth.

As they entered we all looked at each other silently. Then the lady announced that she had only come to keep her hubby happy but didn't want to stay, so she trundled off to the bingo. As always, Jada got everyone in the mood by taking Yvette into a room and putting on a lesbian show. Very soon everyone was in one room, all going for it. A little later on I got nosy and decided to venture in to see how the orgy was going. As I entered the room I tripped over something and looked down to see a plastic leg lying on the floor. The old guy had one good leg and one stump, but it was in no way holding him back since his backside was pumping up and down like a rabbit's. I went back into the lounge area and sat with Peter, the security guard, and a coffee until the party antics were over.

As everyone was leaving Peter realized that it had frosted over outside and the metal stairs were slippery. I suggested that we might need to assist the disabled guy down: the last thing we needed would be a punter with a broken neck – last seen at an orgy! But, as politely as we suggested it, he seemed really offended, as though we had insulted his powers of mobility, and we had no choice but to watch him on the CCTV monitor as he clambered down the treacherous stairs one by one. About halfway down one of his feet slipped. Peter and I rushed out just in time to see him flip over the side of the stairs – I screamed! Then one hand, followed by the other, snapped onto the side rail as he clung on for dear life. He was dangling twenty feet up in the air when his taxi pulled round the corner. Peter ran to the phone for help but before he got to it the guy dropped off the rail feet first, landed upright and jogged to his waiting taxi! Those early parties always were like a bloody circus and we never knew what would happen next!

Not many of the women who are attracted to prostitution are balanced, or sensible, but some are very clever. One girl who called herself Sophie nearly fooled everyone – with disastrous consequences. She was an amazing manipulator but not just of clients. Sophie wasn't your usual sauna girl and at first we were all taken in. Her magical combination of intellect, sharp wit, a plum in her mouth and an air of mystery and sophistication went down well with the clients – she was an instant success.

When she contacted me she told me a story about how she was a former chemistry-degree student with thirty grand's worth of debt to pay off. I was totally impressed by her stunning six-foot frame, endless legs and masses of dark-blonde hair, the whole package smacked of something elusive and expensive. Her eyes, an unusual murky grey-blue, were as fascinating as the rest of her. Despite the fact I knew she had amazing potential I tried to talk her out of starting work. I felt strongly that she could earn more in the business world, but she'd already called several other brothels and had made up her mind.

Sophie was a rapid learner, listening intently to every piece of advice that I gave her. I felt appreciated and so I went that extra mile for her, including loaning her classy outfits and accessories until she got on her feet. She became the hottest thing on the Leeds sex circuit, so it was no surprise to me that the other ladies became jealous and began bitching about her behind her back.

Alarm bells started to ring one day when I visited her

at work. The client she had just seen was leaving. I'd known him for years but he didn't even say hello to me, just brushed straight past. Suspicious, I followed him outside. At first he didn't want to talk but eventually he agreed to call me and a few hours later he did. It seemed that 'Sex-on-Legs' wasn't quite all she was cracking herself up to be. He'd had suspicions about her background story and had tested her on the basic chemical elements. Sophie didn't know any of them. It turned out that she'd picked chemistry for her façade; a smart move because not many of us knew anything about it so she was unlikely to be caught out. But, as the client and I both agreed, a science degree wasn't a necessary attribute for hooking. I just shrugged it off as part of her stage act, a sort of protection for her real identity. But then he went on to tell me something much more worrying.

It seemed that Sophie had borrowed a large sum of money from him. She'd agreed to 'work it off' rather than make cash repayments, but suddenly she had become cold, moody and hostile – when he'd challenged her she'd put it down to the way she was being treated at work.

I didn't like what I was hearing but decided it might be more prudent to help Sophie get a private flat to work from on the better side of Leeds, where she could have more independence and would not have to work with the others. We talked about it extensively and she was keen to give it a try. Getting cash up front in large lumps was a bad idea for her as she admitted that she used it as a comfort when she was feeling low. She promised to make a go of sorting herself out.

We found a clean, tastefully decorated apartment and

Sophie moved her work base there. It was certainly a more conducive environment for a lady who could command high fees and a clientele of the highest fliers. I even asked one of my best mates to pack in her part-time job in sales to be Sophie's receptionist, which was a smart move in one way as my pal was great at the job. Sophie built up a selection of fine clients who hung on her every word and simpered and whimpered around her like whipped puppies. But, unbeknown to me, she had once again borrowed thousands of pounds from one or two of them.

Then one day a rather hostile client rang me and told me that one of the other girls at the sauna had assaulted Sophie at the time she'd been working there. I might have believed it if the accused had not been one of the sweetest girls. I went to see the girl in question and she started to cry: she told me that in fact it was Sophie who had assaulted her, a story that was backed up by the receptionist. Worse still, when I reported back to the client he told me he'd expected me not to take Sophie's side as I was clearly an old hag who was jealous of her! I had a fair idea who would have given him that idea.

By now I knew that Sophie was more than a shit-magnet – she was shovelling it! She had a knack of making herself look like a victim and anyone she hurt came out looking like the exploiter. I realised that our lady was a little unbalanced, to say the least.

When my receptionist mate started to back Sophie and challenge my views, I wondered what was coming next. I warned my pal not to get involved but she did and we argued for months. I'd advised her to keep her distance but she and Sophie had become close outside work and yet again I was perceived as the one with a bad case of the green-eyed monster.

Then one day the flat was raided, right out of the blue. The police arrested Sophie and the receptionist but later let them go without charge. Normally you get a warning of impending trouble such as neighbours' hostile attitudes or letters from the council, but this time we'd had no idea it was coming. I smelled a rat. Sophie had disappeared with the outfits I'd loaned her, as well as with some of the furniture. It later turned out that it was a client who'd made the call to the police after she'd extracted a rather large sum of money from him and then had me ban him from the flat for alleged abuse.

Sophie had played one last ace card, and it seemed that someone else had learned a lesson from all this too. It turned out that my pal had sold her a car. Sophie had no licence or insurance and had then gone out and had an accident a few days before the raid. Of course she hadn't bothered to tell any of us, especially my pal, whose name was still registered to the car, which Sophie then dumped back outside my pal's house. I couldn't help but wonder if the timing of the raid was more than just a coincidence.

Yvette, the sauna's former owner, was a popular worker there. She formed a strong bond with some of the other women, including the girl I'd worked alongside for two years. Managing the girls was not easy for me because tact and diplomacy were never my strong points, and after a few years I employed someone else to do it. Yvette then set herself up as a bit of a union rep.

As time went on and we became more and more

successful, I guess that Yvette decided it was mostly down to her. It came as a genuine surprise to me that she'd grown jealous and bitter. She regretted selling up to me, even though she was now making more money than she ever had as the owner. Finally she plotted my downfall, took half of my staff and opened a new place down the road. It came as no surprise to me when it flopped after only a few weeks. Yvette just couldn't compete with us and still hadn't got it. It was a difficult time. At first I was angry but she didn't really damage me in the end.

By this time I was running dozens of girls in saunas and private flats, making me one of the biggest operators in the area. I couldn't complain about the way the business was going. I was undoubtedly a success but I still wanted to find a way to have Lucy back with me. I was now seeing her regularly at weekends and making sure that I helped Mum in any way I could, but it wasn't the same as being a full-time mum and I knew it. The problem was that I was becoming seriously addicted to my new champagne lifestyle and couldn't think of any more 'respectable' way in which I could possibly maintain it.

24

ALL THE WORLD'S A STAGE

....

'Our tastes greatly alter. The lad does not care for the child's rattle, and the old man does not care for the young man's whore.'

Samuel Johnson

While I was running the saunas and working myself I was also privileged to travel to many exotic places. This was all part of the sort of lifestyle I had craved from the start: exciting, glamorous, luxurious and stimulating. They say that travel broadens the mind, and it certainly taught me a thing or two. Apart from anything else I ended up with a very different view of the way brothels should be regulated and run. England, I discovered, is a long way behind the times.

Holidays with clients were always fabulous and the yearning to discover the world for myself grew stronger with every destination I visited. I went to Egypt, China, Australia, the Maldives, and most of the Caribbean, as well as many parts of Europe including Portugal, Spain, Italy and France, sometimes for a break and sometimes on a 'busman's holiday'.

On one trip I went to China on my own. Tiananmen

Square, Beijing was my first stop. I wandered around among a mass of grey-clad locals on their bicycles. The air was full of dust and faded Communist signs still adorned the walls. There were poignant reminders of the 1989 student riots and it felt like an alien place to be.

That evening I attended Puccini's opera *Turandot*. (Even non-opera fans may remember its most famous aria – 'Nessun Dorma' as sung by Pavarotti at the World Cup.) It was held in the royal courtyard of the Forbidden Palace Gardens in Beijing, a very different place from the square. The sky was a blaze of crimson and gold. The wind carried soft drifts of blossom. I gazed around as the light faded on the many ancient red, green and gilt structures. Row upon row of chairs teetered on uneven cobbles. In front of us, one of the palace buildings was lit up and decorated as a stage.

The story of the opera was set in the palace gardens we were sitting in – even though Puccini had never been there and it was his last opera, finished by his apprentice, which might explain its uncharacteristically more cheery ending. Zubin Mehta (frequent conductor for The Three Tenors) battled with the authorities for years to stage the opera in this, its natural setting. The real Cultural Revolution had finally arrived, some thirty years after it had been supposed to begin.

I wore a full-length claret-coloured ball gown with hand-sewn beads, perfectly matching satin shoes and one solitary striking ring (a gift from my latest client), which had a ruby the size of a small cherry. I always loved dressing up for events like this. Back in England I would sometimes go to the opera with a girlfriend and we would get all togged up in ball gowns and jewels, even though we knew most of the audience would be American tourists in white trainers and anoraks. I loved the feel of heads turning to look as I came in – I had done ever since that first party where I'd made heads turn in the dyed second-hand dress and pearl earrings.

I looked around to see who else might be at such an auspicious occasion and noticed that I was only a few seats down from Michael Heseltine MP and his wife.

I'd paid to get the best seat possible – the only two rows in front of me were reserved for the local Chinese dignitaries, although you would not have guessed that was who they were. In direct contrast to all the immaculately attired foreigners they were dressed in a low-key manner – the man in front of me wore a very loud 1980s zigzag jumper and his hair had not been combed. The Cultural Revolution might have reached Beijing but fashion hadn't.

Nothing could have prepared me for one thing during that trip – a visit to the Great Wall. A girl I'd met out there and I went on an expedition to see how far we could get. We were out of breath when we reached the top of the stairs but it was well worth it: the view was truly exhilarating. In among the mists the wall snaked away into infinity. It was very lonely up there. The wind howled and we walked for two hours without seeing a soul. Previously we'd been two lively women, chattering loudly, but now we were silenced in awe. In the distance we could just make out one of the small temples that broke up the great long expanses of wall. We walked for another full hour. As we approached, we heard the strangest grunting noises.

'Surely they don't keep pigs up here?' I said.

Then, as we turned the corner, my friend covered her mouth with her hand and whooped: 'Oh my God!'

Ten or so previously slumbering Chinese postcard sellers leaped up like Mexican beans and a chorus of bicycle bells and hopeful greetings penetrated the echoing walls.

Poor bastards were gutted when we apologetically, held up our previously bought postcards.

A few days later we ended our trip in style, with a flight to Xian to see the world-famous Terracotta Army.

On another trip – to Australia – six months later, I was determined to get to work in Sydney's notorious twenty-four-hour area: Darlinghurst Road, a melting pot of colourful people who walk, stalk and generally hang out. I'd heard a lot about how well organised the brothels were out there and I wanted to see for myself. Maybe I could pick up some tips on how to improve the services I was offering back home.

The pavements were peppered with leather-clad dykes on bikes, camera-clutching Japanese tourists, junkies, whores, johns and pimps. Seedy strip joints, bold brothels and all manner of entertainment were on offer in grand buildings lit by burning neon lights. It all seemed very open and honest, unlike our own furtive approach to the business.

Smells of all descriptions, but mostly of food and pot smoke, wafted over me as I walked past bikers and hippies and became intoxicated by the odours of sandal-wood and ylang-ylang.

Harleys littered the sidewalk. As I walked past a group of their owners I felt intimidated and held on to my bag a little harder. As I passed by them something tickled my shoulder and out of the corner of my eye I saw a huge tarantula! As I screamed and ran I heard their laughter as the tallest one of the group retrieved the plastic toy from a piece of wire hung over a bar sign. I looked back and laughed with them – served me right for being so judgemental!

I was on a mission – job-hunting – and it wasn't long before I was successful. The next day I arrived at work, walking into a huge reception area with signs that read 'Time-locked safe on these premises'. I was searched for drugs and weapons by one of four burly security guards. The staff were perfectly friendly but I felt overwhelmed by the sheer size of the operation: the illegal UK brothels are never so big and bold. I had received a formal interview the day before, conducted by a very professional suited lady who now showed me through to a large theatre-style dressing room.

I'd noticed that there were a lot of Chinese girls working in the area. But none of them wore their traditional national dress, which I thought was a shame and might indicate a possible gap in the market. So with that in mind I carefully pulled on a short tight bright-turquoise silk Chinese dress that I'd fallen in love with in the market. My hair was piled up on top of my head and I placed two chopsticks in it. I looked at my reflection in a Hollywood-style mirror with bulbs all around it and painted on my work face, emphasising my eyes to look Chinese.

My legs were encased in tan silky stockings and I slipped my recently pedicured feet into high-heeled silk-printed strappy Chinese shoes. My costume complete, I walked nervously into the ladies' lounge. Most of the brothels in the UK would never have even considered a separate area but it worked and meant there was a sanctuary where the ladies could relax between clients. Thirty or so ladies were milling around, like nervous contestants for the Miss World crown. They were all different nationalities, all beautiful and all available – at a price. I made myself a sandwich in the well-stocked kitchen. Then I heard a buzzer.

We all looked up to a board that had different-coloured lights – a green light was flashing. A loud receptionist came in, clapping her hands to awaken us all into action.

'Come on, ladies – green lounge, please! Gold-card holder and this one's for a full hour.'

At that time it was common for UK brothels to have an itemised menu of charges for individual sexual services. A working girl would reel prices off like a chip-shop menu – 'So much for chips, so much for fish and extra for vinegar on top and I don't do ketchup!' Looking back, it all seemed very clinical and unromantic.

But in the legal parlours of Sydney, rather than buying specific services the clients bought time. It was closer to providing them with the 'girlfriend experience'.

The pantomime then began. We filed into the green lounge one by one. Protocol demanded that we placed our hands behind our backs and turned sideways. Then we had to introduce ourselves.

'Hello, I'm Taneal from Brazil.'

'Hello, I'm Meera from India.'

'Hello, I'm Chrissie from England.'

So the parade continued. Eyes front, chins up, stomachs in and chests out. The client didn't even notice me. I went and sat back in the lounge with the cheese sandwich that I'd made earlier. Five magazines, three coffees and a word-search game later, another receptionist came in. By now I'd endured thirteen curtain calls and not had a single strike.

'Come with me, sugar,' she said.

She took me into a room that smelled of mothballs.

'You're a pretty girl, but we need to do something different with your image. An English girl dressed up as a Chinese girl is not what the clients are after, even though you do look stunning!'

Two other receptionists were already in the room and picking out outfits from a wardrobe for me. They stuck me in an old evening dress, let my hair down and blushered my cheeks up like an old whore's. I felt degraded and defensive but I didn't say a single word; I wasn't there to sit on my backside all day so I was willing to try anything at that point. A few minutes later and the yellow light glowed. We all reassembled in the yellow lounge. It worked – this time I was the chosen one.

A suited and bespectacled guy handed me a plain white token. Just my luck: this one was for a minimum time and a basic room. I looked at the plain man and smiled, not knowing whether to be relieved or disappointed. I took him gently by the hand and smiled graciously.

This wasn't like any sauna in England. It was a well organised, orchestrated, managed, packaged, marketed, all-singing, all-dancing cabaret. Although the surroundings couldn't have been more different, the needs of the clients were exactly the same as in the UK. The things that men like women to do for them are the same the world over: they like screwing, they like hand jobs and they like blow jobs, and they like it all dressed up as romantically and sexily as possible. Once I had found the trick of getting them to choose me, I had no trouble sending them away with smiles on their faces.

My favourite Sydney after-work hang-out was the Beef-steak and Bourbon. It was a twenty-four-hour place and in twenty years it had never been closed for one day. For several weeks I went there most nights. One night I walked in to join the throbbing hive of drinkers, diners and other revellers. Behind a large dark-wood and mirrored bar, the barman John grinned as he recognised me.

'Jack Daniel's on the rocks?' He stared at me with big brown eyes, framed with heavy eyebrows. He looked moody but actually was pretty even-tempered. I knew we would meet later when he'd finished, and would indulge in each other until the early hours. He didn't care that I was a whore, he liked that I was warm and wild, not needy and inhibited like other girls he'd dated. It was not a complicated set-up: the only commitment would happen in a cool hotel room with a well-stocked minibar.

This was the sort of relationship I was used to. In recent years, having been unable to sustain an emotional relationship with any one man, I had become addicted to sex since it was the only way I seemed to be able to get the love and attention I craved. I was good at it, but I was still terrible at anything to do with emotions or relationships. I even enjoyed sex with some of my clients, but I enjoyed it all the more when I got to choose *who* it would be with. Sometimes the men I would go to bed with would stay around afterwards for a while, but never for long. I didn't know how to do it any other way. Part of me would have liked to have a long-term relationship, but another part of me would always sabotage it in some way. Usually I would do it by storming off and sleeping with someone else at the slightest sign of any trouble. I seemed to be incapable of sustaining a monogamous relationship with anyone. Often drink was a factor in my bad behaviour and when I sobered up I would always realise, too late, how ridiculous I was being. The men I'd met before going to prison had been as bad as me at monogamous relationships, but since coming out I had met one or two good men who had fallen for me. But I always messed it up, as if in some way I didn't think I was worthy of their love. I can also sometimes become violent during sex, nipping and biting, and some of the guys I tried to have relationships with didn't like it.

The ice clinked as it melted in my glass. The bar manager walked over to us and flirted with me, without noticing or caring for the chemistry surrounding John and me. John scratched my hand playfully as I stared into the bottom of my now-empty glass.

271

'Busy day?' he enquired, lifting my chin gently so that our gazes met.

'Yeah, I learned a thing or two today.'

'You? I thought you would be the teacher!'

I smiled and stared at the bar. Behind rows and rows of bottles were mirrors and I could see rowdy customers jostling in the background. The general manager walked over to John, nodded and then walked away again. John polished a glass and gestured towards him.

'He can fix you up with a better set-up – send you good business clients in a nice apartment. I know a few girls who work for him.'

I looked at him, smiling. 'I won't be staying that long.'

At the back of the room were lines of slot machines. John went on a break and I decided to have a gamble. The noise was deafening: coins dropping, electronic music, people shouting and the occasional clattering of change into metal trays. I sat on a high stool next to a stunning blonde. Her make-up and outfit were so perfect that I couldn't help but stare. She looked out of place, sat alone pumping change from a bucket into the slot like there was no tomorrow.

'Will you save my seat, please?' she whispered and disappeared.

I put my bag on her stool. She came back a few minutes later, thanked me and resumed play. After this had happened two or three times my curiosity got the better of me.

'Do you keep running to the cash machine? It must be costing you a fortune!'

She laughed a deep throaty laugh, taking me by surprise.

'I take men down alleys, give them a blow job and come back.'

It was then that I noticed her hands. They were twice as big as mine and I almost choked on my fresh drink as I realised my faux pas – 'she' was in fact a he. The more I learned in Sydney, the more I realised there was to learn . . .

25
QUEEN OF TARTS

....

'As for me, it is my profession, I do not pretend to anything better.'

Nell Gwyn

After three months in Sydney I returned to England, filled with enthusiasm and eager to apply all the things I had learned to my own business. Having reached the top end of the market back in Leeds, I now had managers running my operations. This left me able to act merely as a coordinator, overseeing everything and swanning in and out of the brothels and flats when it pleased me. I always insisted on high standards: the places had to be spotlessly tidy – no personal effects littered about and the girls immaculately turned out. I would frequently make newer girls laugh by running my hands up their legs and insisting that they should have stockings or baby-smooth legs by the next time I saw them.

Whenever I entered a premises everything was always running smoothly. But the managers told me that when they knew I was coming everyone would be rushing around like in a silent movie, getting things ready. After I left, apparently, it always looked as if a mini-hurricane had hit. But I enjoyed my visits and bumping into the brothel regulars who would treat me like visiting royalty. I would live up to the image of the grand matriarch by wearing stunning outfits and lush cashmere coats.

I was now working out of an exclusive apartment myself, as well as providing escort services. I found clients (or clients found me) who filled my life with precious treasures – and not all of those were material. To those clients I gave a little extra, a little piece of me, and sometimes it was returned with outstanding, unconditional generosity.

Of course, I paid a price for having my working life spill over into my private life. I didn't have time for serious relationships, but now that I was working at the better end of the market the lines between work and play were a little blurry with some of the clients. I was letting them get a little piece of the real me, letting them inside my head as well as snogging them as if they were my boyfriends and hanging on their every word as if I was actually interested. But the rewards were so extraordinary that I didn't question it. Sometimes the client and I would both become simultaneously encapsulated in our intimate fantasy bubble, forgetting for a while the truth of our arrangement.

I never did anything without protection: I always made that clear from the start. Many girls build up trade by taking risks in slow times. While I might not have taken unnecessary risks with my health I sold my soul instead, an infinitely more dangerous gamble. I remember my mother once telling me, 'Well, if you're going to sell your soul to the devil, make sure it's to the highest bidder.' In the end that was what I had done.

Now that I was being well paid, working in a safe environment and with the clients treating me decently, it became less of a transaction and more of an art form. I was proud of my art. The original geishas weren't prostitutes: they would recite poetry and perform tea ceremonies for their clients. I felt that my role as a high-class whore was about entertaining the client and keeping him stimulated, appealing to him on many different levels. Sometimes the sex was monotonous for me when I was having it several times a day. But at other times, when I liked the customer or found him attractive, it was wonderful and exciting, particularly if we were able to take our time and indulge ourselves in foreplay and role-playing.

I'd never dreamed that I would become so exclusive. But I was getting busier and the hours I could physically or mentally cope with didn't get any longer, so the only way to balance it was to charge as much as possible. As I became more expensive, my discerning regulars found ways to pay the difference, but some of my newer clients came from a world I'd never tasted before. I like to think that I wasn't so much greedy as ambitious. Making a lot of money was just another way for me to measure my success.

The more the gents treated me like a queen, the more I strived to live up to the image. No detail was overlooked. I bought the finest imported Parisian lingerie and always wore stockings and suspenders. I knew this was a dying art in the age of hold-ups but it was a small detail that the clients adored. I wore different fabulous cocktail and evening dresses for every social occasion, and then they became part of my work attire. I moved in upmarket circles, attended society balls and was often mistaken for a society wife.

Now, you can put any pretty young girl from a humble background into a fancy frock and call her a 'high-class hooker' but she will plummet like an out-of-nest fledgling if she can't adapt to her surroundings. Being sophisticated and cultured started as an act but over time I became all that I aspired to be. None of this came instantly. A parcel did not arrive one day that read 'Transformation pack: move financially and emotionally to middle-class status.' To make the change complete it wasn't enough just to be in the same financial bracket as my clients – it was a mental journey too. It's not an established fact that working with high-fliers will change you: I had to desire it passionately, communicate it subtly and work hard to achieve it.

The roles of a high-class whore are many: geisha, nurse, courtesan, strict mistress and even, occasionally, a pillow-based confidante. Many clients needed a place to escape and unload, mentally as well as physically. I went from streetwalking strumpet to thinking man's crumpet, an expert in the arts of cerebral masturbation – the art of seducing the mind without fucking the head!

I can see how some clients become involved with girls and end up getting fleeced in the process; guards sometimes drop soon after trousers. I pride myself on knowing that I didn't rip clients off, even when they laid themselves wide open, but I must admit to turning a couple of willing customers into 'sugar daddies'.

Basically, if they were keen I would stop charging them by the hour and they would 'look after' me instead.

When someone you like but don't actually fancy has feelings for you, feelings that you know you can never reciprocate, the emotions they go through become complex, ranging from sadness to bitterness and on to anger and resentment. It was always really uncomfortable being around men who lost sight of reality and became infatuated, especially when some of them were strong, powerful business types.

I was used to being worshipped by my slaves during domination but this was quite different. Don't get me wrong: it's a nice feeling knowing that someone would walk over hot coals for you, give you anything they possibly could just to have you say you love them, but I never could bring myself to lie to them. I never deliberately misled any of them into believing anything was more than it was. I could have married for money more than once and then would have had to sleep only with the one guy instead of with many, but that would never have done. It would not have been honest. Pretending to enjoy sex with someone is one thing, pretending to love them quite another.

I also loved my independence and the freedom to fall in love with whomever I chose, whenever they came along. Yes, after all I have experienced, even now I'm still a hopeless romantic, searching for 'Mr Right'. At this level there was the odd client I fell for, which is unusual with most working girls, intimacy being something that is usually avoided. Rarely in such situations was I lucky enough for it to be a mutual feeling, even briefly. After all, most clients were married and had come to me rather than have affairs: they specifically wanted sex with no strings attached – they had more than enough emotional baggage already. They were quite capable of separating the very genuine feelings of love they had for their wives from their sexual needs, which I could fulfil for them. These men became as intimate with me as it was possible for them to be and there was always a danger that one or other of us would get involved. It was a very powerful feeling for me if they were the ones who became emotionally involved, and occasionally it was my guard that slipped. Such things would never have happened in the saunas or on the streets.

More than with any individual, however, I was really in love with the whole lifestyle. I would wake up in the morning and my maid would bring me my breakfast in bed. I would get ready slowly, putting on all the won-derful clothes and jewels I'd bought. Guys would bring me presents all day and drool over me, and I was getting (sometimes fantastic) sex all day long – and being paid well for it.

One client, who I will call Pete, became more than just a customer. He was single and a similar age to me and we quickly developed a strong friendship that morphed into a fake relationship. He didn't pay me by the hour any more. I got confused somewhere, it felt so natural – he loved me so much that I thought I would catch up. We were the same age and quite compatible. I really did enjoy his company but just didn't fancy him. He even met my mum and Lucy; I didn't feel guilty about it as I presented him as a boyfriend – for by then that was what he was. Of course, at the time I didn't admit to them how I'd met him.

Pete was an incredibly generous man. Since I had just moved house he bought me a new bathroom, complete with jet-spa Jacuzzi. He even took Lucy and me to Alton Towers; he would have treated her as his own, given a chance.

We both shared a love of scuba-diving and Pete took me on the ultimate diving vacation. I'd first got a taste for diving in Australia on the Great Barrier Reef, where I'd been determined to overcome my fear of the water and was quickly seduced by the beauty of everything I saw beneath the surface. Pete took me to a magical honeymoon-type location: endless white sandy beaches, a turquoise ocean with lapping white horses – Paradise, via the Maldives. We had a private island and were waited on like royalty, arriving from the mainland in a helicopter. Our love nest was a huge bungalow on stilts over the sea and our bed was covered in rose petals every morning.

But it was all a crock, because I knew I was leading him on. I knew I could never feel the same as he did and I felt like a fraud. One morning we chartered a yacht and I spent most of the time flirting with the captain while Pete was on the back deck, reading a book. I longed to fall headlong in love, or at least lust! But I couldn't do it to order. I would have loved to give him the love he so badly craved, for his selfless, generous heart truly deserved it. But I just couldn't and in the end even having sex with him felt awkward.

Pete was nervous around women and he had already told me that I was his 'first proper girlfriend'. He followed me around (usually ten paces behind) like a lovesick puppy. When we went into a restaurant, it was me they'd bring the wine to taste and it was *me* they'd bring the bill to (even though he always paid it), as if they knew I was wearing the trousers.

I was grateful for all he'd done for me and I knew how privileged I was to be there, so I tried to fulfil his fantasy for as long as I could.

A year later, the money had gone and so had Pete. He'd never been rich at all; it turned out that he'd been made redundant at the place where he'd worked since school and he'd spent the entire packet on me. I'd had no idea.

Was he a victim? Well, I never set out to hurt him. He just couldn't buy the one thing he wanted. But he gave me so much – of his material wealth and of himself.

Another client, who I will refer to as Mark, taught me the gift of giving in so many different ways. All his cards, gifts and trips were peppered with subtle signs of his affection. He knew that I loved Pre-Raphaelite art and so he would research all the galleries for related exhibitions. All of this would be tied in with a fabulous dinner, followed by theatre or opera.

Mark was a wonderful client and I still remember him warmly. When he first came to visit me he was an absolute gent, which meant he was already special. He had a few strands of strawberry-blond hair swept across his otherwise bare head and was bursting out of his tweed suit and mismatched shirt and tie. He said he was embarrassed about his weight and appearance. I told him, and I meant it, that I didn't mind, because he was so lovely. I told him only to change for himself, knowing how unhappy he was.

One year Mark excelled himself and gave me a price- less dream day. He knew all the things I loved and organised everything down to the tiniest details. The day started with the horse race of the year, the Grand National. I was incredibly excited; as Mark knew, I adored the races. The throb and buzz of the racetrack was exhilarating and we cheered and jumped around in the members' enclosure like well-dressed kids on a trampoline! We must have looked quite mad.

Then in the evening we went into Liverpool to see one of my favourite Puccini operas, *Tosca*. Mark even had a pressed cotton handkerchief ready for my gentle tears. It was a well-presented show and the whole experience was breathtaking. Just when I didn't think it could get any better he took me for a candlelit dinner in a small exclusive restaurant, with exquisite food and a scintillat- ing atmosphere and waiters who looked like butlers straight from the 1920s. The whole setting was divine and to top it all he gave me a rare CD by Maria Callas, as a memento of our day.

Mark then suggested an impromptu visit to my then- favourite local vice den – the casino. It always set my adrenalin racing to walk through those doors. I loved the attention and the chance to wear nice gowns. I knew all the staff by name and would tip all the valets extra- ordinary amounts so that they would look after me like I

was royalty. I would do the rounds first, greeting all the
staff by name and kissing all my friends. I was always
happy and bubbly in the casino. I was addicted to the
buzz. I even had a little fan club of older guys, regular
casino punters who would sometimes ask me to sit with
them for luck. I started by playing roulette and eventually learned blackjack and was reasonably successful at
it. Initially I won huge amounts of money, which I
proceeded to lose over the next five years, plus a lot
more. Like most things with me it eventually became an
addiction, but it wasn't so much the gambling as the
casino life itself that I was addicted to.

I was a bit of a celebrity in my local casino; everyone
would stop me to see what I was wearing, the girls
grabbing my hands to admire my nails or look at my
jewellery. I walked around with my head high, present-
ing myself as a dignified lady. It was my place to show
off, like the Transport Club had been for my grandmother, Ethel.

Mark seemed so eager to please me. For months he
watched his weight and went to the gym with real
determination to reach his goal. I guess winning me
was part of it. One day, a year after I'd first met him,
he came to pick me up and I realised then that he was a
totally different man. Dressed in an outfit he had picked
that was simply stunning, he was slimmer and fitter,
with short well-groomed hair. He could have had a string
of love interests. The physical transformation was wonderful and, thankfully, he stayed the same sweet guy.

Then he surprised me by making the biggest change of
his life. After two decades of raising a family he left his

loveless marriage, but once our arrangement came to an end he went back.

Mark's tastes in music still leave footprints on my CD collection. He shared his love of classical music and helped me develop my taste for opera. He actively sought out new music, and then bought it for me. We went to live-jazz nights, theatres and galleries, and to fine, unique restaurants up and down the country. He worked so hard to make our times together special and he spoilt me beyond belief. Anything I expressed an interest in, he sought out, encouraged and arranged. Once he asked me about my childhood dreams. I told him how I once got on my bike and chased a hot-air balloon for miles, wishing I was in it. I was so moved that I cried tears of joy when he told me he had bought me a champagne balloon flight.

I cared deeply about Mark and I seriously enjoyed his companionship. But in the end I couldn't reciprocate his intense love for me, no matter how hard I tried, which left me feeling sad. I wondered if there was any hope that I would ever fall in love with the sort of man who would treat me well. But the way we grew together, and what we shared, was truly amazing. He was my dream-maker.

I broke all my own rules with another special client, a builder; I'll call him Harry. His special magic was making me laugh. He was only a few years older than me and we clicked immediately. I had never met anyone who made me so happy, which was intoxicating.

On his first visit Harry told me that he'd never been to see a prostitute before. The word itself sounded so harsh as it left his lips and he looked a little embarrassed so I rescued him gently by correcting the term to *working girl*.

As he reached into his wallet to pay me, he proudly showed me photos of his beautiful children. He seemed so open, unlike many of my other clients. Sometimes the clients are so private that they even give a pseudonym and create a secret identity, just like the girls do.

Over the forthcoming weeks Harry came to explain (in his own time, I never asked clients about the personal stuff) all about his situation. He loved his wife but wasn't *in love* with her. They had been together since school. He described her as being like a sister and told me that people often mistook them for siblings as they even looked alike. Like most long-term relationships, especially ones where kids and businesses are involved, the sparkle and excitement that were there in the beginning had been replaced by routine and security.

The chemistry that we shared was amazing. What started as good sex quickly became intense lovemaking. Tell-tale signs that we were in deep started to emerge. The hour that Harry would usually spend with me started to become several hours, until we both knew this could no longer be a business arrangement. We started to have songs in common, places we'd visit secretly. He would send me gifts and notes that would blow me away.

In the beginning the fact that Harry was unavailable just fuelled the flames. As time went on things became unbearable and we both started to fall to pieces. I realised I was finding it difficult to work on the days he'd been to see me, and he had started to drink during the long nights he was at home. We couldn't continue the way we were: he could see the crumbs that he could offer me after his business and family were no longer enough, but there wasn't much he could do about it unless he changed everything.

One afternoon we arranged to go for a drive in the countryside to discuss the impossibility of it all. Not that it did much good – we both ended up in floods of tears, knowing that we couldn't go on but unable to stop.

I knew that Harry was in pain and he could clearly see mine. He mumbled on about not being able to leave till the kids had grown up, but we both knew he wasn't being honest with himself. Of course he reminded me of all he would lose. He had a huge house, cars and a big company that would all have been at stake, as well as the tender hearts of his boy and girl. His wife had never even slept with another man and had devoted most of her adult life to what had previously been a happy marriage. Success had come hard for both of them. Harry's father had been a painter and decorator, and he had originally followed in his dad's footsteps, expanding the firm and getting into the construction side, taking on more men and bigger and bigger contracts. They had started life on a council estate and his biggest fear was losing it all and ending up back there.

I was so envious of what Harry and his wife had together: knowing each other since school, sharing a house and kids – it made me painfully aware of everything I had missed out on. There were always moments when I wished I was someone's wife, being a good mother to his kids. But I knew I would never have been able to do the domestic side of the job. I would have dreaded becoming a bitter housewife like my mum.

Harry had made me feel happy, and the thought of sharing that happiness with his family seemed impossible. I was greedy for more of him. After months of feeling as though my heart was splitting I tried ending our affair, hoping that would end the pain. But we got back together within a matter of days, both of us emotionally worn out. One night I got drunk. I couldn't take it any more. I rang his mobile – it was switched off. Well, it would be – after all, it was gone midnight. In a moment of emotional turmoil and in an act of sheer madness, I did the unspeakable and committed a sin so great and unthinkable that every woman will hate me for what I'm about to reveal: I called him at home.

It was Harry who answered . . .

'Please, please don't do this.'

It was too late. The damage was done. In one split second I'd shattered his wife's world. She had trusted him implicitly and he'd come to me in the first place so he wouldn't have an affair – now look at the mess we were in. Every betrayed wife must consider her husband's mistress a whore so it must have seemed twice as tough that I quite literally was one.

She rang me the next day. She seemed so unnaturally calm and positive that I was suspicious of her motives. I expected, and deserved, a screaming banshee. She said she wanted to meet me, to see what I was like, and maybe I would answer some questions for her as Harry had clammed up. I was physically shaking and feeling pretty disgusted with myself. When she turned up she was armed with a huge bunch of flowers. She said she wanted to show me that the meeting was to be 'non-confrontational'. I couldn't believe her incredible strength and generosity and dignity.

'Just like her,' Harry said later.

I was so moved and so damned sorry. I didn't dare indulge myself in any self-pity. I knew I was a marriage-wrecker and I was disgusted with my own behaviour.

Ironically, the last time I bumped into Harry it turned out that he'd taken on a major construction project that had gone belly up. He had returned to running a small decorating business and his lifestyle had changed dramatically. He was still with his wife and his children had grown up. He seemed happy and settled and so neither of us lingered for long. Harry had chosen a good, ordinary life. He had realised what was important and he had made a deliberate choice. I couldn't help wondering if I had left it too late to achieve a happy family life myself and whether I was just doomed to wreck everyone else's. Might I have to acknowledge that my chosen lifestyle was a liability?

26

THE QUEEN IS DEAD.
LONG LIVE THE QUEEN.

....

'*Once a newspaper touches a story, the facts are lost for ever, even to the protagonists.*'

Norman Mailer

Even from when I was little, everything in our house was a fucking secret. Everything was always none of my business. I never knew anything till *after* it happened. In all the years at home, I'd never even seen my foster-mum naked. When things were told to me there was always a big dramatic announcement: nothing got to creep up on you – it was always more like being hit by a bus.

So the one thing I never wanted was to have secrets from Lucy. I never lied to her about what I did, because she didn't ask any questions. But I was glad about that, since I didn't feel she was old enough to understand just yet.

I always intended to sit her down when she was the right age and explain everything but at the same time I wanted to protect her from reality for as long as possible. For now we were living in two different cities, she in Sheffield and me in Leeds, two different worlds, so it wasn't too hard for my mum to shield her from the truth. Had we lived in the same town I don't suppose it would have been long before someone would have felt it their duty to inform her of her mother's reputation.

As Lucy had been getting older, I'd been thinking that the time was probably right to start telling her a bit about the past and about the life I'd lived, easing her gently into the whole truth. But my mum was adamant that my daughter should know nothing. I think Mum and the rest of the family thought that if they didn't talk about it, then it didn't exist. I went along with it because she'd done such a great job bringing Lucy up and I didn't want to rock the boat unnecessarily, but it was beginning to feel as if there were more secrets than I was comfortable with.

I'd spoken several times on the phone to a female Leeds journalist who wanted to do an article about me and I felt there was a rapport building between us. I wasn't proud of how I had obtained my incredible lifestyle but I also refused to be ashamed of it. I agreed to do an interview and, as it wasn't money that motivated me, I did it without charge, naming only one condition, which I thought the journalist had agreed to: not to let their sister paper in my home town of Sheffield run the story.

I didn't want to put my family through any more – especially as the press coverage during my trial had been bad enough. I rang Mum and explained that there was nothing to worry about because the piece would run in Leeds and not in Sheffield.

The Leeds paper ran a two-page colour spread inside the middle of their women's supplement – complete with several colour photos, including one of my face covering the front of the supplement. It was well written, empathetic and non-judgemental. It portrayed me as a survivor who had pulled herself up from the gutter into a good lifestyle. I was very pleased with it and grateful that the journalist had repaid my trust and not let me down.

The day after the article came out in Leeds I got a phone call from my foster-mum, screaming hysterically at me. At first I couldn't understand what she was saying, but gradually her words began to make sense to me and the horrible truth dawned.

'How could you do this to me?' she wailed. 'How could you do this to the family? What about your daughter?'

A very different article had burst onto the pages of the Sheffield paper, whose editor had lifted the photos from the Leeds article and put together all the shit he could find on me, from my going to prison to my football-pitch streak, splashing it all into one huge seedy story. My foster-family were rightly disgusted, but not with the paper: with *me*. I begged Mum to let me come to Sheffield and explain everything to my girl that night, before anyone else did. But in a temper with me, and quite possibly hurt by what she felt was a betrayal, my mum threw the paper down in front of Lucy.

'This is who your mum really is!'

I still can't believe she did that. It must have been really hard for my baby to understand what was going on, a bit like when I was first told the truth about my own birth family.

It choked me when my mum put her on the phone.

'Oh, Mummy,' Lucy said. 'I'm so disappointed!'

Her quiet, brave attitude somehow made it harder. I felt truly ashamed of myself. Later my mum told me that Lucy kept a photo of me in a frame in her room. It was from a rare modelling shoot where I was allowed to keep my clothes on.

'My mummy's a model!' she would say proudly to anyone who saw it. No one had corrected her, until now.

Both the journalist and I had been very naive to think that we could control where the story went once it was published.

I'm convinced that secrets and lies destroy families – because when unpleasant things are eventually exposed – and they always are – the fact that they have been hidden makes them a hundred times more damaging.

Realising that I had yet again disappointed Lucy so badly was devastating. It seemed to be yet another warning of why I needed to re-examine my life and my priorities once and for all. The pressure to make some major changes in my life seemed to be building – and there was more to come.

I never considered myself a royalist or anything and I'm not one for trite sentimentality. But something deep down inside me stirred the day that Princess Diana died and the shock of it triggered a change in my outlook on life. Hearing of that tragic accident and seeing the way in which so many people responded to it, I started to ask myself a lot of questions. Like: what had I ever done for anybody? If I died tomorrow what would it be that I would be remembered for, if at all? I didn't much like the answers I came up with.

My journey through the sex industry had started out from a place of desperation. I'd initially been trapped by poverty but now I had become addicted to the wealth. In my pursuit of money and love and attention, however, I had let Lucy down for years, and she was the person I cared about the most.

Watching the crowds gathering outside Buckingham Palace and in Kensington Gardens on the television somehow challenged everything that I thought was making me happy. I realised that something was going to have to change.

Not long after Diana's death, a friend of mine who worked in the local gym, got a lump on the back of his hand and was diagnosed with cancer. A couple of months later, by Christmas, he was dead.

I went to see him at the hospice late one night, just before he died. He was on my mind and I couldn't sleep. We joked about maybe his wife might get the wrong idea and I told him I should jump under the covers if we were going to be accused anyway! I sat with him for a while and listened to him trying to breathe. I dared to ask him, 'What's it really like?'

He turned his head slowly away and closed his eyes for a moment.

'The worst thing,' he said eventually, 'is that I will never be able to hold my baby daughter again.'

He died at twenty-nine and left behind a wife, a daughter and three stepchildren. The seed that had taken root inside me when I'd had to have that terrible conversation with Lucy in the wake of the news story now began to sprout, making me look again at my own life and what I was doing with it.

Then, out of the blue, I received another disturbing phone call. My foster-mum had gone into hospital for surgery. I immediately went to visit her. I was told she was tired and understandably worn out and that I mustn't stay long. I walked into the ward, holding back the tears.

I knew I must be strong for her, but I didn't feel it. The glowing lime-coloured strip lights buzzed and the acrid smell of disinfectant hurt my nose; everything seemed to be white and green, a pale imitation of life. I pushed open the door to the ward, my heart in my mouth. I was in shock.

There she was, laid up and helpless. I tried to fight back the tears – this moment should not be about my own feelings. She hadn't even told me that she was ill – more secrets – let alone that she was having a breast removed because of cancer, cancer that had by now spread through her glands. She tried to sit up and I could see clearly, despite her pain, that she had found the strength to be angry with me about my work and the number of brothels I ran. I was trying not to cry but my heart was breaking.

'Mum,' I pleaded, 'I really do want to get out of it.'

'Well, do it, then – soon! Do it for your daughter if you won't do it for yourself!'

I couldn't understand why she'd chosen that moment – but it will be burned into my mind for ever. I felt as if the cancer was my fault and that maybe she wouldn't have developed it if I had been a different person. I made Mum a promise that day that I would quit prostituting myself and walk away from the businesses.

A year later, in 1998, after more comebacks than Shirley Bassey, I finally hung up my stockings and quit working as a whore for ever. I swore it would not be long before the brothels too would become history.

27
THE START OF THINGS TO COME
········

'*Treat a whore like a lady and a lady like a whore.*'
Wilson Mizner

In 2001 I stepped out of a first-class railway carriage at
Bath's quaint station, having concluded a series of successful talks in London about a high-profile six-part
documentary, in which I would be taking part later in
the year. Although I'd decided I was leaving the sex
industry behind, I hoped that it would give me a good
platform from which to launch my other pursuits and
would also contribute towards my new mission of
making sure none of my experiences had been in vain.

I had also just completed several satisfying days with
one of my writing mentors; I was determined to hone my
writing skills until they were good enough to earn me a
living. Despite not getting results at school, I could see no
reason why I shouldn't be able to catch up if I worked
hard and listened to the right people.

While in Bath I planned to pursue another of my great
passions: photography. It was a passion that had stayed
with me ever since Ethel gave me my first camera for
Christmas as a child and I took my first-ever picture of

her coming down our drive in the snow in a fake-fur coat and white block heels. Years ago at school I'd tried to tell my careers teacher about the lunchtime photography club, and ever since then I had been photographing Lucy and my travels. That weekend I was brushing up my skills with a course organised by the Royal Photography Society. This had been another long journey I never guessed would turn out so well, from a snap-happy kid at ten with a simple camera to my first commercial contract and online exhibition.

The Priory Hotel was like some place I'd only ever seen in period dramas or *Homes and Gardens*. In the lounge a chandelier provided the central focus, the sunlight from the large glass balcony doors splitting into dozens of prisms of light, floating around the room like miniature rainbow butterflies.

Sofas in rich colours and fabrics were dotted about. Lamps, tables and interesting knick-knacks filled the rest of the space. A low picture rail divided the room, with portraits mainly from the 1920s scattered and hung as if in a museum. A French-style mirror on a solid marble mantelpiece was framed by candlesticks and a jet clock – it was three in the afternoon and time for tea.

I could smell the coffee long before the French waitress brought it in. She carefully set down a tray with a cafetière, a jug of cream and a bowl of sugar lumps. Home-made biscuits stared at me temptingly. She was polite and quiet, dressed in black and white, and she seemed genuinely taken aback when I asked her name.

After my coffee I stepped through the balcony doors into the magnificent gardens and drank in the view. Although it was only April the sky was Wedgwood blue and the sun lit the whole scene like an Impressionist painting. The hush was broken only by the soft cooing of a wood pigeon. A breeze brought me the scents of lavender, jasmine and magnolia. Shapes and splashes of crimson, violet and magenta and a palette of many greens adorned carefully manicured lawns, with small cherub statues keeping guard. A clump of bushes, trees and an ornamental cherry blossom carefully concealed a deserted outdoor pool. A small pond reflected brilliant white rays and minnows gently nipped at its cool surface, sending out ripples. A Lebanese cedar imposed itself on the scene, with its branches stretched out like tabletops. The beds in front of the window teemed with forget-me-nots and orangey-yellow tulips. The walls were crawling with ivy, bright yellow glory vine and thick, fluffy lilac wisteria.

My life seemed as busy and vibrant with possibility as the garden itself. But with the new excitement had come feelings of apprehension. Perhaps this year I would walk away from the very industry that had afforded me this wonderful lifestyle. Could I trust that my writing, photography and other interests would carry me through to that new life I dreamed of? My cynical side reminded me that I'd been here before – straight after prison. Back then it had all ended in bitter disappointment

Up in my bedroom I stared into the mirror at the new woman I saw looking back nervously. A classier lady than I had once been, more refined than before, with a few gentle lines of experience just starting to show on her face. Was that really me – a successful businesswoman?

I was scared that if I asked too loudly someone might shout back: 'No! It's only that old whore.'

A few days later I was back in Leeds, in the middle of Roundhay Park, where the rain was coming down faster than a punter's trousers. The television crew had me marching up and down picturesque valleys with the backdrop of the city in the distance.

I traipsed happily up and down the crunchy autumnal carpet. I was getting more soaked by the second and my new suede boots and trousers were coated in fresh mud, but I had to focus on the task ahead. They'd just snapped me back down to earth by telling me look 'reflective', because this scene was going to be dropped over emotional footage of me candidly confessing the horrendous events leading up to my imprisonment.

I gazed into the distance as if it were the future itself and, as the rain slid down my nose and throat, I sensed a feeling of cleansing. Filming, mooching and moodiness finished, I walked back to the car, leaving the crew behind. There was a strange feeling of completion. It was the last bit of filming for the series and I was not going to let the damp atmosphere put me off.

The film crew were packing up. As I approached the car my pace quickened slightly as I flashed back to a call earlier from a girl who had once worked for me.

'Be quick – I'm filming, darling!' (A newly adopted phrase of mine, delivered in my best *Ab Fab* voice.)

'Okay,' my friend said, 'I'll cut straight to the chase. I heard you sold one of your parlours – I want to buy the others.'

And so that rainy September afternoon I finally had confirmation that my 'psychic stomach' was right. That tightening in my solar plexus never lets me down. An amazing chain of events had unfolded: it was the end of an era and the start of things to come.

A week later I sold off all my parlours. It was a scary moment, like standing on the edge of a cliff – ready to jump but not knowing if I'd land safely, or how far I would drop.

I'm not scared of change – it thrills me. It's just that feeling of the unknown and, let's face it, I decided a long time ago that I would rather be dead than dull. The way things were finally heading, it looked as if I might have an exciting but risk-free future, for the first time ever.

28
FULL CIRCLE
....

'I don't think a prostitute is more moral than a wife, but they are doing the same thing.'
Prince Philip, Duke of Edinburgh

My relationship with my daughter had blossomed since Lucy had become a teenager and come to terms with the truth of my past. Instead of occasional weekends and short breaks, we now spent a lot more time in each other's company and had made real progress in getting to know one another. She was fast becoming a young adult who needed to express herself. I could relate to her now more than I could when she'd been a child; she was good at communicating her needs and I felt more able to respond.

But at the same time I felt a mixture of excitement and apprehension. If my daughter was ever going to come and live with me, was I now capable of being a *good* mother?

We had already had a 'dry run' when there had been an incident during Christmas 1999. I had received an angry phone call from my mum; she and Lucy had had a row. Despite the fact that it was Christmas, I was asked to fetch Lucy and all her belongings immediately. I guess Mum thought that she could make Lucy behave better by threatening her with having to live with me, but she and I bonded well over the Millennium celebrations. Then, in the New Year, just as we were both adjusting to our new situation, my mum realised that her ruse hadn't worked and that she was in danger of losing Lucy for good. She demanded that I return Lucy, and had the legal paper-work of a residency order that we had agreed some time before (supposedly for my mum's peace of mind) to back her up. I had no option but to let her go back, and I didn't want the same thing to happen again.

Many months after the last showdown Mum had said that although she wanted the best for Lucy, if a similar situation ever arose again she would not stand in our way. But I strongly suspected that wouldn't be the case.

Isn't it funny how fate sometimes deals you a second chance, and how all things come full circle? I had been wanting for so long to have Lucy back with me full-time and I had been trying to see a way to do it that would cause her the least amount of disruption. I knew it would be unfair of me to think I could steam in and uproot her just because I wanted to. Then, when I was least expecting it, on Father's Day 2002 I was offered my chance when Lucy announced that she now wanted to come and live with me.

So when Lucy finally decided it was time to come home I tried to stay cool while my mum went through every emotion, ranging from pure anger and rejection to sheer emotional exhaustion. I tried to tell her how I saw through her anger and that Lucy and I both still loved her. I tried to tell her that we needed her and would need her even more now if this was going to work, for Lucy's sake more than mine. But none of this was enough.

My mother said she felt a failure and asked where she'd gone wrong, admitting that somehow she'd felt that raising Lucy through her teenage years would put right the wrong at the point where she felt she'd left off with me. I told her, as lovingly as I could manage, that it was wrong to compare the two. I held her hand as I told her what an amazing parent she'd been to Lucy: she had to take full credit for a bright well-spoken articulate young lady. I also told her that I was sorry she felt I was such an unsuitable person to take over my daughter's care, that I'd turned out to be such a disappointment.

I tried my hardest to understand my mum's pain and to reassure her. But by the following day she had drawn up battle plans and I was back to being her enemy. I dare say the cancer made her more vulnerable and more insecure. I'm certain that the illness also had a bearing on Lucy's choice to stay with her as long as she did. Even after she left, although she knew that the move was right, Lucy felt guilty, as if she had caused her Nan suffering. I tried to tell Lucy not to take these feelings on board.

My foster-mum's reaction was to try and shut the door on Lucy immediately with no winding-down period. My daughter had to leave her house as soon as possible. She said that the longer Lucy stayed the more difficult and painful it would be for her. Before I had even had time to sort out a school or her room or anything, Mum had packed up all Lucy's things and I got a phone call telling me to pick her up. When I arrived my mother had gone to a neighbour's house as we carried all my daughter's possessions to the car. After putting the last items in we knocked gently on the neighbour's door, wanting to say goodbye, to give her a hug. But the neighbour opened the door, keeping it on the chain. I offered to leave so that Lucy could say goodbye, but there was nothing doing. We had no choice but to do as we were told. Mum must have been in so much pain that day and I was powerless to do anything to help.

Now I was no longer to be the sisterly part-time mum. Despite my misgivings about my own suitability, I was very excited at the prospect of being given another chance. I felt privileged that Lucy would even consider coming to live with me after all I'd done to mess up her young life so far. I was well aware of just how big the responsibility was going to be and I didn't need the reminders that followed from my well-meaning foster-relations who hadn't spoken to me for over a decade but were now ringing to give me lectures on the well-being, safety and happiness of my girl.

I had considered all the potential pitfalls that lay ahead, which would be even more difficult with my foster-mum's *you've made your bed – now lie in it* attitude. Lucy and I both desperately needed her support as we stepped into unknown territory together, but she'd withdrawn it. I could imagine how hard it must have been to go from being the main mother figure to suddenly having to revert to being just the grandmother. I dare say that Mum thought it would be less painful to cut us off completely. Some of the damage of the previous months felt irreparable. Would we all get on again one day? Would we ever want to try?

I had convinced myself that my foster-mother hated me and that the only reason she'd tolerated me at all had been for Lucy's sake. She'd told me several times since her illness had been diagnosed that she did love me, but I found it hard to believe that when she acted the way she did. Shouldn't a mother's love be unconditional? I struggled with my feelings, reminding myself that, to give her full credit, as well as doing a brilliant job of raising Lucy, she had never once denied me as her true daughter.

The first few days were the hardest emotionally. I tried my best to deal with Lucy's feelings sensitively, to let her know how loved and secure she could be with me.

The next thing was to sort out the more practical matters, like a decent school and making her feel at home and in her own space. With a sense of fun and a genuine desire to make this work, together we started to heal and move on.

My whole world had changed overnight, as on the day when Lucy was born. All the feelings flooded back. Once again she became the centre of my universe, my first priority. Ironically, all this happened just at the time when I was feeling that I'd pleased myself for long enough and needed to lead a less selfish life.

I had no idea how I would square full-time motherhood with my need to make a living. Nor did I know how Lucy would adjust. But life seemed to be settling into a wonderful new pattern. I was excited about the future and felt proud of myself for the first time in years.

29

LIFE IS A BEACH

....

'I can enjoy her while she's kind;
But when she dances in the wind,
And shakes the wings, and will not stay,
I puff the prostitute away.'

John Dryden

The filming of the TV series *'Personal Services'* (not to be confused with the film of the same name), went brilliantly. It was an honest, ground-breaking documentary that showed how some women can work safely in brothels. I was proud of my contribution and still think it was an excellent piece of TV. I spent nine months of my life being followed around by a film crew, during which time there were many adventures. Just when I didn't thnk it could get any more exciting I received some sensational news: LWT wanted me to be the programme's figurehead narrator! We had to overcome many hurdles to confirm this. It was important that the viewing public should not think that the programme was biased or that it condoned prostitution, by using an ex-madam as a presenter. Then there was the fact that under the series rules I couldn't profit in any way from my life as a madam. At first I was going to waive the fee altogether. Then I had a better idea and asked for it to be donated to Cancer Research.

In preparation for my first attempt at narration, the series producer arranged for Lucy and me to watch an expert at work. This turned out to be more than just an education – it was an amazing experience in itself. We were transported around in a limo, put up in a swanky London hotel and given the full VIP, no-expenses-spared treatment, and I can tell you it suited us both very well! Finally we got to watch Andrew Sachs (a.k.a. Manuel from *Fawlty Towers*) doing the voice-over for *Shoplifters from Hell*.

A couple of weeks later I was doing it for real. I sat in the booth with headphones on, watching myself and all the other ladies in the programme. On the screen in front of me was a scene from my huge birthday bash back in April. Wow, that was some party! I transformed the back garden into a fake beach, complete with several tons of sand, forty square feet of decking and – of course – palm trees. I even found some amazing garden furniture – solid teak hand-carved crabs! I hired a huge marquee, complete with a desert-island mural, had a live band, a disco, a separate drinks tent and a veritable banquet. Of course, it all went marvellously on the night. But as usual in my life the run-up to it was an adventure in itself.

All my friends fell in to help out and we only just pulled it off. Although I'd planned the bash for weeks, the workmen who were completing my house were behind schedule so we were in the midst of landscaping the garden, having a new kitchen fitted and all the while being followed around by a TV crew! The kitchen floor was still being laid on the morning of the party and I was doing my best headless-chicken impression.

It was probably the most memorable party I'll ever throw, and we were all still talking about it months later. It's so appropriate that, although it was the first footage we filmed over a nine-month period, it was screened in the last episode, including my walk away from the parlours and the finale of the party – a spectacular twenty-minute firework display. So I guess in the end I really did get to exist the industry with a bang! Or, as you might say, *in a blaze of glory . . .*

After the TV series, I continued to work with the media as a specialist in 'adult issues', figuring that my journey would never be wasted if by communicating my experiences to others I could make a positive difference. Recently I've spoken at national conferences and in 2005 I contributed to the Government's paper – 'Paying the Price' – on tackling prostitution issues. Ironically, I predicted on my website many years ago that any politician championing the rights of prostitutes would have to be squeaky-clean in order not to have his trousers pulled down. I was actually quite sad, though, when David Blunkett, the then Home Secretary, fulfilled this prophesy in such a spectacular manner and I'm almost certain that this will affect the final outcome of policy decisions. Only recently I heard a minister saying the Government's plan was to challenge the view that prostitution was inevitable, a position that would almost certainly serve only to push it further underground and make it even less accountable than it is now. But on a more positive note, I'm over the moon that those who are involved in facilitating child prostitution and trafficking women are going to be hit hard.

So, my lifestyle had to change, but with that came a new sense of achievement and I'm slowly regaining my self-esteem. For the longest time I thought there was only one thing I was any good at and it is only now I realise that I have more going on between my ears than my legs. I just hope I can convince everyone else of the same thing. My wish for the future is that I will be able to lead a more stable but nonetheless interesting life. I'm already starting to get bookings for more public speaking events and after several enjoyable radio experiences, I have realised I would love to host a late night phone-in show. My long-term dream is of running a live music venue abroad.

I'm still single but have never lost hope in finding someone special to share my life with. On the family front, sadly my relationship with my mum is still an up-and-down affair. I've always thought of her as my true mother – not Doreen, who only gave birth to me. I know that my foster mother has been steadfast in her love and has told me many times that despite all I have done I am still her daughter. I love her deeply for that. I'm sorry for all the pain I've caused her and the rest of my foster-family, and that for a long time I was such a big disappointment. I know they hated me being a prostitute and my mum especially felt frustrated as she saw it coming and sensed the dangers I faced. I love her for bringing up Lucy. She did a marvellous job for love, and Lucy is a real credit to her.

*　　*　　*

Lucy has grown into a beautiful, articulate young lady and thankfully she has remained undamaged by my past. She enjoyed observing my media work so much that she now wants to do something similar herself. I was able to get her into a private girls' school during her teenage years and she has blossomed beyond all my expectations, achieving a stack of high-grade exam results and a forthcoming university place in media and related studies – so different to my own start in life just seventeen years before.

Now, when I look back on everything that has happened, my only regret is that I didn't do better by Lucy when she was younger and that I was too young, selfish and reckless to raise her myself. She is my most priceless treasure and will always remain so. Within a few months of having her home, I was looking proudly at my beautiful daughter fast approaching the scarier side of womanhood. I knew I'd made the right decision in giving up the business, even though the pain of the transition was still having an effect on all three of us – my daughter, my mother and myself.

I'm not proud of my past, but I refuse to be ashamed of it. I set out to live a life that was different from that of most other people, and in that I have succeeded. I made some terrible choices and decisions along the way and have paid the price every time. But I've also learned to turn a lot of the negative experiences into positive ones. Now Lucy and I have made it safely to the other side and I can't wait to see what will happen next. I have made the transition from feeling totally worthless to becoming expensive, to eventually realising that life itself is priceless.